CANADA

Author

Garry Marchant began his writing career as a copy boy and reporter for the *Winnipeg Tribune* but abandoned it for a decade of travelling around the world. After working for small weeklies on the BC coast for a year, he hitchhiked to Rio de Janeiro, where he became editor of the *Brazil Herald*, the country's only English language daily. Later, he spent several years in Hong Kong working as a reporter for the *South China Morning Post* and as an editor for the *Far Eastern Economic Review*.

For ten years, he worked as a freelance writer based in Vancouver, BC, writing a monthly travel column for *Vancouver Magazine* and contributing to publications in Canada, the US, Australia, Hong Kong and Singapore. His work has also appeared in two anthologies: *Away From Home, Canadian Writers in Exotic Places*, 1985, and *Our American Cousins*, 1987. He has received numerous awards for writing and photography.

Garry Marchant now lives and works in Hong Kong.

Photographer

Kenneth John Straiton was born in Toronto in 1949. He moved to Vancouver, British Columbia, in 1973 to study architecture but soon left to pursue a career as a photo-artist. He has worked as a carpenter, taught photography, and travelled extensively. His 1982 series 'Quiet Idols', has been shown in Japan, Europe and North America.

Ken Straiton has been living and working in Tokyo since 1984.

CANADA

Garry Marchant

Photography by Ken Straiton

British Library Cataloguing-in-Publication Data
A catalogue record for this book is available from the British Library

Distribution in the United Kingdom, Ireland and Europe by Hi Marketing Ltd, 38 Carver Road, London SE24 9LT, UK

Grateful acknowledgement is made to the authors and publishers for permissions granted:

David Donnell for
'The Canadian Prairies View of Literature'

McLelland & Stewart Inc for
Men for the Mountains © Sid Marty 1978

Alfred A Knopf Inc for
Joshua Now and Then © Mordecai Richler 1980

Editor: Stefan Cucos
Illustrations Editor: John Oliver
Maps: Tom Le Bas
Photography by Ken Straiton
Additional illustrations courtesy of Paul Harris 12–13, 53, 75; National Archives of Canada 40, 128–29

Production House: Twin Age Ltd, Hong Kong
Printed in China

A heritage home in Oakville, an affluent Toronto suburb

Contents

INTRODUCTION 11

HISTORY 21
The First Inhabitants 21
The Viking Interlude 21
The First Europeans 22
Early French Colonies 22
Indian Wars 26
French-English Rivalry 26
British North America 27
The American Revolution 30
Internal Problems 31
Confederation 33
Early Expansion 33
The Prairies 33
The Pacific Coast 34
Into The 20th Century 35
World War I and Beyond 35
World War II and Beyond 38

GEOGRAPHY 41
Arctic Tundra 41
Cordillera 42
Interior Plains 42
Hudson Bay Lowlands 43
Canadian Shield Forest Lands 43
St Lawrence Lowlands 43
Appalachian Region 45

ADVENTURE 46
Fishing 46
Hunting 47
Whale Watching 50
Game Watching 50
Water Sports 51
Horse Riding 54
The North 55
Winter Adventures 55
How To... 55

FACTS FOR THE TRAVELER 58
Getting There 58
Passports and Visas 58
Customs 58
Money 59
Health 59
Getting Around 59
Climate 62
What to Pack 63
National and Business Time 63
Holidays 64
Language 64
Hunting and Fishing Licenses 64
Telephones 65
Electric Current 65
Further Information 65

(preceding pages) Golden hay bales during harvest in Alberta

BRITISH COLUMBIA 67
History 67
Vancouver 68
Victoria 83
Vancouver Island 88
The Interior 93

THE PRAIRIES 100
Alberta 100
Saskatchewan 114
Manitoba 122

THE NORTH 134
Northwest Territories 134
Yukon 149

ONTARIO 155
History 155
Toronto 158
Niagara Falls 169
Ottawa 170
The Province 175

QUEBEC 183
History 183
Montreal 185
Quebec City 198

The Laurentians 203
The Eastern Townships 204
The North Shore 206
The Gaspé Peninsula 210

ATLANTIC CANADA 215
Prince Edward Island 215
New Brunswick 226
Nova Scotia 233
Newfoundland 245

FESTIVALS 259
Old Time Fairs 259
Ethnic Festivals 259
Food Celebrations 259
Seaside Races 263
Rodeos 263
Loggers Contests 266
The Unusual 266
Northern Fairs 266

CANADIAN CUISINE 268

HOTELS 274

USEFUL ADDRESSES 292

RECOMMENDED READING 293

INDEX 296

SPECIAL TOPICS
A Canadian Identity   19
Canadian Indians   23
Northwest Passage   71
The Calgary Stampede   112
Old-Time travel   130
Outdoors in the
    Great White North   136
The Klondike Gold Rush   154
Ontario Rail Journeys   182
Quebecois Culture   189
Vive La Différence   202
Rail Hotels   212
The European Connection   250
Newfies   256
Canadian Sports   264

EXCERPTS
David Donnell on prairie prose   14
Sid Marty on park wardens
    and their wives   28

Frederick Whymper on the
    Yukon winter   148
Peter Kalm on Canadian ladies   197
Stephen Leacock on
    the perfect hostelry   214
Kildare Dobbs on
    running to paradise   236
Mordecai Richler on a
    marriage fiasco   260

MAPS
Canada: physical   56
Canada: climate, population, land
    use, natural vegetation   60
British Columbia   69
Alberta   119
Saskatchewan   123
Manitoba   138
Northwest Territories   150
Yukon   150
Ontario   156
Quebec   186
Prince Edward Island   218
New Brunswick   227
Nova Scotia   240

Introduction

Most of the world knows Canada for its stunning scenery and its outdoor activities. The country's physical attractions are unequalled anywhere. This broad land spanning a quarter of the world's time zones has every variety of landscape, except for extensive deserts and tropical jungles. Here are space and magnificent settings to charm any outdoorsman, photographer or nature lover. But in this land of many peoples, the country's human geography equals its scenic wonders, so the lesser-known urban attractions almost match those of the outdoors.

In the east, Atlantic waves crash against sheer rocky headlands, just as Viking explorers saw them, while in the west, rumbling Pacific surf pounds hard-packed, sandy beaches lined by dense rain forest. Within this immense land, scenic spectacles include thundering Niagara Falls, diamond-blue glaciers creeping down mountainsides, fjords cutting deep and narrow into the coastlines, and the jagged horizon of the Rocky Mountains. So many shimmering lakes splash across the green forests that from the air it looks like a watery maze. The broad central prairies, as vast and awesome as the steppes, veldt or pampas, spread like a gilded sea into the sunset. In Canada, there is room enough to appreciate the land without being crowded in by others.

Canada should be approached as not one but at least six distinct nations. The world's second largest country has such a variety of geography, history and people that it cannot be grasped in even a dozen visits. With its strong sense of regional identity, Canada often seems to be a collection of nations sharing the same currency, post office, public broadcasting system, armed forces and central government.

The Atlantic provinces, among the first settled, retain old-time values and the stolid, serious demeanor of their Gaelic ancestors. Even the major cities, such as Charlottetown, Prince Edward Island, and Moncton, New Brunswick, are small-town quiet, as though comfortably back in the 1950s. (In Newfoundland, always an exception to everything, St John's, the capital, is lively, energetic and as singular as an offshore Ireland.)

Quebec, a distinct social and cultural entity, is the defender of the French civilization in North America, a nation within a nation. Unique in language, architecture, cuisine and customs, it provides Americans, especially, with a convenient vacation substitute for Europe. There is nothing reserved about the warm, lively Quebecois, those 'Latins of the north' whose exuberant spirit infuses the streets of Quebec City and Montreal.

Ontario, the economic, political and cultural giant which regards itself as the heart of the country, is businesslike, conservative, somewhat austere. The values of

(following pages) Toronto's financial district

The Canadian Prairies View of Literature

First of all it has to be anecdotal; ideas don't exist; themes struggle dimly out of accrued material like the shadow of a slow caterpillar struggling out of a large cocoon; even this image itself is somewhat urban inasmuch as it suggests the tree-bordered streets of small southern Ontario towns; towns are alright; Ontario towns are urban; French towns are European; the action should take place on a farm between April and October; nature is quiet during winter; when it snows, there's a lot of it; the poem shimmers in the school-teacher's head like an image of being somewhere else without a railway ticket to return; the novel shifts its haunches in the hot reporter's head and surveys the possible relationship between forms; sometimes the action happens in the beverage rooms and cheap hotels area of a small town that has boomed into a new city; Indians and Metis appear in the novel wearing the marks of their alienation like a sullen confusion of the weather; the town drunk appears looking haggard and the town mayor out ward-heeling and smelling women's hands buys him a drink; a woman gets married and another woman has a child; the child is not old enough to plow a field and therefore does not become a focus of interest except as another mouth; they sit around with corn shucks in the head and wonder who they should vote for, the question puzzles them, vote for the one with the cracked shoes, he's a good boy, or the one who jumped over six barrels at a local dance; the fewer buildings they have, the more nationalistic they become like a man who has stolen all his life accused of cheating; above all, they dislike the east which at least gives them form and allows their musings and

discontents to flower into rancour; musing and rancourous, I turn down the small side streets of Galt, Ontario, afternoon light, aged twelve, past South Water Street, not quite like Rimbaud leaving Charleville, my hands in my windbreaker pockets like white stones, and promise myself once again that when I get to the city everything will happen, I will learn all of its history and become the best writer they have ever dreamed of, I'll make them laugh and I'll even make them cry, I'll drink all their whiskey and make love to all their wives, the words tumbling out of my mouth as articulate as the young Hector, the corn under my shirt awkward a little rough light brown dry and making me itch at times.

David Donnell

the United Empire Loyalists, who remained true to the British crown during the American Revolution, still set the tone in this bastion of the Canadian establishment. Despite claiming to be Canada's cultural center, Ontario has its most rigorous censorship, and frets over the perceived evils of Sunday shopping, long after most of the country has adopted it.

A hearty, outgoing friendliness characterizes the western provinces, which many Americans find most familiar to their own open, cordial style. The prairie provinces in particular are Canada's least British, least formal region. Even its sophisticated cities exude a fresh, vigorous pioneer attitude.

British Columbia, blocked by the Rockies, developed later than, and separately from, the rest of the country, and it shows. Vancouver is a more West Coast American than Canadian city. The Pacific province is the the country's most unconventional. Here, social aberrations appear first, are more extreme and last longest. Even the politics, which attract the extremes of right and left to the endless amusement of the rest of Canada, borders on the bizarre. Victoria, the westernmost city and the capital, is an exception, an enclave of tea-sipping, crumpet-crumbling royalists.

Canada's northern territories, the Yukon and the Northwest Territories, are the size of Europe—with a population that would snugly fit into a domed football stadium. To northerners—rough, tough pioneer types in the most rugged climate inhabited by man—all southern Canadians are effete wimps.

Despite its great chunk of real estate, Canada is largely an urban country. More than 70 per cent of the population live in cities that are safe and often lively, with attractive shops, restaurants, theaters and nightlife.

Canada's cities, especially, have a rich ethnic diversity. Canada, perhaps the least homogeneous of all English (and French) -speaking countries, boasts of its 'cultural mosaic', unlike the melting pot to the south. One UN report claimed that Toronto was the world's most cosmopolitan city, and visitors frequently remark on the variety of human form they encounter across Canada. Especially in the larger cities, immigrant groups—Italian, German, Ukrainian, Dutch, Portuguese, Greek, Chinese, Indian, Jewish and many others—add their language, cuisine and culture to that vague and still developing entity that is Canada.

In recent years, the original inhabitants, the many different groups of native Indians and Inuit, have become more visible across the country. Distinctive native paintings, carvings and crafts are displayed in museums and sold in galleries in major cities. Native dancing and music are performed during festivals and celebrations, while Indian activists have become politically vocal, particularly concerning land claims.

With its sparse population spread over a vast area, its great variety of people and its powerful neighbor, perhaps Canadians have not evolved a clearly distinctive national

(preceding pages) Quebec City's lively Winter Carnival swirls around a snow palace sculpture

A Canadian Identity

The overwhelming economic and cultural influence comes from across the border. The benign, but overpowering, giant neighbor, the US, is a dominant force on all aspects of Canadian life—and this influence has increased with a new Free Trade Agreement with the US introduced in 1989.

Culturally, living next to the world's most dynamic, powerful nation has its drawbacks. If young people from Tehran to Tokyo wear Levis and T-shirts and listen to rock'n'roll, a young nation one-tenth the size across the 'world's longest undefended border.' can hardly resist assimilation.

As former Prime Minister Pierre Trudeau said in a speech in Washington, DC in 1969: 'Living next to you is in some ways like sleeping with an elephant; no matter how friendly and even-tempered the beast, one is affected by every twitch and grunt.'

Yet there are substantial differences between the two countries, and anyone who notices no changes when crossing the border is simply unobservant. Canadians are generally quieter, less aggressive, less excitable and more reserved. There is a certain social gentility and less crime (Urban Americans are astonished to see people walking the streets at nights in Canada's largest cities).

A newsman once observed that Canada is like vichyssoise; cold, half French and difficult to stir. A Canadian Broadcasting Corporation television crew examining the Canadian character supposedly approached a man on the street in downtown Toronto.

'We understand that Canadians are apathetic.' they said. The man thought about it, shrugged, and said, 'Who cares?'

Canada's cultural contributions tend to get swallowed up into a kind of Northern American blend. The temptation for a Canadian artist, writer, musician or performer to step across the border, where wealth and acclaim await, is irresistible. With the differences in accents only discernible to other North Americans, the world sees them all as American. In fact, many popular 'American' cultural figures are Canadian.

Curiously, Canada has long supplied father figures to the US, men of quiet authority such as Lorne Greene's Ben 'Pa' Cartwright of the TV series *Bonanza*, Raymond Burr's Perry Mason and William Shatner's Captain Kirk of *Star Trek*. Canada also provides the US with many of its fantasy figures. Joe Shuster conceived of Superman while working at the *Toronto Star*, and in the earlier stories, Clark Kent worked for the *Daily Star*, not the *Daily Planet*. More recently, the ultimate American hero Rambo came from the novel *First Blood* by David Morrell, of Kitchener, Ontario. (Coincidentally, the first Rambo movie was filmed outside Vancouver, BC, with stars and stripes bunting displayed to make it look American).

Traffic signs in Riveriere-du-Loup, Quebec, come in both official languages

personality. But lacking such national traits, they tend to be more individualistic—one reason why Canadian travelers do not gather in clans overseas like so many others.

Although Canadians supposedly brood over their 'identity', this is mainly a harmless intellectual exercise of underemployed journalists, tenured academics and bored bureaucrats. You will travel far and wide in the country, visiting cafes, coffee shops, beer halls and bars, without running into the confused Canadian staring into his drink, wondering 'Who am I?' Yukon-born author Peter Berton's observation, that a Canadian is someone who knows how to make love in a canoe, is as good as any of the weightier pronouncements.

Canadians complain that their American neighbors, and the rest of the world, know so little about them. When Chicago mobster and bootlegger Al Capone said 'I don't even know what street Canada is on', he was only kidding. Because good news is no news, this peaceful, non-violent country rarely makes international headlines—yet these characteristics make it a desirable place to live and visit.

Finally, very few Canadians have seen all ten provinces, and only the more adventurous have been to the Great White North. When visiting Canada, restrict your travel to one or two regions. Then you have good reason to come back and see the rest.

History

To understand Canada, think of it not as one country, but as several separate nations co-existing in reasonable harmony. Canadian history does not have a single, cohesive pattern, but is a patchwork of separate stories. Different peoples in disparate and widely separated regions developed along unrelated lines, only coming together as a nation a century ago. In fact, the borders were not set until 1949 when Newfoundland joined the country. Canada remains a somewhat Balkanized nation of competing ethnic groups and regions that seems to survive and prosper almost despite itself. It is this great variety of peoples and places that makes Canada so interesting and lively.

The First Inhabitants

Prehistoric Asians crossed to North America over the land bridge that is now the Bering Strait perhaps 25,000 years ago. Gradually moving south, these people developed advanced, distinct cultures long before the coming of the Europeans. An estimated 250,000 of their descendants, the Indians and Eskimos (now more commonly called Inuit in Canada) occupied what is now Canada when the Europeans arrived.

The impact of the Europeans, who began arriving in Canada in the 18th century, was rapid, drastic and near fatal to the native people and their cultures. The late Canadian actor and Indian spokesman, Chief Dan George, emotionally described their plight: 'My culture is like a wounded deer that has crawled away to the forest to bleed and to die alone.'

The Viking Interlude

According to Norse Sagas, Leif Ericson reached Vinland, a legendary place where grapes grew somewhere along the Atlantic Coast, in about AD 1000. Certainly the Vikings were the first Europeans to reach North America, arriving 500 years before Christopher Columbus, by way of the Faeroes, Iceland and Greenland.

The roving Norsemen established a settlement at L'Anse-aux-Meadows in what is now northern Newfoundland and explored far to the south, perhaps to present-day New England. However, they suffered from the long, harsh winters and harassment from the Indians. Viking attempts to found permanent colonies failed, and they had no influence on the New World.

The First Europeans

Some historians believe that Basques and Englishmen fished the North Atlantic off Canada as early as the 14th century. However, exploration did not begin in earnest until the late 1400s when adventurous mariners, aided by European governments, came in search of the Northwest Passage, a fabled route to the riches of the East (see page 71).

Italian explorer John Cabot, sailing under the British flag, is often credited with being the first European to sight Canada. In the summer of 1497, Cabot landed on a beach in either Cape Breton Island or Labrador, claiming the 'new-found land' for England. Although he did not find the passage (it does not exist), his voyages inspired new explorations, established England's claim to North America and led to the opening of the North Atlantic Grand Banks, one of the world's most fertile fishing grounds. English, French, Spanish and Portuguese fishing fleets were soon making huge profits from Grand Banks cod, but England, the most aggressive, soon controlled the rich fishing grounds, justifying its authority in part because of Cabot's discoveries.

Early French Colonies

In 1534, explorer Jacques Cartier landed on Prince Edward Island, which he named Ile Ste Jean, and on the Gaspé Peninsula. Following what he thought was the ever-elusive Northwest Passage, he sailed down the St Lawrence River as far as present-day Montreal, claiming the area for France. Cartier called it *kanata,* the Huron-Iroquois word for settlement or village. For decades after Cartier's discoveries, France largely ignored the New World. But when King Francis II started the craze for felt hats, hatters needed a new source for beaver, for long the most valuable of all furs, and Canada had plenty of beaver. The beaver is today Canada's national emblem.

France established commercial monopolies to promote colonization in return for control of the lucrative fur trade. In the early 17th century, these companies established trade settlements in Acadia (Nova Scotia) and at Quebec City.

Samuel de Champlain, explorer, cartographer and writer, and the Father of New France, was the major force in Canada's early history. In 1603 he traveled up the St Lawrence as far as Montreal Island, writing a detailed account of the countryside. The following year, he joined an expedition to establish a trading outpost in Acadia (now Nova Scotia, New Brunswick and Maine). After a disastrous first winter on an island on the St Croix River where many of the colonists died, the survivors moved to a better location on the Bay of Fundy. Port Royal (now Annapolis Royal, Nova Scotia) became the first permanent European settlement in Canada.

CANADIAN INDIANS

Eastern woodlands Indians, the Algonquin-and Iroquoian-speaking tribal groups, inhabited the forested lands stretching from the Maritimes to Ontario in the St Lawrence Valley and around the Great Lakes. These warlike people were hunters, trappers, fishermen, gatherers and farmers. They lived in palisaded villages of rectangular, bark longhouses seven meters (23 feet) wide and up to 90 meters (295 feet) long. Extensive cultivated fields of beans, corn and squash surrounded these semi-permanent fortified farm settlements which were moved every ten to 15 years when soil and firewood were exhausted.

Transportation through the forests was by birchbark canoe, snowshoe and toboggan. Woodlands Indians dressed in deerskins and furs decorated in quill-work and beads and with moosehair embroidery in colorful floral motifs on black-dyed hides.

Nomadic, militant Plains Indians—Blackfoot, Blood, Cree, Assiniboine and others—were hunters, foragers and warriors. Horse raiding was the most common form of intertribal warfare. They roamed the prairies from the North Saskatchewan River as far south as Texas in search of the great buffalo herds, stalking and killing them with bow and arrow or stampeding them over steep cliffs.

Plains Indians lived off the buffalo, drying and pounding the meat into pemmican (a preserved staple of ground meat, fat and berries). They made robes, moccasins and shields from the skins, and tools and utensils from the horns, hooves and bones. These are the Indians that Hollywood depicts, living in teepees (large conical birch-bark or buffalo-hide tents) and dressing in brightly decorated buffalo- and deer-skin clothing. They embellished fringed deer-hide moccasins, jackets, dresses, leggings and shirts with porcupine quillwork, beads and feathers and painted buffalo robes with abstract, or representational, images. Teepees, which took up to 40 buffalo hides, were often lavishly painted with naturalistic or geometric images.

Life was easier for Pacific Coast tribes such as the Tlingit, Salish, Nootka, Tsimshian, Haida and Kwakiutl. The climate was relatively mild and food plentiful. There were deer, elk and mountain goat in the forests, shellfish, seals, whales and porpoises in the sea and plentiful salmon in the many rivers flowing into the Pacific. With more leisure time, the coastal tribes developed a rich culture, and North America's finest indigenous art—considered by anthropologists such as Claude Levi-Strauss to equal that of Greece and Rome. Especially impressive were visual arts, the cedar carvings of totem poles, ceremonial dishes, masks and longhouse doors.

Coast Indians lived communally in huge, ornate post-and-beam longhouses covered by split cedar planks, constructed and decorated in distinctive regional styles. Giant dugout war canoes provided transportation on the rivers and the open sea.

In 1608 de Champlain established a settlement at Quebec. From this base, he created an extensive trading network by forming alliances with tribes such as the Hurons. While this was good business, it later involved New France in the bloody Indian wars (see below).

Champlain was determined to make Quebec the center of a thriving colony. Back in France, he convinced Louis XIII's ambitious chief minister Cardinal Richelieu of the importance of North America to French colonial ambitions. In 1627, the Cardinal founded the Company of One Hundred Associates to create a French empire based in Quebec. Under this short-lived company, and later the Community of Habitants (1645–63), New France took its own distinct shape, based on European feudalism, along the banks of the St Lawrence.

Although the French government encouraged emigration (Catholic of course, the Protestant Huguenots were forbidden to settle), growth was slow. Settlements were founded at Trois Rivières in 1634 and Montreal in 1642. Although originally a missionary colony, Montreal quickly shed its sacred role to replace Quebec City as the fur trade center. Montreal remained Canada's commercial center until Toronto replaced it in the middle of this century.

While many immigrants remained as habitants down on the farm, hundreds of young men disappeared for years to trade with Indians far in the interior. This was a period of tremendous energy, of one of the world's great ages of exploration. From the late 17th century, *coureurs des bois* (literally, runners of the woods), adventurous, illegal fur traders working outside company restrictions, set out across the continent in search of furs and freedom.

Traveling mainly by canoe, these merchant-adventurers explored and traded as far west as the Rocky Mountains and south to the Gulf of Mexico. Pierre Radisson and his brother-in-law Medard Chouart Des Groseilliers traveled far beyond Lake Superior where they heard of the Bay of the North Sea. Unable to interest the French in this quicker, cheaper route to Europe which eliminated the long canoe trip from Lake Superior to Montreal, 'Radish and Gooseberry' (as the English called them) sold the idea to London merchants, and changed the course of Canada's history. The 45-ton ketch *Nonsuch* sailed into Hudson Bay in 1668, returning the next year with a rich load of furs. In 1670, the Hudson's Bay Company was formed to trade for furs, outflanking the French to the north.

To the south, Louis Jolliet and Father Jacques Marquette discovered the Mississippi in 1673 and Robert Cavalier de La Salle named and claimed Louisiana for King Louis XIV in 1682, thus encircling the New England states. In the early 18th century, the La Verendrye family explored and set up trading posts over much of the Prairies. In 1742, while searching for a fabled 'western sea', two La Verendrye brothers were the first white men to see the Rocky Mountains, somewhere in present-day Montana.

Totem poles are the most dramatic forms of West Coast Indian art

Indian Wars

New France's early years were marked by bloody conflict with the Indians. Champlain made allies with the Algonquins and Hurons, who accepted the missionaries and became partners in the fur trade.

To the south, the Hurons' traditional rival, the Iroquois confederation, was aligned with the Dutch in New Amsterdam and later the English who supplied them with guns. The fierce Iroquois attacked fur convoys en route to Quebec and the French settlements. In 1649, while almost annihilating the Hurons, they tortured and killed several Jesuit missionaries. They then turned on the French settlers, nearly overrunning Montreal in 1660 and threatening the colony's existence.

In 1663, King Louis XIV and his finance minister Jean Baptiste Colbert reorganized it as a crown colony instead of a private trading enterprise. Control was placed under a military governor and an intendant based in Quebec City, under orders from Paris. The 1,100 strong Carignan-Salieres regiment sent out in 1665 built a series of forts and finally quelled the Iroquois. When the regiment was recalled to France in 1668, some 400 officers and men remained as settlers, thus strengthening the colony's defenses and economy.

Attempts to make it a self-sufficient rival to the British colonies failed despite increased immigration and a diversification of the economy. New France remained almost medieval, with no representative government and all authority under the governor, intendant and bishop.

French-English Rivalry

By the late 17th century, North America was settled like a pioneer's patchwork quilt, with rivalries between New France and New England reflecting those of the mother countries in Europe. The period from 1689 to 1815 was one of almost constant warfare in North America, part of a global struggle affecting Europe, the West Indies, India and the Pacific. King William's war (1689–97) was followed by Queen Anne's war (1702–13), and the King George's war (1739–48), with the English launching raids against the French in both Acadia and Quebec.

In the 1713 Treaty of Utrecht, Britain won recognition of its claim to the Hudson Bay region, Newfoundland and Acadia, while France retained Ile Royale (Cape Breton Island) and Ile Saint Jean (now Prince Edward Island).

To retain a foothold on the Atlantic, the French built the massive Louisbourg fortress in Cape Breton. In 1745, during King George's war, a joint British-New

England force took the fort with the aid of the Royal Navy. Three years later, it was returned to France at the Peace of Aix-la-Chapelle, to the dismay of its captors.

By the crucial French and Indian War, an extension of Europe's Seven Years' War (1756–63), France had refurbished Louisbourg, built a series of forts in the Ohio Valley and made new treaties with Indian tribes. But New France had a small population and France dispatched only token reinforcements against Britain's considerable military and naval forces. When Anglo-French hostilities broke out in the Ohio Valley in 1754, the British sent more than 23,000 troops to North America.

Four years later, they again conquered Louisbourg, gaining control over the sea approaches to the St Lawrence River, and to New France. In June the following year Major-General James Wolfe sailed up the river to Quebec City with a large force of 9,000 men. Although British artillery shelled the lower town for weeks, the well-placed citadel and upper town, protected by steep, high cliffs, proved a strategic stronghold. By September, the besieged French were running out of provisions while the British feared being trapped by the icy river throughout the winter.

One dark night, Wolfe, with about 4,000 soldiers, rowed past French river patrols to a point west behind the city and crept up the cliffs in the dark. On the morning of September 13, 1759, the British general assembled his troops on the Plains of Abraham. Montcalm rushed his forces out of the fortified citadel to confront the British, but the battle was over in half an hour. Both generals lost their lives in perhaps Canadian history's most famous battle. Although there were other battles later, this marked the end of France as a force in North America.

Montreal surrendered to a British fleet in 1760, and by the Treaty of Paris (1763), the British finally controlled New France.

British North America

After the Treaty of Paris, British North America (BNA) consisted of several distinct areas. Sparsely populated Newfoundland was a string of unconnected fishing villages; the west and north, known as Rupert's Land and the North-West Territory, was a vast, largely unpopulated but fur-rich area run by the Hudson's Bay Company; Acadia was populated mostly by New Englanders, with some immigrants from Britain, following the expulsion of the original settlers, the French-speaking Acadians, in the 18th century. New France, still dominated by French settlers, became the fourth distinct region of British North America.

In the Quebec Act of 1774, Britain placed authority for the colony in the hands of a governor and appointed council while maintaining the Quebecois' traditional language, civil law and religion. The act allowed Roman Catholics to hold civil office

A Good Woman is Hard to Find

So one May morning I sat in an office in Calgary across the table from three careful and dedicated men. Two of them asked irrelevant questions about the life cycle of the hoary wood bat. The other, veteran Chief Park Warden Mickey McGuire, said nothing, but listened carefully, while looking me over as if he would have loved to examine my teeth and hooves.

'Which theory do you think Parks Canada should be following?' one of the two asked me, 'for the purpose of managing the environment? The evolutionary concept, with all its unpredictable connotations? Or a more dynamic approach, with active manipulation of the ecosystem?' And he settled back in his chair.

'That's a good question,' I began, and tried to fend it off as best I could. It was a good question, because nobody in the entire parks service had the slightest idea how to answer it. McGuire gave me a grim smile. He had decided to rescue me.

'In other words,' he began ironically, 'in other words, if you looked out the window of the Athabasca Hotel and saw a fire coming for town at about thirty miles per hour down the side of Tekarra Mountain, would you throw a bucket of water at it, or order another round?'

The other two interrogators stirred uncomfortably in their chairs.

'I like to keep things simple,' said Mickey, nodding his grey-haired head. Then he asked a few questions about my work in Yoho Park, while he leafed through my application form.

'I see that you're a married man now', he said. 'You know, if I had my way, I'd have the wives in here with the man at these interviews. No sense hiring a man if his wife doesn't like the bush.'

One of the bureaucrats cleared his throat with impatience. The Chief Warden had made a heretical statement, since under the new system of centralization, wardens and their wives were supposed to be moved out of the backcountry and into town. Their wives no longer had to have the slightest interest in the backcountry. But this chief Warden fought the new system every step of the way and in his park there were still wardens living in the backcountry districts, which suited me fine.

'Does your wife ride?' he asked.

'Yes,' I answered cautiously. After all, he never asked what.

'Can she shoot straight?'

'Like Annie Oakley.'

'Split wood?'

'She's deadly with an axe,' I answered.

'I don't see the point. . . ,' one of the others put in, but Mickey silenced him with a distasteful glance and turned back to me.

'Kid, it's always entertaining to be bullshitted by an expert. But, tell me the truth now. Is she a city girl? Would she like living in the bush?'

'She's right off the farm,' I told him, stretching the truth by about six years. 'She loves wood-stoves. She likes cold weather, prefers it to hot. She's one of those people who likes to get wet in the rain. She likes the wind on her face. Loves to hike, ski, ride, you name it. She's strong and she's tough.' And this was all true.

Mickey eyed me with new respect and sat back in his chair, considering. Then he shot forward as if to catch me off guard.

'How tall is she?'

I wondered what this had to do with anything, but answered honestly. 'Five foot ten.'

McGuire was impressed. 'Good,' he grinned. 'She'll be able to carry waterpails over the snow drifts without spilling them.'

The interview was over and a few days later I got a letter telling me the job was mine. Somehow, though, I got the impression that my shrewd choice of a mate had at least as much to do with my success as my knowledge of ecology or my previous experience.

Sid Marty, Men For The Mountains

and collect tithes while confirming the *seigneurial* landholding system. It also won a degree of loyalty, if not affection, from the French-Canadians.

By the late 18th century, Britain's 13 original North American colonies had grown strong enough to question the authority of the Mother Country. However, both Nova Scotia and Quebec declined invitations to attend the first Continental Congress in Philadelphia in 1774. While the 13 colonies declared their independence to form the United States of America, these two remained part of Britain. For the first time, the two countries became distinct entities.

The American Revolution

In their revolutionary fervor, the Americans believed that the two northern colonies would gladly join them in seeking independence. Feeling themselves liberators rather than conquerors, an American army marched to Canada. In November 1775, the Americans captured Montreal and Trois Rivières but were defeated trying to take Quebec and their army was forced to retreat.

The most important effect of the American Revolution was the mass migration of some 50,000 United Empire Loyalists into Nova Scotia and the upper St Lawrence valley. While many were genuinely loyal to the crown, others were attracted by the free land offered. The areas they settled developed quickly, changing the political as well as physical nature of the country as the new settlers soon began agitating for rights they had enjoyed in the American colonies.

In response to Loyalist demands, Britain created New Brunswick out of Nova Scotia in 1784. In 1791 Quebec was split into mainly French-speaking Lower Canada and English-speaking Upper Canada, now Ontario. In the following decades, more immigrants from the US, Britain, and Scotland (refugees from the 'clearances' of the highlands) arrived. Farms, towns, industries and cultural institutions such as schools and universities developed. The economic base widened, with timber and grain added to fur and fish as important exports. Throughout this period, the country was ruled largely by an established aristocracy of rich merchants.

Peace had not yet come to North America. For several reasons, including British interference with American shipping on the high seas, the US declared war on Britain in June 1812 and struck at its closest possession, Canada. The Americans burned York (Toronto) and Newark (Niagara-on-the-Lake). In retaliation, the British torched Buffalo, New York and Washington, DC

Although badly outnumbered, Canadians rallied round the British to repel America in the War of 1812–14. The Americans were more successful in naval battles on the Great Lakes, and the Treaty of Ghent on December 24, 1814, ended the conflict.

While nothing was resolved, the War of 1812 gave Canada its first real sense of community and identity.

Minor skirmishes continued for several decades until the boundaries were finally set between Maine and Canada (Quebec and New Brunswick) in 1842. From then, the two nations could proclaim the cliché about sharing the world's longest undefended border.

Internal Problems

With the fears of war reduced, Canada's attention turned inward; during the 1820s, agitation for political reform increased and the powerful Anglican ruling class was challenged.

The Rebellions of 1837 were two separate conflicts. In Quebec, it marked a resurgent French-Canadian nationalism, with the francophone middle class challenging the power of the established Roman Catholic church in education and the growing anglophone merchant class in business and politics.

In 1837, the Parti Patriote under lawyer and politician Louis-Joseph Papineau launched a short-lived uprising. British troops crushed the Patriotes in several small skirmishes and Papineau fled to the US. In six battles, more than 300 people, mainly rebels, were killed. Papineau, who lived in exile in Paris for a time before returning home, remains a hero to many Quebec nationalists.

The Upper Canada rebellion was a more limited, almost comic-opera, affair. In this colony, a small Church of England group controlled the government. The Reform Party, under a hot-headed Scots journalist William Lyon Mackenzie, turned from debate, boycotts and public protest to open rebellion over political and economic grievances.

From December 5 to 8, about 1,000 men gathered at Toronto's Montgomery's tavern. On December 5, more than 500 of them bearing rifles, staves and pitchforks marched on Toronto where they encountered a force of about 20 Loyalists. After a confused confrontation and exchange of gunfire, both sides fled. Casualties were two rebels, one loyalist. After another small outbreak a few days later, the 'rebellion' collapsed, and Mackenzie fled to the US.

The following year, American supporters marched on Canada, and though the border raids were once more repelled, the US and Britain came close to war.

The zealots had failed, but moderates continued to push for reform. Following a report urging the reunification of Upper and Lower Canada and economic changes, the British Parliament passed the Act of Union in 1840, the first step to self rule. Responsible government, with Canadian control over domestic affairs, came in 1848.

SACRED
To the Memory of
HERBERT MAYNARD
Who Departed this
Life on the 30th Day
of Novemder 1816 at
the Innocent and
Interesting Age of four
Years Eight Months
and Eight Days

Confederation

Partly motivated by a fear of US military and economic action following the Civil War (Britain openly supported the south), and hoping to strengthen the colonies, both the Colonial Office and Canadian politicians agitated for a unification of all of British North America. In September 1864, provincial representatives met in the Charlottetown Province House to discuss union, and by July 1, 1867 the British North America Act had created the Dominion of Canada. At this time, Prince Edward Island and Newfoundland refused to join.

The frail, divisive and disparate country included a mere 3.7 million people (compared to 40 million Americans), mainly French and Irish Catholics, and English, Scottish and Irish Protestants. Immigrants from Germany, Switzerland and other European countries who arrived throughout the 19th century moved the country towards greater cultural diversity. The only real cities were Halifax, Toronto, Montreal and Quebec, there was a limited, though growing, rail and canal communications systems and a lot of empty real estate. Its future was certainly not guaranteed.

Early Expansion

The late 19th century was a period of nation building, of binding these parts together, and of rapid expansion. The first leader, Conservative Sir John A Macdonald (prime minister from 1867 to 1873 and 1878 to 1891), was one of Canada's most important political figures, and one of its great visionary characters. His greatest achievements were in promoting western settlement and a transcontinental railway to link Canada to the Pacific and bring British Columbia into the fold. By purchasing Rupert's Land and the North-West Territory from the Hudson's Bay Company in 1870, partly to block further American expansion, he extended Canada's control as far as the Arctic.

Manitoba became a province in 1870; British Columbia, somewhat unwillingly, in 1871; and Prince Edward Island in 1873. However, violence marred Canada's spread to the west as resentful Metis people already living on the Prairies twice revolted against the eastern government.

The Prairies

At the time of confederation, the Prairies were the domain of Indians and Metis (mixed European-Indians, many being French-speaking Catholics) who lived off the

Early pioneers lie buried in St Paul's cemetery, Halifax

great buffalo herds. They felt they formed a separate nation which was threatened by the land purchase, the advancement of a rail line and the arrival of settlers from Ontario in their traditional hunting lands.

In 1869, government surveyors began mapping the Red River Valley, a major crossroads, while ignoring the 6,000 Metis already living along the banks. The Metis declared a provisional government, touching off the Red River Rebellion of 1869–70. Led by Louis Riel, the Metis took Fort Garry at the juncture of the Red and Assiniboine rivers where Winnipeg now stands.

When Macdonald sent a joint British-Canadian army west to restore peace, Riel escaped to Montana and the rebellion collapsed with little violence. The federal government created the province of Manitoba in 1870, with French language and cultural rights guaranteed. Today, Manitoba is a distinct western province, with a strong French flavor.

Conscious of the bloody Indian wars in the American West, Canada signed treaties with the natives, gaining control of their lands by the end of the 1870s. The new North-West Mounted Police (NWMP), the red-coated paramilitary force that became the Royal Canadian Mounted Police, maintained the peace. Generally, in the Canadian west, law and order preceded the settlers, which made for a less exciting, but less violent, history.

It wasn't all peaceful, though. The arrival of thousands of homesteaders seeking free land again provoked the Metis, many of whom had moved from Manitoba to northern Saskatchewan. Louis Riel returned from Montana to lead another attack, the short-lived North-West Rebellion.

The government in Ottawa acted quickly, mobilizing a militia and dispatching it west on the almost completed railway. The Metis were outnumbered and armed only with primitive rifles against light artillery and a new weapon used for the first time in war, the machine gun (a Gatling gun). On May 12, at the Battle at Batoche, the army overran Metis defenders who were reduced to firing nails and stones out of their rifles, and the rebellion was crushed. Louis Riel was hanged in Regina on November 16, 1885, which outraged French-Canadians from Manitoba to Quebec and the Maritimes.

The Pacific Coast

In the far west, meanwhile, what is now British Columbia was developing as a separate colony far removed from Canadian events. English explorer Captain James Cook landed on Nootka on the west of Vancouver Island in 1778, and in 1792 Captain George Vancouver explored and charted the coast. British merchants came by sea to trade for furs with the coastal Indians, thousands of miles from their counterparts farther east. For many years, the coast, of interest only to these traders, was controlled by the Hudson's Bay Company. Meanwhile, European explorers and traders were also approaching the Pacific overland from the east. In 1793, Alexander Mackenzie of the North West Company (Hudson's Bay Company's main rivals) was the first European to reach the interior of the province and cross the Rocky Mountains to the Pacific. Other North West Company members followed him into the interior. The Hudson's Bay Company (which merged with the North West Company in 1821) controlled all of the west as far as present-day Washington and Oregon. The Oregon Treaty in 1846 set the border at the 49th parallel.

The discovery of gold on the Fraser River in 1857 rapidly changed that, with fortune seekers pouring in from around the world—particularly from the California gold fields. The population rapidly expanded, as prospectors moved inland along the rivers, throwing together tent camps and shack boomtowns. The British established the colony of British Columbia in 1858, merging it with the island in 1866. In 1871, the 12,000 white residents reluctantly agreed to join the new confederation on the condition that the federal government begin building a railway linking it to the east within two years and complete it within ten. Constructing the Canadian Pacific Railway (CPR) across the Canadian Shield and Prairies and over the Rockies to the coast was a major engineering feat. On November 7, 1887, the western and eastern lines met and Canada at last stretched, as its motto says, *A mari usque ad mare*, from sea to sea.

Into The 20th Century

Under French-Canadian lawyer Sir Wilfred Laurier (prime minister from 1896 to 1911), Canada grew and prospered. Offers of free land in the Prairies attracted homesteaders from Britain, Europe, Eastern Canada and even the US, where available land was rapidly running out. In 1901, the federal government issued a booklet to entice immigrants, romantically titled The Last Best West. Alberta and Saskatchewan became provinces in 1905.

World War I And Beyond

Considering its size, Canada made a major contribution to 'the war to end all wars.' A country of just eight million people spent $1.67 billion and raised an armed force of more than 600,000, first under British, and later Canadian, command. Canadian

(following pages) The Coast Mountains loom over Vancouver, BC

Expeditionary Force (CEF) casualties were 48,000, and Canadian army action in battles such as Passchendaele and Vimy Ridge became part of the country's mythology.

There were political costs at home as well, with many French-Canadians resentful of fighting what they saw as Britain's war. Military conscription became a bitter issue in the election of 1917, with every French-Canadian member of parliament opposed to it and most English-speaking MPs in favor. The Military Service Act was passed in 1917 and 124,000 men were conscripted. By the end of the war, the CEF, which started as a colonial contingent under the British Army, became Canada's national army. The war increased Canada's presence in foreign affairs and its sense of national identity. The country participated in the Paris Peace Conference on its own rather than represented by Britain.

In the inter-war years Canada took further steps toward full autonomy under Liberal Prime Minister William Lyon Mackenzie King, the most influential, lasting Canadian politician of the mid-20th century. King demanded that Canada have full control of its domestic and foreign policies, and that Britain and her dominions be constitutionally equal. This was achieved at the Imperial Conference of 1926 and confirmed by the British Statute of Westminster in 1931. Power to amend the Canadian Constitution remained with the British parliament until passage of the Constitution Act in 1982. The worldwide depression of the 1930s was made even worse by a dreadful drought on the Prairies and a dramatic drop in grain prices. By 1933 some 20 per cent of the population was unemployed, and men took to riding the rails across the country. Memories of the 'Dirty Thirties' still haunt older Canadians. World War II finally ended the depression that several governments were unable to control.

World War II And Beyond

Although, like the US, Canada was isolationist throughout the 1930s, when Britain declared war on Germany in 1939 it followed suit a week later. Again, the contributions were considerable for a nation so removed from Europe. Expenditure reached some $2 billion, and of a population of just 12 million, 1.5 million served in the armed forces. More than 42,500 Canadians died in the war.

Following the war, a period in which it had taken a higher profile in international politics, Canada again entered a period of prosperity. The economy diversified, manufacturing expanded and modernized. Also in 1949, Newfoundland voted by a very narrow margin to become Canada's tenth province. And, while links with Britain gradually weakened, Canada became increasingly tied to the US economically and culturally.

Canada also became more active in foreign affairs. In 1941, it joined the North Atlantic Treaty Organization (NATO), and fought in the Korean war (1950–3). Its main international influence was as a 'middle power' peacemaker. During the Suez Crisis in 1956, Canada proposed a United Nations Emergency Force. Canadian troops participated in UN peacekeeping actions in the Middle East and Africa. Also throughout the 1960s and 70s Liberal Prime Minister Pierre Trudeau was recognized internationally, where he was more popular than at home.

In the latter part of the 20th century, Canadian politics remain as divisive, confusing and entertaining as always. French-Canadian separatism resurged as a major threat to Confederation during the 1960s, abated, then grew again by the end of the 1980s.

In October 1970, following several kidnapings by the terrorist Front de Libération du Québec (FLQ), the Quebec government requested the Canadian Armed Forces to assist local police. Canadians, so accustomed to living in an orderly society, were shocked by the sight of armed soldiers on Quebec's streets. On October 16, Trudeau, a forceful leader, proclaimed a temporary state of 'apprehended insurrection' under the War Measures Act, banning the FLQ, suspending civil liberties and detaining more than 450 suspects. While civil libertarians and editorial writers were appalled, a large majority of Canadians, including Quebecois, supported the strong reaction. They point to the disappearance of terrorism in Quebec as proof of its success.

Although the province voted 'non' to separatism in a 1980 referendum, this did not mark the end of Quebec nationalism—the provincial government vowed to prevent what many Quebecois fear as the erosion of French language and culture in North America. As the decade of the 80s neared an end, disputes arose over a number of issues, such as Quebec's and the federal government's interpretation of abortion rights, and especially over language and education issues. In 1989, in a controversial move, Quebec introduced an 'inside-outside' sign law; business signs must be French on the outside, but could be bilingual on the inside, provided the French lettering was larger. As usual, the compromise pleased no one, and squabbling continued. However, these disputes were largely on a political and business level, and personal relations between French and English remained civil and without rancor.

Canada faced another crisis in the summer of 1991 when the Meech Lake constitutional agreement, which recognised Quebec as a 'distinct society', was defeated. Against the opposition of most Canadians, who were ignored when the agreement was drawn up, Prime Minister Brian Mulroney attempted to push it through. When two provinces, Manitoba and Newfoundland, refused to ratify the agreement, the future of Canada seemed once more thrown open to debate.

Once again, the country survived the 'crises', although Mulroney and his once-powerful Conservatives did not. In the 1993 general election, the ruling party was destroyed, winning only two seats in the entire country.

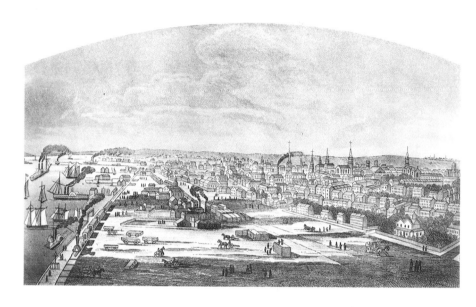

City of Toronto, from a cleared space on the Esplanade near the Don river,
engraving, 1869, courtesy of the National Archives of Canada

That election saw a resurgence of Quebec nationalism, and regionalism, reflected in the success of the Bloc Québecois and the Western-based Reform Party. But in the crucial September 12, 1994 Quebec provincial elections, the separatist Parti Québecois (PQ) won with just 44.7% of the vote compared to 44.3% for the Liberal Party. The Liberals claimed a moral victory, while the PQ said it was a step towards independence for the province. Quebec politics remained as equivocal and entertaining as ever. Meanwhile, an unpopular Free Trade Agreement (later expanded to NAFTA, the North American Free Trade Agreement, with the US and Mexico) bound the American and Canadian economies even more closely together.

The mid-1990s is as interesting as ever, with the lively disputes over language, culture and native rights, and another large influx of immigrants, many from Asia and the Caribbean, altering the character of the nation still more. Canada, as a nation, is still not defined.

Geography

'...If some countries have too much history, we have too much geography.' (Prime Minister W. L. Mackenzie King, 1936.)

When it comes to geography, Canada has more than just about any place. The western hemisphere's largest and the world's second largest country (only Russia is bigger), Canada covers nearly ten million square kilometers (3.9 million square miles). This is a country of extremes and a variety of physical features, with vast forests both deciduous and coniferous, jagged mountains, soft hills and bald prairie, fresh and saltwater beaches, and so many lakes that from the air much of the terrain resembles a maze of land and water. Canada has more freshwater lakes and rivers, an important resource, than any other country—about 25 per cent of the planet's total. It shares the Great Lakes, the world's largest body of fresh water, with the US and has 32 other lakes more than 1,300 square kilometers (500 square miles) in area.

The country covers the northern half of the continent, with an irregular, broken coast of almost 240,400 kilometers (150,500 miles) on the Atlantic, Pacific and Arctic oceans. The giant Hudson Bay, an enormous gulf gouging deep into the continent from the northeast, almost forms a separate ocean.

Stretching from its southernmost point at Middle Island in Lake Erie, to Cape Columbia in the north and Ellesmere Island in the Northwest Territories, Canada covers some 4,600 kilometers (2,734 miles). The east-west expanse is even greater: 5,500 kilometers (3,400 miles) from Cape Spear, Newfoundland to the Yukon-Alaska border. Atlantic coast cities are closer to Europe than to West Coast communities, nearer to Caracas, Venezuela, than to Dawson City, Yukon. The enormous scope of the country can only be truly grasped when crossing it by road or rail, or even flying over it tens of thousands of meters up at hundreds of kilometers an hour.

Ice Age glaciers, earthquakes and volcanoes sculpted this broad land into seven distinct geographical regions.

Arctic Tundra

About a quarter of the country is frigid, barren Arctic; it comprises a corner of the Yukon, the Northwest Territories and many islands including three of the world's ten largest, Baffin, Ellesmere and Victoria. More than 900 plant species cover the mainland tundra like a soft, spongy rug. Approaching the North Pole, vegetation thins out to rock and surface moss or bare rock and soil with patchy vegetation. Lakes are frozen from November to May in the south Arctic, September to June in the north and glaciers cover about five per cent of the area.

More than half the precipitation falls as snow. Groundwater exists as permafrost, permanently frozen ground ranging from tens of meters thick to 500 meters (1,650 feet) in the far north. Here, prevailing winds form wave and ripple patterns on the hard-packed snow. Though much of the land is flat, Arctic terrain also includes uplands, deep coastal fjords and mountains such as those found on the Parr Islands, as well as the jagged peaks of Ellesmere Island.

Cordillera

The Canadian stretch of this mountain system running the length of the Pacific Coast of the Americas, from Tierra del Fuego at the southern tip of Argentina to Alaska, is about 800 kilometers (497 miles) wide, extending more than 2,000 kilometers (1,240 miles) from the 49th parallel border with the US up to Alaska. While most of the Canadian portion of the range lies within BC and the Yukon, it also extends into southwestern Alberta and the Northwest Territories.

The Cordillera covers 16 per cent of the country and includes its most varied and dramatic scenery, with plateaus, valleys, plains and rugged mountains, rushing, glacier-fed rivers and clear alpine lakes. The range has five distinct sub-regions; the Rocky Mountains with nine peaks higher than 3,353 meters (11,000 feet), the interior basins and plateaus, the Coast Mountain Range, the deeply indented Inside Passage along the Pacific Coast, and the outer system of fog-enshrouded, rainforest-covered islands. Besides the well-known Rockies, there are formidable mountain ranges such as the Cariboo, Selkirk, Stikine, Mackenzie and Franklin.

Its great lateral extent gives the Cordillera a wide range of climates and vegetation. In the Coast Mountains, heavy rain and snow produce luxuriant forests, while interior vegetation ranges from low grasslands to alpine tundra.

Interior Plains

The plains, extending from the US border to the Arctic Ocean, form 18 per cent of the land surface, including the southern third of Manitoba, half of Saskatchewan, most of Alberta and the far western stretch of the Northwest Territories. Plains terrain includes glacial lakes and deposits, treeless tundra, coniferous forests, semi-arid grasslands, rolling, hummocky hills and large, fertile flatlands. Giant lakes such as

Winnipeg, Athabasca, Great Slave and Great Bear separate the plains from the Canadian Shield. Eroded badlands of dramatic plateaus, gullies and wide valleys add geographical variety, especially in southern Alberta. Extreme cold limits agriculture in the far north, but the south forms an extensive flat plain ideal for farming. Here waving golden wheat fields stretch out to the limits of the earth, and this 'Big Sky Country' gives a sense of space found only on calm oceans or the world's great deserts.

Hudson Bay Lowlands

This small area of 320,000 square kilometers (123,520 square miles), or 3.5 per cent of the country's land surface, lies on the Hudson and James Bay coasts (mainly northern Ontario and a corner of Manitoba) and entirely within the Canadian Shield. Hills of glacial till near the shield level off to peat-covered plains, low, forested ridges, and marshes, swamps, bogs and gravel beach near the coast.

Canadian Shield Forest Lands

This great shield of 4.6 million square kilometers (1,775,600 square miles) covers almost half of Canada, sweeping like a giant horseshoe from the Northwest Territories above Alberta through northern Saskatchewan and Manitoba to cover most of Ontario, Quebec and Labrador. The high, rugged terrain, sparsely covered with soil and deeply eroded by glacial action, encompasses rocky outcrops, rolling plateaus, shallow lakes and rivers.

The severe landscape of rock, bog, lake and woodlands, rich in minerals, forest and water resources, is popular with hearty outdoorsmen for hunting, fishing, canoeing and camping (see Adventure, pages 46-55). Most tourists experience the region through driving or taking the train between Winnipeg and Toronto, or on the last half of the rail trip from Winnipeg to Churchill, Manitoba. Then, the shield is like an endless Christmas tree farm interspersed with lakes.

St Lawrence Lowlands

The relatively small lowlands, stretched along the St Lawrence River from the Great Lakes to the Atlantic covers less than two per cent of Canada (180,000 square kilometers or 69,500 square miles) river, supports the nation's greatest population density

and about 80 per cent of its manufacturing industries. It covers the southernmost edge of Ontario and a narrow strip of Quebec along the river. It is defined by undulating and level plains, limestone plateaus and low hills with barren, dry or boggy surfaces. The rich soil and relatively mild climate of the plains make them ideal for farms, orchards and market gardens.

Appalachian Region

Slightly larger than the lowlands and sometimes included as the same region, the Appalachian lies between the St Lawrence Lowlands and the Atlantic Continental Shelf to the east and southeast. It includes part of Quebec as well as New Brunswick, Nova Scotia and the insular Newfoundland. This extension of the American Appalachian chain combines lowlands and eroded upland mountains lower than those in the US.

The Canadian mountains are flat to rounded in shape, with a few sharp peaks never exceeding 1,280 meters (4,200 feet). Lowlands, formed where glacial lakes deposited rich soil, include fertile plains areas such as Prince Edward Island and the Annapolis, Restigouche and Saint John River valleys. The area also encompasses coastal beaches and sand dunes, forests, farmlands and rocky highlands.

For Mackenzie King and other federal politicians, Canada may have 'too much geography'. For ordinary Canadians, as well as visitors, all those rivers, mountains, forests, lakes and beaches make for one colossal, bountiful playground.

Fall foliage along the St John River, east of Fredericton, New Brunswick

Adventure

In the general world view, Canadians are great outdoorsmen. They are seen as paddling birch-bark canoes down swiftly flowing streams singing 'Rose Marie,' squatting before camp fires munching pemmican (dried buffalo) and bannock bread, riding into untrekked mountains with pack trains or treading fearlessly among the giant mammals of their land, the moose, the cougar, the polar bear. In fact, most Canadians are city dwellers, 75 per cent living within 240 kilometers (150 miles) of the US border. Yet, in this huge, unpopulated country, even the largest, most sophisticated cities are within a few hours of a wild frontier unknown to most Europeans, Asians, even Americans.

Commercialized adventure travel in Canada started in the late 19th century when the Canadian Pacific Railway set up great lodges along its line through the Rockies. Fishermen and big game hunters from the Eastern US and Europe seeking grizzlies, bighorn sheep and mountain goat joined grand expeditions into the mountains, expeditions equivalent to the great African safaris of the day.

So Canada is synonymous with adventure travel. This may be as individual as a quiet hike along mountain trails or as organized as a whirlwind flight to sip champagne at the North Pole, as placid as watching the sun set across an isolated lake, or as exhilarating as scaling sheer cliffs or dog-sledding across the pack ice.

In recent years, adventure travel has come of age. Outfitters around the country operate canoe, horseback, hiking, sailing and rafting trips, or rent equipment to do-it-yourself adventurers. Options for adventure travel, organized or individual, are as numerous as the lakes that dot the north.

Fishing

With its immense resources of fresh water and its long coastlines, Canada is the world's finest fishing spot—as visiting sportsmen from the US, Europe and Japan well know. Every province has its piscatorial attractions, from cod in Newfoundland's rich waters to salmon off BC's coast, from bass in southern Ontario and Quebec to grayling and pike in the Yukon and the Northwest Territories' rivers and lakes.

In much of Canada, fishermen can pull over to a stream by the side of the road or throw their canoe or boat into a river or lake, drop a line and get a bite (provided they have a license, of course). Fishing is also a highly developed industry with boat charters and well-equipped lodges and fishing camps. In luxury camps, wine is served with meals and brandy sipped near a blazing hearth. These wilderness lodges provide meals, accommodation, bedding, motorboats and experienced guides and do everything to pamper the sportsman except hook the fish.

More basic outfitters provide only cabins with a wood-burning heater, stove and utensils, while guests bring their own sleeping bags, food, fishing gear and expertise. Some outpost fly-in camps are no more than a tent site and cooking pit.

In the Atlantic, deep-sea charters for mackerel, cod, swordfish and especially giant bluefin tuna depart daily in summer and fall, with fishing improving up until about October. Freshwater fishermen will find Atlantic salmon and brook trout in all Maritime provinces and Newfoundland. Quebec's rivers and lakes hold pike, bass, trout and ouananiche, a landlocked salmon. Its northern waters are rich with lake and brook trout and Arctic char.

Ontario, with more than a quarter of a million lakes, plus countless streams and rivers, claims 80 per cent of the world's trout fishing waters. Here you'll find sporting game fish such as muskellunge (muskie), trout, bass, perch and pickerel. The Prairies claim so many lakes, many are unnamed and seldom see fishermen. Those that do go find northern pike, walleye, Arctic grayling, and rainbow and brook trout. BC's streams, rivers and lakes hold abundant whitefish, bass, perch and char. The provincial specialty, though, is its unmatched salmon fishing.

For the well-heeled sportsman, fly-in fishing has opened remote areas that once required days to reach by canoe or on horseback. Across northern Canada, float planes drop fishermen onto perfect, empty lakes where they cast for lake trout, northern pike, walleye and Arctic grayling. Fish and game laws are a provincial jurisdiction, with bag limits and licensing regulations set by each government. Provincial fish and game departments provide information, aerial photos, provincial park guides and brochures listing fishing camps and the best spots.

Hunting

Hunting is also strictly regulated in Canada, with each province issuing licenses and setting its own rules, bag limits and firearm regulations. Gun regulations are stricter than in the US, with handguns and automatic weapons banned. However, sportsmen may bring in any type of legitimate shotgun or hunting rifle.

In many provinces, hunters must be accompanied by licensed Canadian guides. The variety of game and fowl is extensive, with hunting in every province. (Even Prince Edward Island has some small game). Big game hunters may bag bear (black, grizzly and polar), moose, caribou, mountain sheep and goat, white-tailed deer, wolf, cougar and musk-ox. Game birds include duck, pheasant, grouse, ptarmigan, partridge and goose.

(following pages) A river rushes through the mountains near Hedley, southern BC

Whale Watching

It is becoming more fashionable to spot wild game from horseback, on foot or from a canoe, and shoot with a camera instead of a gun. Whale hunting as a major industry has given way to whale watching on Canada's east, west and north coasts. Fast, inflatable Zodiacs, sea kayaks or spacious, comfortable mini-cruise ships with whale experts aboard sometimes come close enough to these great, frolicking mammals to stare them in the eye and smell their gamey breath. Some boats are equipped with hydrophones to pick up sounds of the whales communicating with high-pitched songs and clicking noises. In places, the giant mammals can be seen from shore. Whale-spotting ventures range from as low as $25 for several hours up to $2,000 for several-day excursions.

Whale watching is a seasonal pursuit. During the summer feeding season, thousands of beluga, killer and right whales come to eastern Newfoundland's spectacular bays, to Manitoba's icy Hudson Bay or along BC's shores. Eighty per cent of the world's narwhals, those strange creatures with two-to three-meter (six-to ten-foot) 'tusks' (actually protruding upper teeth) live in Canadian waters. In July and August, sightseeing ships set out to view these 'Sea Unicorns' traveling in pods of ten or more north of Hudson's Bay, near Pond Inlet and Iqaluit (Frobisher Bay). Beluga are also spotted in summer in Hudson Bay, outside of Churchill.

July and August are best for killer-whale watching in BC waters. In spring (mainly March and April), Pacific gray whales migrating from Mexican feeding grounds to Alaska are seen alone or in pods along the West Coast.

Late summer (August and September) is the prime whale-watching time in eastern Canada. Although September weather is often foggy and stormy, with big waves, cetacean authorities say whales get closer together, feed more often and breach more frequently at these times.The Department of Fisheries and Oceans' *Guide to Whale Watching in Canada* is a useful manual on whales, and where to find them.

Game Watching

Anyone driving through national or provincial parks, or along the highways in less populated areas, is almost certain to spot some wildlife. (In many parks warnings are posted not to feed the bears, who have learned to panhandle from friendly—if foolish—tourists.) Specialty tours in the Rocky Mountains focus on hiking and wildlife viewing—stone or bighorn sheep, moose, mountain goat, grizzly bear, caribou, wolf and fox. An Indian tribe near Alberta's Jasper National Park provides accommodation in authentic tee-pees, an introduction to Indian culture, lessons in crafts such as moccasin making, and visits to Indian historical sites. Indian guides also take guests to study wildlife such as buffalo herds.

From Prince Edward Island, each March, helicopter tours operate to the vast Gulf of St Lawrence ice fields where more than 100,000 once-threatened baby harp seals gather.

Water Sports

Canada, with the world's greatest reservoir of fresh water and more than 240,000 kilometers (150,000) miles of coastline, is ideally suited for marine recreation. Boaters can drift along silent lakes in the early morning mist or plunge through raging whitewater in a kayak (one of Canada's contributions to the boating world), while scuba divers may probe the bottom of an ocean or lake.

Houseboating, the gentlest of waterborne adventures, is found in a number of provinces. In BC's central Shuswap Lake district or the Okanagan, houseboat companies rent roomy, comfortable floating homes that even amateurs can pilot. Companies give a short lesson on how to operate the boat and use the galley, and boaters then explore the thousands of kilometers of navigable waterways, sandy beaches and peaceful little marine parks.

Ontario's extensive network of historic canals, the 'highways' built in the 18th and 19th centuries, has been taken over by yachting and houseboating in recent years, with boat rentals available by the day, week or month.

WHITEWATER RAFTING

Whitewater rafting on inflatable boats, a relatively new but rapidly growing sport, is found in most provinces. Packages cover a wide range of rivers, with day excursions or long camping trips through remote areas.

Canada's most popular run is on the Ottawa River where small, paddle-powered inflatables bounce through foaming rapids on one- and two-day tours.In BC, where the water runs high and heavy, 'Western-style' motorized 11.5 meter (38-foot) rafts are needed to brave the rapids of rivers such as the Fraser and Columbia.

Oar-, paddle- or motor-powered rafts drift past semi-desert and sagebrush country, deep canyons, old farm settlements, historic Indian villages with tall totem poles (in the north), native Indians netting and drying salmon along the river, abandoned log cabins overgrown with moss as well as wildlife such as bear, deer, eagles and bighorn sheep.

Even Manitoba, northern Saskatchewan and Alberta, despite their flat, dry, prairie image, are dipping tentative toes into the swirling white waters. From Edmonton, outfitters go whitewater rafting on the Red Deer River, a two-and-a-half-hour drive away, while Klondike jet boats take day or weekend trips on the North Saskatchewan River. In Yukon, oar-powered Zodiacs run rivers traveled by trappers and prospectors for 200 years.

SCUBA DIVING

The international underwater set, accustomed to tropical oceans, is just discovering first-rate, year-round scuba diving along BC's uncrowded, clean coastal waters. Local divers, using six-millimeter (1/4-inch) wet or dry suits, find the unusually clear water, with visibility up to 30 meters (98 feet), excellent for photography. Just off the coast of the Pacific Rim National Park on Vancouver Island, dozens of wrecks, including ships not yet found, lie in the shallow waters of the 'Graveyard of the Pacific'.

West Coast marine life includes wolf eels, ling cod and more than 325 species of fish, 180 types of sponges and 90 different sea stars. Divers encounter great, barking sea lions, giant spotted sea anemones, coralsand 50-kilogram (110-pound) octopuses. International divers rate the waters off Pender Harbor and Powell River along the Sunshine Coast (just north of Vancouver) as among the world's top diving spots.

Diving in Nova Scotia's Atlantic waters adds the anticipation of possibly discovering a wrecked ship or even a lost fortune. Only a few of the province's more than 3,000 wrecks, some dating back hundreds of years, have been found. Some are 'treasure ships' still carrying gold and silver coins and other valuables. From Tobermory on Lake Huron, north of Toronto, inland scuba divers explore Fathom Five Marine Park, an area rich with wrecks and caves. The exceptional clarity of Georgian Bay waters, which helps preserve the 50 known wrecks in the area, is ideal for underwater photography.

CANOEING

The country's favorite form of boating, canoeing, can be an hour's paddle around a local lake or an arduous month-long journey across seldom explored territory. Many outfitters give preliminary instruction in basic paddling techniques and flatwater skills before letting their clients strike out on a wilderness camping trip. Some also teach fundamental and advanced whitewater canoeing and kayaking.

Guides are not required, so experienced canoeists can strike out on their own with provincial government maps and pamphlets which outline planned routes, campsites and portages. Outfitters provide complete canoe and camping gear, pre-trip briefings, detailed route descriptions and inch-to-the-mile maps of most areas. Canoes can be

Berg Lake, Mount Robson Provincial Park, BC

rented in parks in every province. Even prairie-flat Saskatchewan has 50 mapped and documented canoe routes, from basic to advanced, including whitewater. Many follow historic fur-trader routes.

Horse Riding

While horse riding is popular across the country, it is at its best in Western Canada where rank greenhorns and hardened horsemen can ride into unmapped mountains with trail riding outfitters. Horses haul riders, food and gear across rushing streams and up steep slopes, and trail cooks prepare meals and set up camp. More experienced riders can take challenging packhorse expeditions, some running for up to three weeks. On shorter trips, overnight stays are usually at comfortable campsites or tent houses. Day trips often explore areas accessible only on horseback.

Guest and dude ranches feature hiking and fishing, real cowboys and ranch activities such as trail riding, breakfast rides, roundup and branding—as well as hot showers, clean beds and cold drinks. At most, novices can take riding lessons in the corral before, high in the saddle, they set out into the open range.

Those who have an aversion to the saddle can still get out on the range by horse power. In southern Alberta's Kananaskis cowboy country, covered wagons carry campers along mountain and valley roads that are closed to motorized vehicles.

The North

The 'Great White North' is opening to organized adventure travel, although it is pricey. With increased international interest, there are now hundreds of travel tours in Yukon and Northwest Territories, including more than 50 to Baffin Island alone. There are short snowmobile and sledge jaunts and dog-sled wildlife safari tours to view and to photograph bear, narwhal, seal, walrus and whale in their natural habitat.

Some dog-sledding expeditions start with instructions on driving. Other tours include lessons in seakayaking with the Inuit (Eskimo), camping on historic Ellesmere island, and backpacking in Ayuittuq National Park, the 'land that never melts'.

Those with limited time and tolerance for camping can take short fly-in tours to northern communities and Inuit camps, attractively set among tundra carpeted with Arctic flowers, mosses and lichen. All-night native craft shops in the Land of the Midnight Sun, where in summer it is light for 24 hours, sell soapstone carvings, embroidered hats, mitts and parkas and frozen Arctic char.

Winter Adventures

Canada has plenty of winter, when adventure travel continues, with snowshoeing, cross-country skiing, dog sledding, snowmobiling and ice-fishing for the hardy.

The most popular sport, and a true passion for many city-bound sportsmen, is downhill skiing, especially in Quebec's Laurentians and the Alberta and British Columbia mountain chains. Most resorts, from upscale to rustic, are within a day's drive of major cities.

The greatest thrill on the slopes is helicopter skiing, especially in BC's Bugaboos, Cariboos and Monashees, which claim some of the world's finest deep-powder skiing. Away from lift lines and crowds, setting off alone down these previously untouched slopes, is the ultimate ski experience.

How to ...

Many provinces publish guides specifically on fishing, hunting, adventure or outdoor travel, listing operators and outlining trips and costs. For free copies, write to the individual provincial tourist bureau (see Useful Addresses, page 292).

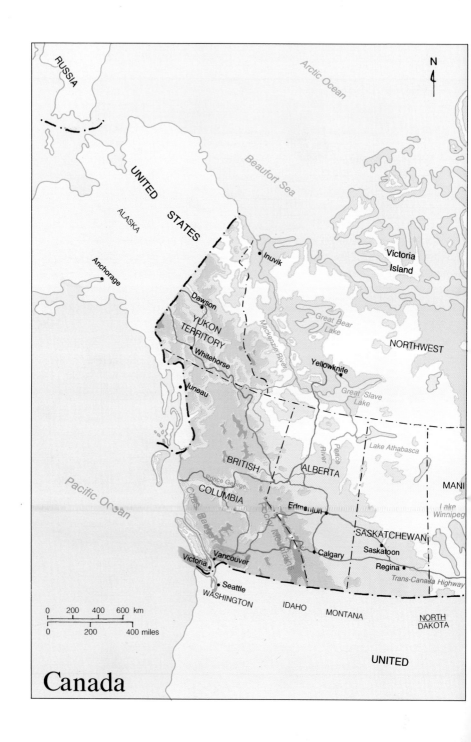

Canada

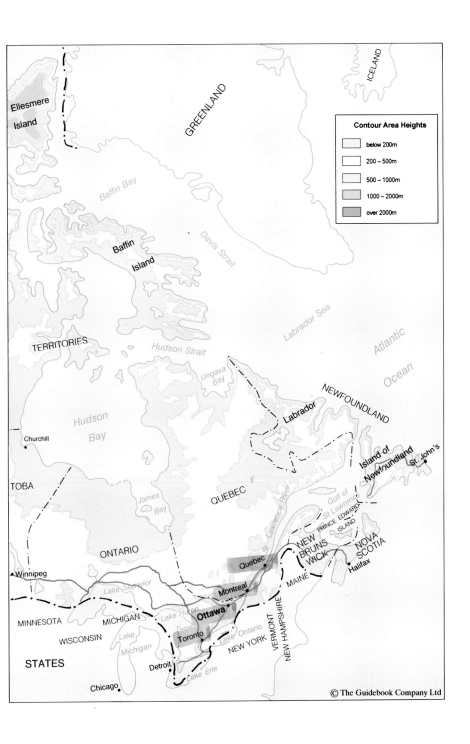

Contour Area Heights

below 200m
200 – 500m
500 – 1000m
1000 – 2000m
over 2000m

Facts for the Traveler

Getting There

Most of the world's major airlines fly to Canada. Connections to the US, Europe, Asia and the Pacific are particularly good. There has been a great expansion of air routes into the country across the Atlantic and Pacific oceans in the past ten years.

National carriers Air Canada and Canadian Airlines International Limited have extensive international and domestic routes. Major international gateways are Montreal, Toronto and Vancouver, although Halifax, Ottawa, Winnipeg, Edmonton and Calgary also have flights from overseas. Many airlines fly from the US to smaller Canadian communities. The largest number of visitors are motorists from the US, crossing at points all along the border where entry formalities are minimal but where lines can be long on summer weekends. The Greyhound Bus Company connects Canada and the US along many routes. There are offices all over the US.

Passports and Visas

US citizens do not require passports or visitors' visas for visits of up to 90 days. Longer stays are allowed if they first report to immigration. They do require official identification such as a birth certificate, social insurance card, proof of citizenship or other document. Others not requiring visas include citizens of Australia, New Zealand, Great Britain and most other European countries and Hong Kong. It is best to check with the nearest Canadian embassy, high commission or consulate where visas can be obtained if needed.

Customs

Visitors can bring in 50 cigars, 200 cigarettes and one kilogram (two pounds) of tobacco. Those of legal drinking age (depending on the province, usually 19) may bring in 1.1 liters (40 ounces) of wine or spirits or 8.1 liters (288 ounces) of beer.

Visitors may import sporting equipment for personal use as long as it is declared at the border. Equipment includes fishing tackle, boats (with licenses), outboard motors, golf, tennis, camping, skiing and other recreational equipment, radios, portable televisions, typewriters, musical instruments, cameras and film.

Canada Customs can restrict any of these items if they do not comply with federal regulations, so check first.

Money

The Canadian dollar is divided into 100 cents. US dollars are easily exchanged, as are most major currencies in the cities. However, smaller places will be a problem so it is best to carry some Canadian money and travellers' checks in Canadian or US funds.

Banks and foreign exchange offices give the best exchange rates. Exchange services are available in the shopping districts of major cities, at airports and at some tourist information offices along the Canada-US border. Many hotels, restaurants, department stores and other shops will accept US currency, but at an unfavorable rate. Major credit cards such as American Express, Carte Blanche, Diners Club and Visa are widely accepted—although in out-of-the-way places it may be better to have cash. A broad-based (and highly unpopular) seven per cent Goods and Services Tax (GST) on everything from food and souvenirs to haircuts, taxi rides and hotel rooms was introduced on January 1, 1991. A complex rebate plan for tourists was included, which seemed to many to be more confusing than helpful. Non-residents can get a refund by completing the form in Revenue Canada's pamphlet 'GST Rebate for Visitors'. For more information call (in Canada only) 1–800–66VISIT.

Health

Health standards in Canada are excellent and the public health system is the envy of many. You can drink the water and eat the food anywhere. There are no health hazards in the cities. In the national parks, beware of mosquito bites and do not feed the bears.

Generally, vaccinations are not needed and no special health precautions are required. Smallpox, cholera and yellow fever shots are necessary, however, for those coming from infected areas.

Getting Around

The only practical way to cross the country quickly is by air. Besides the two major Canadian airlines, which have frequent flights between all major cities, a number of

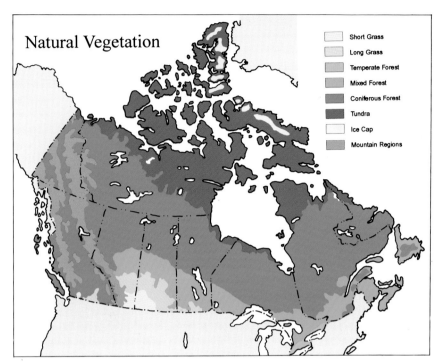

Natural Vegetation

- Short Grass
- Long Grass
- Temperate Forest
- Mixed Forest
- Coniferous Forest
- Tundra
- Ice Cap
- Mountain Regions

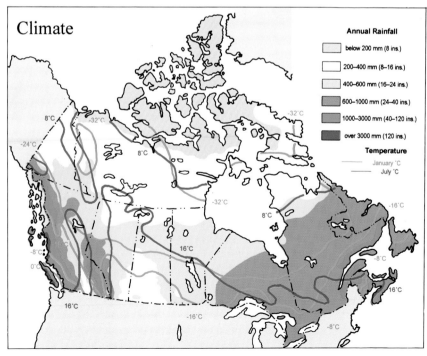

Climate

Annual Rainfall

- below 200 mm (8 ins.)
- 200–400 mm (8–16 ins.)
- 400–600 mm (16–24 ins.)
- 600–1000 mm (24–40 ins.)
- 1000–3000 mm (40–120 ins.)
- over 3000 mm (120 ins.)

Temperature

- January °C
- July °C

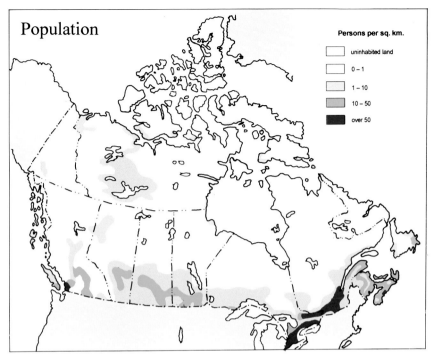

Population

Persons per sq. km.

- uninhabited land
- 0 – 1
- 1 – 10
- 10 – 50
- over 50

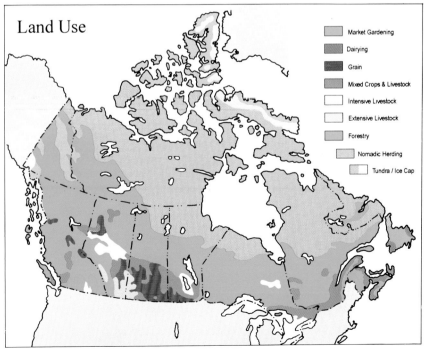

Land Use

- Market Gardening
- Dairying
- Grain
- Mixed Crops & Livestock
- Intensive Livestock
- Extensive Livestock
- Forestry
- Nomadic Herding
- Tundra / Ice Cap

smaller subsidiaries serve the regions. In peak season, especially July and August, flights can be heavily booked. For those with more time, Canada has some fine train trips although long distance service was seriously curtailed in the late 1980s. VIA Rail's transcontinental journey, from Halifax to Vancouver, is one of the world's greatest, although it is advisable to break up the four-day, three-night trip along the way. A number of other lines penetrate Canada's wilderness: Winnipeg to Churchill (on Hudson Bay), Vancouver to Prince George, and Edmonton to Prince Rupert are particularly attractive. Rail travel is as expensive as air, but if you have the time it is far more enjoyable (see pages 182 and 212).

Comfortable and convenient buses crisscross the country, reaching into most communities. Different companies serve the regions, while Greyhound spans the nation. Bus stations are usually conveniently located in city centers, and departures between larger centers are frequent. Only the hardy budget traveler would consider crossing the country by bus in one go, but taken in steps it is a most pleasant trip.

Even small communities have rental cars. All of the main companies, Avis, Budget, Hertz and Tilden, have offices at the airports and in the cities; and you can pick a car up at one location, drop it off at another. A valid driving license and a credit card are usually required. All foreign driving licenses are valid throughout Canada for a period of six months. The minimum age for renting a car or recreational vehicle is 21 years. Driving is on the right, road signs in metric. The road system is excellent and in the countryside, where traffic is usually light, driving is pleasant. Montreal and Vancouver have Canada's worst traffic—and drivers.

Speed limits on city streets and provincial highways are posted in kilometers per hour (90 kilometers equals 55 miles, 50 kilometers is 30 miles), and vary throughout the country. Regular, unleaded and diesel gasolines are available throughout the country and sold by the liter. There are 3.78 liters to a US gallon.

Drinking and driving is a serious offence nationwide and the laws are strictly enforced, even with visitors. The punishments are severe. Jail terms, even for first offenders, are not unusual. On first conviction, an offender may be liable to imprisonment of up to five years. Seat-belts are compulsory for driver and passenger in most provinces, as are helmets for motorcyclists. You can rent bicycles in many cities and resorts.

Climate

Temperature is measured in degrees Celsius rather than Fahrenheit, but the conversion is simple for those used to Fahrenheit: simply double the Celsius temperature and add 30. During the summer, days are usually hot, particularly inland, while the coast is much cooler. Since the country is so vast, temperatures vary greatly. Generally, the West Coast is temperate with moderate rainfall. The Prairies and the eastern provinces have extremes of temperature from very cold in winter to hot in summer. Summer is the best time to visit the extreme north, while May, June, September and October are the most pleasant months nationwide. Winter months are increasingly popular with skiers and other outdoor types.

What to Pack

Canada is generally more conservative than the US, less formal than Europe. Yet Toronto follows Europe's fastidious fashions more than Vancouver which favors casual, laid-back styles. For day-to-day summer wear, pack as you would for the US or Europe. The weather varies across the country, but it is usually warm to hot most of the summer and extremely cold in the winter. Coastal cities get deluged with rain, so be prepared. Toiletries, film, medical supplies, books and any extra clothing you might need are available everywhere except extremely isolated outposts where only the experienced outdoors type would venture.

National and Business Time

Canada spans six time zones, from Newfoundland Standard Time in the east to Pacific Standard Time in BC. The zones do not follow provincial borders. In summer (from the end of April to the end of October) most provinces go on daylight saving time, advancing the clock one hour. Newfoundland is always a half hour out of synch with the rest of the country (or vice versa), prompting the local apocalypse joke: 'The world is coming to an end at noon, 12:30 in Newfoundland'.

Generally, office hours are nine to five. Most banks are open from 10 am to 3 pm Mondays to Fridays, although many branches now stay open until 5 pm. In some cities, a few centrally located banks open Saturdays as well. Recently, currency exchange booths and bank machines, open seven days a week, have cropped up in major cities.

In shops and department stores the hours vary among regions. In Quebec, BC and other provinces, they are open seven days a week, while in Ontario, which generally lags behind the rest of the country, Sunday opening remains controversial. Liquor outlets are also a regional matter. Laws have been greatly liberalized in recent years, with many provinces now allowing bars, beer parlors and lounges to open Sundays. Quebec has the most enlightened licensing hours with clubs serving drinks until 3 am.

Holidays

Canada observes ten federal holidays: January 1; Good Friday and Easter Monday; May 23 (Victoria Day); July 1 (Canada Day); first Monday in September (Labor Day); second Monday in October (Thanksgiving); November 11 (Remembrance Day); December 25 (Christmas Day); and December 26 (Boxing Day).

Most provinces have their own civic holidays, usually in the summer. Newfoundland observes St Patrick's Day on the Monday nearest March 17, St George's Day on the Monday nearest April 23, Discovery Day on the Monday nearest June 24, Memorial Day on the Monday nearest July 1, and Orangeman's Day on the Monday nearest July 12. Quebec celebrates St-Jean-Baptiste Day (also known as Fête Nationale) on June 24. The first Monday in August is a civic holiday in Alberta (Heritage Day), BC (BC Day), Manitoba, New Brunswick (New Brunswick Day), Nova Scotia, Northwest Territories, Ontario (Simcoe Day) and Saskatchewan (Saskatchewan Day). Yukon Discovery Day is the third Monday in August.

Language

Canada's official languages are English and French, although the latter is spoken mainly in Quebec and parts of New Brunswick.

Hunting and Fishing Licences

Anyone wishing to hunt or carry firearms in Canada must obtain a licence from the relevant provincial fish and wildlife office. Bag limits and firearms regulations vary from province to province, but handguns and fully automatic firearms are prohibited entry into Canada. Non-residents hunting big game must be accompanied by a licensed local guide. Regulations and licenses are available at provincial fish and wildlife offices, or the provincial tourism body.

Separate licenses are required for fresh and saltwater fishing. Saltwater licenses are issued by the federal Department of Fisheries and Oceans and can be obtained at some sporting goods stores, department stores and marinas. Freshwater licenses, issued by provincial governments, are also available at sporting goods outlets and marinas. Freshwater licenses are usually valid only for the province of issue. National park fishing licenses can be purchased at park headquarters.

Telephones

Coin-operated telephones are widely available and local calls cost 25 cents. As in most countries, charges for local calls from hotels range from free to outrageous. Even the most remote community has direct dialing with the rest of the world, often through satellites.

Electric Current

Canada uses the same 110 volt electrical system and plugs as the US so appliances from south of the border work here. Those arriving from other countries must use convertors.

Further Information ·

Tourism Canada maintains offices in Sydney, London, Paris, Frankfurt, Tokyo, Mexico City and The Hague.

British Columbia

In size, geographical variety and physical isolation from the rest of Canada, British Columbia, known to Canadians simply as BC, could be a separate country. Frequently it behaves as though it is, with its politics and attitudes often out of step with eastern Canada.

The third largest and westernmost province covers nearly 1,040,000 square kilometers (400,000 square miles) of forests, ten separate mountain ranges, mighty rivers and lakes, and 8,850 kilometers (5,500 miles) of rugged Pacific coastline.

History

British Columbia is a mere infant, even in terms of Canada's short history. When Wolfe and Montcalm were scuffling on the Plains of Abraham (see page 27), BC was but a footnote in a few European explorers' reports. Its pre-European history stretches back long before that, however. For more than 9,000 years, the eight tribal groups living between Seattle, Washington, and Skagway, Alaska, developed a highly distinctive culture and life, expressed in totem poles, spirit masks and long houses, which many art historians and anthropologists place on a par with that of Greece or Rome.

Even today, aspects of the native Indian culture, especially the visual art, are found throughout the province, including Vancouver's Stanley Park, museums, native Indian restaurants and many galleries and shops. Using the abundant soft cedar wood found in the rain forests, and working with knife, adze and chisel, skilled carvers form ravens, eagles, loons, wolves and killer whales that are all part of their mythology. Poles, carved doors, ceremonial cooking utensils, canoes, masks and 'bent boxes' made from steaming and bending cedar are the main art forms. The European aspect of BC's history did not really begin until the late 18th century. Spanish explorers arrived from the south in 1774, claiming the region for Spain and leaving place names such as Quadra, Galiano and Juan de Fuca. Four years later, British explorer Captain James Cook explored west Vancouver Island, establishing fur trading with the coastal Indians. After several skirmishes between the two countries, the British gained control of the area. Captain George Vancouver carefully mapped the coast from Oregon to Alaska in 1792. The British stayed, and gave the province its name. Russian fur traders of the Russian American Company also joined the fray from 1799, coming down the coast from their northern base in Sitka, Alaska.

Lions Gate Bridge links Vancouver with north shore communities

Blocked off from the rest of Canada by the Rocky Mountains, modern BC developed separately. It was not wholly settled by people coming overland from the east, as were the Prairies, but by fur traders, gold prospectors and adventurers who came by the Pacific or, often, the United States. Only when Canada offered to build a transcontinental railway to the coast did BC join Confederation in 1871. But even as late as 1878, a secession resolution passed the provincial assembly, and some diehard British Columbians today still mutter about separatism.

When the Canadian Pacific Railway reached the Pacific coast in 1885, an incredible feat of engineering, the province was bound to Canada forever, first by this slender thread, then by road and air service in the 20th century.

Today, the province's attractions are the vast outdoors, home to moose, grizzly bear, wolf and mountain goat, and the sophisticated coastal communities which have Canada's kindest climate. While easterners freeze through the winter, west coast dwellers complain that the drizzle interrupts their gardening.

Vancouver

The country's third largest city (named after the British explorer) and the continent's second largest sea port in tonnage handled, Vancouver holds a special place in Canadian mythology. The young city only celebrated its centenary in 1986. In part because of the influence of its mild climate and stunning setting, the city is considered by other Canadians to be mindlessly hedonistic and zany. Lotus Land, easterners call it, a place more concerned with the ski slopes and beaches than the bottom line.

Every New Year's Day, while the rest of Canada sensibly recovers from festivities, thousands of Vancouverites, many in costume or formally dressed from parties, flock to English Bay for the annual Polar Bear Swim. In the heady 1960s, the city had an official court jester, complete with cap and bells, who received a government grant for a time. Local events have included the Fraser River Outhouse Race, where rafts topped by fake outhouses drift down the wide river, and also an official, invitational bathtub race where municipal mayors piloted bathtubs on wheels through Vancouver streets. In the World Cannonball and Bellyflop Championships, huge men plopped into a swimming pool, competing for best style and biggest splash.

This is a city dedicated to pleasure, especially of the outdoors, and there are more joggers, skiers, tennis players, sunbathers, sailors, sport fishermen and frisbee fanatics than in any other Canadian metropolis. Within the city limits there are nine miles of public beach, marinas, golf courses and hundreds of tennis courts. Ocean or whitewater canoeing and kayaking, as well as alpine and cross country ski slopes, are all less than an hour's drive from the city center.

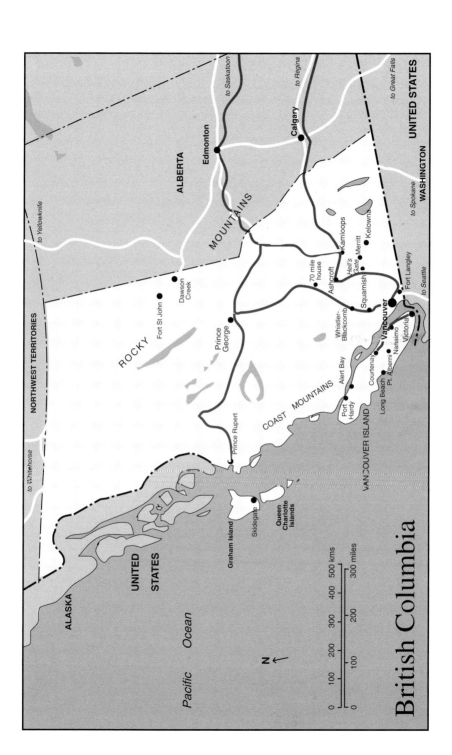

British Columbia

Northwest Passage

The search for the hoped-for Northwest Passage, an Arctic water route to the riches of the East, was a fascinating but futile episode in northern Canadian history. Even with today's modern technology, commercial ships do not cross the top of North America from Europe to Asia — although icebreakers and submarines do occasionally.

For more than 300 years after that annoying North American continent was discovered to be blocking the dreamed-of route to the Orient, explorers probed the icy, dangerous northern lands looking for a passage.

In 1576, Martin Frobisher sighted the formidable obstacle of Baffin Island, but noted possible passages both north and south, blocked by ice. In the 17th century, explorers turned south into the Hudson Strait, with no luck. The British Navy, notably under Edward Parry and John Ross, continued explorations in the early 19th century, mapping the Arctic Islands.

In 1845, British naval officer Sir John Franklin set out with two ships, prophetically named *Erebus* and *Terror,* to sail through the Northwest Passage. He never returned. Franklin's disappearance touched off one of the greatest rescue operations in Arctic history.

The British sent out expeditions in search of the missing flotilla from the east and west, and overland from the south. None found any traces of the expedition. Later, search parties sent out by the government, the Hudson's Bay Company and Lady Franklin all failed. One party did find Franklin's winter headquarters on Beechey Island, but Franklin's fate remained unknown.

These expeditions did, however, define the coastal outline of most of the Arctic Islands and took note of the short ice-free period for ships, in August and September. By then, the prospect of commercial shipping had been forgotten, although the Hudson's Bay Company continued to use part of the water route to its Arctic posts.

In 1854, explorer John Rae was awarded 10,000 pounds sterling for settling Franklin's fate. Piecing together Eskimo reports and evidence of personal effects belonging to the crew, he concluded that all had died on or near King William Island. Later expeditions found more artifacts, skeletons and the only written record.

It was finally concluded that Franklin's ships had been frozen into the ice pack west of King William Island, and Franklin had died in June 1847. The surviving 105 officers and crew members headed south overland, but none made it back. The mystery of Franklin's disappearance, and the many voyages made to solve it, make up one of the greatest stories of northern exploration. (The presence of scurvy, possible lead poisoning from tinned food and probable occurence of cannibalism all form part of the Franklin epic).

The long-sought passage was not traversed until 1906. It was not the British or any other navy, but a remarkable Norwegian adventurer, Roald Amundsen, who finally made the three-year journey on the ship *Gjoa*.

The first west to east passage was made by the RCMP vessel *St Roch* (now in Vancouver's Maritime Museum) under Henry Larsen in 1940-2. In the summer of 1944, the *St Roch* also became the first ship to traverse the passage from east to west in a single year—and to cross the passage in both directions.

In 1969, the American oil tanker *Manhattan*, accompanied by the Canadian icebreaker *John A Macdonald*, traversed the passage from east to west. In the 1980s, the whole question of Canadian sovereignty over the Arctic arose when the American ship *Polar Sea* crossed the passage. Although the US and Canada have reached an agreement dealing with US icebreakers entering the Arctic, the sovereignty issue has not yet been settled.

Vancouver is overwhelmed by the grandeur of its setting: the steep North Shore mountains rising from the sea, ocean inlets and the primeval forest encroaching on residential areas. In some suburbs, game wardens have to chase away the bears that wander into backyards and raccoons attack family cats.

Generally, what man has wrought is not overly impressive, and is not getting better, although there are notable exceptions such as the five sweeping sails of the Canada Place cruise ship terminal. In this setting, even a skyline of ordinary high-rises looks good.

A striking recent development is the change in the human geography. Vancouver is now very much an Asian city, with many Chinese from Hong Kong, Singapore, Taiwan, Malaysia and China, East Indians and Pakistanis from the subcontinent as well as Fijians and a sprinkling of Koreans, Filipinos and Japanese. The new population mix gives the port city an exotic flavor.

SIGHTS AND ATTRACTIONS

At just over one million people, Vancouver is relatively small. Downtown, the West End residential area and Stanley Park are concentrated on a peninsula. Many of the city's attractions—the parks, beaches and waterfront as well as the older districts are within easy reach of most downtown hotels.

■ GASTOWN, WHERE IT ALL STARTED

A small trace of Vancouver's past remains as a reminder of its rough pioneer days. The city was founded as a booze joint when, in 1867, riverboat captain John 'Gassy Jack' Deighton paddled a canoe with his wife, a dog, two chickens and a keg of whiskey to a lumber mill. He set up a plank across two barrels as a bar for mill workers, lumberjacks and gold diggers. In gratitude, his first customers helped him build a shack, and Vancouver was founded.

The initial shantytown which grew up around Gassy Jack's place burned down in 1886, sparking a massive building boom in more substantial concrete and red brick. The city soon shifted west, Gastown became a slum and by the 1960s was destined for the wrecker's ball. However, concern for heritage saved the few blocks of old buildings. The city laid brick sidewalks and cobbled streets to encourage pedestrian traffic, planted trees and installed fancy street lights patterned on the 19th-century originals.

The civic effort worked, and Gastown is now a favorite tourist spot—too touristy, some locals complain. The few blocks along **Water Street**, as well as **Blood Alley** and **Gaoler's Mews**, are ideal for a leisurely stroll. Here are many good restaurants and night spots, quality boutiques as well as shops selling trinkets and gewgaws of the east. Lively street scenes of jugglers and stetson-hatted Western singers, hot dog stands and 1960s-type hawkers displaying I-made-it-myself cheap jewelry, make for a holiday atmosphere.

A bronze statue of **Gassy Jack** stands before the location of his first saloon, **the Globe**, at one end of Water Street in Maple Tree Square. Several blocks west is Gastown's popular symbol, the world's first **steam-powered clock**. Unveiled in 1977, it is an intricate granddaddy affair of chains, pulleys and steel weights wound by a one-cylinder steam engine. Each quarter hour, a steam whistle modeled on the old paddle-wheeler type wheezes out the Westminster chimes. On the hour, the main whistle blows. Designer and creator Ray Saunders still builds clocks in Vancouver.

■ CHINATOWN

Southeast of Gastown, Vancouver's Chinatown is North America's second largest (or third or fourth, depending on who is counting) and the most authentic, residents claim. On busy weekend afternoons, Chinatown streets are crowded with recent Asian immigrants. It could be Hong Kong except for the wider roads. Local gourmets also boast that Vancouver restaurants serve the best Chinese food this side of the Pacific.

Here in this Asian corner, glistening brown ducks and slabs of barbecued pork hang from butcher shop windows, to the despair of city health inspectors. Strange vegetables like *bok choy* and *gai an* and exotic fruits such as lichees and durian spill over onto the sidewalks, and herbal medicine shops display strange and wondrous potions of the East, of dried lizards, coiled snakes and unrecognizable oddities. Here are the gaudy souvenir shops, Chinese department stores and movie theaters, *wonton* noodle shops and *dim sum* restaurants—though rarely a parking spot.

Here, too, are a few traces of old Vancouver, the original buildings with Chinese-tiled roofs and decorations and Chinese social clubs. Dr Sun Yat-sen lived in an apartment on the northwest corner of Pender and Carrall while plotting the future of China. *The Chinese Times*, at 1 East Pender, North America's largest circulation Chinese-language paper and Chinatown's oldest, no doubt reported news of his efforts. Also on Pender, kitty-corner to *The Times*, the recently completed Dr Sun Yat-sen Classical Garden, the only one of its kind outside of China, commemorates his efforts.

At 29 meters (96 feet) wide but only 1.3 meters (six feet) deep, the world's narrowest building is found at West Pender off Shanghai Alley, according to Ripley of Believe-It-Or-Not fame. Now a newly renovated two-story office building, it was the result of one man's successful battle with city hall at the turn of the century. In 1903, when the Sam Kee Company bought the land, it was a standard-sized lot. But a decade later, when the city widened Pender Street, the owners were left with only 1.3

meters (six feet). Partly on a bet, they built the unusual, long narrow building that was then known as a mini-skyscraper.

■ GRANVILLE ISLAND
Two decades ago, Granville Island, across False Creek south of the city center, was a dirty, desolate industrial area of grungy factories, warehouses and railway sidings. Now, the small island under Granville Street Bridge (actually a peninsula connected by a road) is a thriving area of houseboats, condominiums and the pleasant Granville Island Hotel located in a renovated warehouse.

Several theaters, the Emily Carr College of Art, art galleries and craft shops, and boat equipment stores for fashionable yachters are found here, as well as many of the city's trendiest restaurants and bars.

The centerpiece is the lively **public market** in a massive converted warehouse with a neo-brutalist decor of skylights, exposed pipes and tin sheeting—nothing fake here. The vast, barnyard structure is dedicated almost entirely to the pleasures of the palate, with fresh-from-the-farm produce stalls, butchers and bakers (the candlestick makers are in the craft shops outside), fishmongers selling fresh salmon, oysters, trout, clams, crab and the local specialty, geoduck (pronounced gooey duck). This shellfish, with an appendage resembling a long neck coming from its shell, is popular with Japanese diners. Lining these crowded aisles are delicatessens and fruit stands, flower shops and a French specialty shop selling pâté, patisseries and croissants.

On fine days, you can buy an inexpensive lunch of salads (fruit or vegetable), fresh baked croissants or muffins, Greek kebabs, Italian pastas and pizzas, delicatessen sandwiches, or fish and chips. You can sit inside or go out on the wharf to watch the kayaks, sailboats, yachts and tugs skim by several feet away and the Coast Mountains rising snowclad over the city across False Creek.

Granville Island is a short taxi ride from downtown, or you can scoot across the inlet in little rowboat-sized ferries departing from under the Burrard Street Bridge. The hundreds of parking spaces are almost always taken.

■ STANLEY PARK
Stanley Park, 405 hectares (1,000 acres) of natural rain forest leased from the federal government for $1 a year, is North America's largest urban park and the city's favorite playground. Encompassing the whole western tip of the downtown peninsula and near most major hotels, the park has miles of hiking trails and sandy beaches. There are recreational facilities such as tennis courts, cricket pitches (an anachronism in North America) and pitch and putt courses, a zoo with polar bears, picnicking lawns, a children's miniature train, pony rides, and summer theater under the stars. Brockton Oval provides joggers with a regulation-size cinder track, hot showers and changing rooms.

Vancouver skyline

English Bay Marina, Vancouver

At the park entrance, Canada Geese and rare Trumpeter Swans nest on Lost Lagoon, bordered with bullrushes and weeping willows. Traffic to the park often stops for a parade of geese crossing the road.

Cyclists, wheezing joggers and casual strollers all circumnavigate the ten-kilometer (six-mile) seawall around Stanley Park. (Bicycles are available for rent nearby.) En route is the bronze **statue of the Girl in a Wet Suit**. Sculptor Elek Imredy, who donated the statue to the city in 1972, says it represents Vancouver's affinity to the sea.

At **Brockton Point Light House** you can see the **Nine O'Clock Gun** which, at the turn of the century, was fired to mark the close of the fishing day. It still fires at precisely 9 pm merely to maintain tradition, and to scare the gulls and lovers. You'll also pass **Siwash Rock** (a craggy island with a lone tree), and the figurehead from the Canadian Pacific Railway's steamship *Empress of Japan* looking out to sea, towering **totem poles** facing Coal Harbor (popular with photographers) and **Lumberman's Arch**. Stand on these shores listening to waves slapping at the barnacled rocks and breathe deeply the ocean air scented with seaweed and freshly-cut cedar, and you will experience Vancouver at its very best.

Prospect Point, where the east end of Lions' Gate Bridge enters the park, provides a sweeping view of the North Shore and of freighters and cruise ships leaving the harbor. A century ago, during a storm, the trading ship SS *Beaver* ran aground on the rocks below, ending a long career in BC waters. A memorial to the *Beaver* is nearby, and a replica with tall wooden masts and guns cruises the harbor and up the deep Indian Arm inlet. The cruises depart from Coal Harbor at the north foot of Bute Street.

Stanley Park Aquarium near the zoo and the Georgia Street entrance to the park is Canada's finest and largest, with more than 8,000 aquatic species. Dolphins and killer whales perform at the mammal complex pool and visitors can handle sea stars, crabs and other creatures which hide under rocks at the touch pools and see sport fish such as Pacific salmon, Arctic grayling and trout in their natural habitats. The **BC Hall of Fishes** exhibits local marine life, including the world's largest species of octopus, the Giant Pacific, which can grow to more than 45 kilograms (100 pounds).

■ UNIVERSITY OF BRITISH COLUMBIA

In Vancouver, going to school is a pleasure. The University of British Columbia is beautifully set on a broad peninsula on English Bay opposite downtown in a natural, primary-growth forest. Information booths at all entrances provide maps and literature to visitors. The campus has a fine arts gallery, botanical garden, geology museum, the **Nitobe Memorial Gardens** (a traditional Japanese garden including a teahouse), and a rose garden with more than 1,500 flowering bushes.

A major attraction, even for those who normally shun museums, is the **Museum of Anthropology**. Dramatically set on the Point Grey cliffs, it houses one of the world's most comprehensive collections of native West Coast art.

The huge concrete and glass structure, a stylized Indian post-and-beam longhouse, is no dusty dinosaur-bones-and-rusty-sword museum. The towering windows, skylights, open spaces and natural tones convey the impression of the outdoors. The 14-meter-high (46-foot), glass-walled, cathedral-like **Great Hall** houses ancient, arrow-straight totem poles salvaged from abandoned Tsimshian and Kwakiutl coastal villages, and some of the largest native pieces ever found.

Displays include a giant carved Kwakiutl house front and a huge three-part bowl, once a potlatch feast vessel in the form of a double-headed serpent which looks like an ornately-carved hot tub on wheels. (The potlatch, great ceremonial gatherings and feasts, were banned in 1884 by the Canadian government which seized the utensils and regalia. The missionaries considered the celebrations unchristian, and denounced the events because the Indians gave away their essential belongings. The ban was repealed in 1951, but the potlatches are no longer the major affairs they once were.) Majestic poles, carved doors, canoes, masks and boxes display the stylized, supernatural figures constant in Coast Indian art: ravens, beavers, frogs, killer whales, eagles, wolves and sharks. Often, they appear partly human or transforming between the natural and supernatural worlds.

Outside the Great Hall's soaring windows and set back in the rain forest, stand contemporary totem poles, mortuary poles and two full-sized, cedar-plank gabled Haida Indian dwellings, completed in 1962 and probably the first of their kind built this century.

Walking along the totem-lined forest paths—with the mist rolling in off the Pacific, the salty scent of the ocean air and tang of pine needles, the squawking gulls and the surf rumbling beyond the cliff—evokes a sense of the spirit of the early coast dwellers.

The concrete searchlight towers beneath the gun emplacements at nearby old **Point Grey Fort** are remnants of Vancouver's largest and longest used coastal fort. Every sunny summer day, thousands flock to **Wreck Beach** beneath the university to gape at these sturdy structures from which a nervous city prepared to defend itself against feared Japanese invaders during the early days of World War II. Or perhaps the people are there because this is also Canada's most famous and popular nude beach, where even hawkers peddling beer and pina coladas are bare.

■ CANADA PLACE
An impressive addition to the skyline, the white-sailed Canada Place, sitting like a trading schooner on the harbor, is the city's newest symbol. This vestige of the suc-

cessful Expo 86, formerly the Canadian government pavilion, includes the Trade and Convention Center, a cruise ship terminal capable of handling several ships at once, the 505-room Hotel Pan Pacific with its impressive views, an outdoor amphitheater overlooking the harbor, a glass-enclosed, two-level restaurant, a weathered totem pole rising into the vaulted atrium, and a giant IMAX 3-D theater.

On the mall-level promenade, shops sell Indian crafts and BC jade carvings. In the adjacent food fair, native Indians who ran a popular food stand at Expo 86 offer a taste of Canadiana—buffalo burgers or salmon on bannock bread.

A public promenade around the entire five-sailed structure provides vistas of the North Shore mountains and the harbor busy with bright red, white and blue SeaBuses shuttling to the North Shore and, in summer, giant Princess, Cunard and Holland America Line cruise ships steaming north to Alaska via the Inland Passage.

Adjacent to the modern center stands a memory of old Vancouver, the restored, high-ceilinged and colonnaded **Canadian Pacific Railway Station**, one of the city's remaining historical buildings. The end of the line of the famous CPR railway, as far west as you can go on the Canadian mainland, it is also the start for both the Sky-Train (an elevated mass-transit system to the eastern suburbs, worth the ride) and the SeaBus to the north shore.

■ SEABUS TO THE NORTH SHORE

Catamaran-hulled 400-passenger ferries provide cheap transport between the North Shore and downtown and the most accessible view of the city from the water. Sea-Buses depart for the 12-minute ride across Burrard Inlet every 15 minutes from the old CPR station to the foot of Lonsdale Avenue in North Vancouver.

A flotilla of sailboats, cruisers, fishing boats, even kayaks head out to sea under the Lions Gate Bridge. Float planes, direct from Victoria, the provincial capital, or from isolated coastal communities, plop down in Coal Harbor like Canada geese.

The **Pan Pacific Hotel**, and the **Sears Tower**, with a viewing gallery and circular rooftop restaurant, dominate the city skyline. The only reminders of early Vancouver, glimpsed between the great square block buildings, are the green-domed **Sun Tower**, once the tallest building in the British Empire, the ornate, art deco **Marine Building** built in the 1930s, the restored **Sinclair Center** and **The Landing** and the verdigrised pyramid of the **Hotel Vancouver**. The Canadian National Railway built this, the last of Canada's great chateau-style hotels, between 1928 and 1939 (see page 275).

■ MOUNTAIN PLAYGROUNDS

Looming ahead are the forested slopes of **Grouse** and **Seymour**, popular ski areas. (You can be on the slopes easily from any Vancouver hotel for a day's skiing, and back for après-ski nightlife.) Mount Seymour has downhill and cross-country skiing, some snowshoeing and a well-maintained access road in winter. The cleared slash up the mountain is the gondola to the popular Grouse Mountain recreation and ski area. As Canada's largest, most modern tramway, the gondola can whisk up to 100 passengers 1,128 meters (3,700 feet) up for a panoramic view of the city below. On a clear day, you can spot Mount Baker and the Olympic Peninsula in the US before heading off for the slopes, hiking trails, lounge, cafeteria, restaurant, gift shops, gardens, outdoor barbecues and chairlifts to higher peaks.

Nearby is a 137-meter (450-foot) suspension bridge swaying 70 meters (230 feet) over the Capilano River. It is an unnerving experience for the faint-hearted, but the view from the footbridge (narrow enough to hang onto the railing on both sides) is worth the palpitations. The rushing river, sometimes braved by inner-tube, kayak or even rafting enthusiasts, cuts through the narrow canyon, to a 61-meter (200-foot) waterfall. There are salmon and trout ponds upriver at Cleveland Dam. A six hectare (15-acre) park of tall firs and cedars surrounds the swaying bridge.

The **Capilano Trading Post** with authentic, restored and painted totem poles, cigar-store Indians, a wishing well and a cardboard cutout Mountie (red-coated Royal Canadian Mounted Police officer), is somewhat Disneylandish in this pristine setting. An authentic native carver who often works outside the building is happy to talk to visitors about his work and Indian art.

Lynn Canyon Park on Lynn Valley Road in North Vancouver is less commercial, and less crowded, than Capilano, although physically they are similar. In Lynn Canyon, there is the rushing river, a suspension bridge over a waterfall and canyon, and trails through 81 hectares (200 acres) of unspoiled rain forest. An ecology center in the shape of the provincial emblem, the dogwood flower, has films and scientific displays on the ecology of plants, animals and man.

■ BACK IN VANCOUVER

Closer to the city center, just south of the Burrard Street Bridge in Kitsilano (once Vancouver's Haight-Ashbury-hippy district), are the **Vancouver Museum**, depicting the city's and province's early history with a permanent collection as well as changing exhibits, the **H R MacMillan Planetarium** and the **Maritime Museum**. The *St Roch*, the first vessel to cross the Northwest Passage both directions and the first to circumnavigate North America, is permanently moored at the Maritime Museum. The short, two-masted schooner, built in Vancouver in 1928 as an Arctic supply and patrol vessel for the Mounties, served in the north for 26 years. It sailed from Vancouver on June 23, 1940 on the treacherous southern route through the Arctic islands. After being trapped in the ice for two years, it reached Halifax on October 11, 1942. It returned via the easier northern route in just 86 days, from July 22 to October 16, 1944.

■ AFTER DARK

The city's nightlife is perhaps the liveliest in English Canada, with elegant dinner-dance restaurants, rock bars, discos, jazz and comedy clubs, even a bar where transvestite waiters glide by on roller skates.

Aficionados of the ecdysiasts' art will find it performed here as perhaps nowhere else in the world, especially in bars along Granville Street north of the Granville Street Bridge. Most popular are the **Cecil**, the **Austin** and **Champagne Charlies**. Such as the **Marble Arch**, on Richards downtown, and, further afield, **Number Five Orange** on Main Street and the **Drake**, on Powell past Japantown.

The most popular comedy clubs, where the talent varies wildly and the crowd lets them know it, are **Punchlines** on Water Street in Gastown and **Yuk Yuk's** on the old Expo site.

There are now casinos open seven nights a week. Although not on the grand Las Vegas scale—no floor shows or even alcoholic drinks—and with fairly low betting limits, these elegant, action-packed, European-style places are popular with the gaming crowd. Blackjack, roulette and Sic Bo, an adaptation of the Chinese game, are particularly favored and can be played nightly from 6 pm to 2 am at about a dozen casinos, including one in the Holiday Inn on Broadway, at Richards and Davie downtown, one near the airport and several in the suburbs. Main companies are **Great Canadian Casino Company** and **Royal Diamond**.

DAY TRIPS

In winter, sporty Vancouverites are preoccupied with skiing. Good downhill slopes and cross-country trails are within 20 minutes of the city center, at **Grouse Mountain**, **Cypress Bowl** and **Mount Seymour**, while excellent resorts are just a few hours away. With the city's mild climate, this makes Vancouver an attractive winter destination.

Fashionable Vancouverites flock to **Whistler-Blackcomb**, just 110·kilometers (70 miles) and a 90-minute drive northwest from the city. A daily train departs North Vancouver's Pemberton station at 8 am, arriving at Whistler at 10.20 am and continuing on to **Prince George** in the interior. The two mountains include 122 ski trails spread over 800 hectares (2,000 acres).

Although known worldwide for its skiing, this resort, near the pleasant Whistler village, offers much more to the summer tourist. There are hiking trails through the mountains and heli-hiking for thrillseekers. Helicopters drop hikers and guides on mountainsides where they can explore alpine meadows and icefields. Some packages include a gourmet lunch. A ski plane also lands on glaciers when it is warm enough in midsummer to play in the snow and ice wearing only shorts or a bathing suit.

Arnold Palmer designed the golf course in the flat valley, claiming it was a mountain golf course you didn't have to be a mountain goat to play. There are tennis courts, a water playland with chutes and waterslides plunging into a hot pool, whitewater rafting, kayaking, windsurfing, horseback riding and good fishing.

■ BY TRAIN

The Royal Hudson, the largest steam locomotive in regular passenger service in North America, operates a popular day excursion up the coast. The refurbished CPR locomotive departs from the North Vancouver railway station at 10.30 am daily from late May until mid-September. The station has free parking and there are buses from the Vancouver Bus Depot, making pickups on the way.

During the six-hour, 128-kilometer (80-mile) round trip between Vancouver and Squamish, the old passenger train steams past mountains, forests, waterfalls, beaches (including a nude beach) and craggy little islands. At midday, the train stops in **Squamish**, a pleasant town of small cafes and fast-food stands, antique stores and souvenir shops. Two hours here allows time for lunch and a short walk or trek to **Shannon Falls**, cascading 213 meters (703 feet) down a cliff. You can take the train (five and a half hours round trip), a passenger ship, the MV *Britannia* (a seven-hour round trip) or a combination of the two. The ship departs from downtown Vancouver at 9.30 am Wednesday through Sunday during July and August and twice-weekly from mid-May to the end of June.

■ WHITEWATER RIVERS

Several Vancouver-based companies run whitewater rafting day trips on both the Fraser and Thompson rivers. Some companies provide bus transportation to the river from Vancouver, while others require that you get there yourself. Check with the Vancouver Travel Info Center (683-2000) for reputable companies. Generally, good walking shoes and raingear are suggested, but outfitters will advise on suitable clothing.

Motorized inflatable rafts, departing from launch points several hours' drive upriver, drift past semi-desert and sagebrush country, deep canyons and old farm settlements, and wildlife such as California Bighorn sheep.

The day is enlivened with heart-stopping runs through foaming whitewater rapids and swirling whirlpools. Highlights of the Fraser River trip are runs through the **Devil's Cauldron** and **Hell's Gate Canyon**, the wildest rapids. In Hell's Gate, the Fraser Canyon's prime tourist attraction, the canyon narrows to a bottleneck, forcing the water through at an incredible speed. Here the flow is greater than the Colorado River through the Grand Canyon. Rafters spend a day in the unspoiled wilderness, shooting wild whitewater rapids and lunching in isolated splendor, and are back in Vancouver in time for preprandial drinks.

Hell's Gate can be seen from the air, too. An enclosed airtram makes the 152-meter (500-foot) journey across the gorge and foaming waters to the opposite bank where a model of salmon fishways and exhibits and a film on the salmon's life cycle are on display. The airtram can be reached by road from Yale, an old goldrush town on the Trans-Canada Highway East 69 kilometers (43 miles) from Hell's Gate.

■ THE FRASER VALLEY

The farming community of **Fort Langley**, a pleasant drive some 48 kilometers (30 miles) east of Vancouver, is the farthest point on the Fraser River that ocean vessels can navigate. Here the Hudson's Bay Company built a fur trade post on the south bank of the Fraser River in 1840, partly to fend off American competition. It served as a supply depot for fur traders and, later, gold miners. In 1858, BC was declared a British colony in the fort's Big House, also living quarters for the chief trader and senior clerk. The fort's buildings, palisade and bastion have been restored and guides in costume demonstrate blacksmithing, barrel-making and period carpentry. The buildings are open from 10 am to 7 pm June 1 to Labor Day (first weekend in September) and 10 am to 4.30 pm the rest of the year.

■ DOWN BY THE SEA

Steveston, a picturesque village south of Vancouver, was home to a Japanese fishing community before World War II and retains an Asian flavor. During the war, everyone of Japanese origin in Vancouver (including those born in Canada and soldiers who had fought for the country in World War I) was removed to work camps in the interior, their boats, vehicles and property seized and sold in what was one of the lowest points in Canadian history. Years after the war, some returned to their homes, although many remained on the Prairies and in Ontario.

Old canneries and wood-frame buildings have been restored, commercial fishing boats line the docks, nets are hung out to dry and fishermen sell salmon, giant red snapper and shrimps right off the boats.

Victoria ❦

Victoria, the BC provincial capital at the southern tip of Vancouver Island, is aptly named. Big city Vancouverites scorn North America's most British city as being 'behind the tweed curtain' but the locals capitalize on their 'Englishness', especially during the tourist season. They play cricket and croquet in the many parks and take afternoon tea; shops sell Wedgwood china, Scottish shortbread and Irish linen; and red double-decker sightseeing buses or horse-drawn carriages ply the quiet streets.

Canada's symbol, the maple leaf, during a brilliant fall

Canada's elderly, here to retire, help set the city's conservative, proper tone—somewhat surprising when you consider Victoria sits on the edge of untamed wilderness and fishing, mining and logging communities. But the city's climate is Canada's gentlest and ideal for retirement, with only 68 centimeters (27 inches) of annual rainfall and an average of six hours of sunshine daily. While most of the country hibernates under a blanket of ice and snow, flowering baskets hang from 19th-century globed lamp posts, and in February local flower enthusiasts officially 'count the blossoms.' The total count is generally over three million blooms.

Victoria's history would not suggest such a genteel end. Spain's Juan Perez reached Vancouver Island in 1774, Captain James Cook claimed it for England four years later and Captain George Vancouver arrived with HMS *Discovery* in 1792 to press the point. Under pressure from the British, Spain finally abandoned claims to the area three years later, but Victoria was not settled until the Hudson's Bay Company, the giant fur trading enterprise, established Fort Victoria in 1843 as its headquarters.

The company was then all-powerful in BC, acting as government as well as the only real business with the governor of the company ruling the land. Interested solely in fur trading, the Hudson's Bay Company did nothing to encourage colonization.

Fifteen years after the company moved in, gold was discovered on the Fraser River and BC's only port quickly transformed Victoria from a frontier trading post to a supply town for fortune seekers heading to the gold fields. Soon after Queen Victoria moved the British Navy's Pacific Fleet from South America to nearby Esquimalt harbor which is now a Canadian Navy base. Victoria has been the provincial capital, and a government town, since BC joined confederation in 1871.

Getting There

Just getting to Victoria from Vancouver is pleasant. You can make the scenic, three-hour trip by car (or bus) and ferry, or take an equally picturesque half-hour helicopter or float plane flight. Contact Helijet Airways, 273-1414 or Air BC, 388–5151 from Vancouver, 688–5515 from Victoria. Car ferries from Tsawwassen, 32 kilometers (20 miles) south of Vancouver, to Swartz Bay, on the island, operate every two hours on the odd hour from 7 am to 9 pm except in summer when sailings are hourly. During peak travel periods, there may be several sailing waits. Regular bus and ferry services with Pacific Coach Lines (385–4411) depart from the Pacific Central Staion (which is also the VIA Rail and Greyhound Bus terminal) on Main Street, and Victoria depot next to the Empress Hotel. There are also good connections from Washington State.

SIGHTS AND ATTRACTIONS

Not as dramatic as Vancouver, this port city has its own gentle beauty. In 1907, Rudyard Kipling said: 'To realize Victoria you must take all that the eye admires most in
Bournemouth, Tourquay, the Isle of Wight, the Happy Valley at Hong Kong, the
Doon, Sorrento and Camps Bay; add reminiscences of the Thousand Islands and
arrange the whole round the Bay of Naples ...'

That 'bay' is Victoria's central **Inner Harbor**, always busy with large ferries from
Washington State, seaplanes from small coastal communities, sleek yachts and work-
worn fishing boats. The well-groomed gardens of the ivy-covered **Empress Hotel** and
the BC **legislative buildings** face the waterfront. Guided tours visit the impressive
neo-Gothic, 19th-century buildings which were built from local granite, copper, slate
and wood. At night, thousands of bright bulbs illuminate Parliament like an elaborate
circus tent.

The Empress, one of Canada's great railway chateau-style hotels (see page 274),
is like a seaside castle with pinnacles and turrets, verdigrised roofs, rich wood panels
and beams, and intricate plaster decoration enriching the lofty ceilings.

High tea, an old Victoria custom, is available in at least 15 establishments, especially in the 'Olde Englande' atmosphere of the spacious, regal Empress lobby. In this
corner of genteel Britain, visitors queue for blend teas in delicate china served with
thin cucumber sandwiches, crumpets with honey butter and scones with jam and
clotted cream presented on fine silverware.

The **Provincial Museum**, also fronting the harbor, displays one of the world's
largest collections of Pacific Coast Indian artifacts. Here, a simulated 19th-century
town and an Indian longhouse are authentically portrayed. Giant cracked and
faded totem poles are moody reminders of the distinctive local Indian heritage.
Outside, at the corner of Douglas and Belleville Streets, more colorful, modern
examples greet visitors to small Thunderbird Park, a grassy area with a collection
of Indian totem poles, many topped with the carved mythical thunderbird so
prominent in tribal legend.

The **Maritime Museum**, housed in the province's first courthouse, includes marine artifacts, uniforms, model ships and a 115-meter (38-foot) Indian dugout canoe
which sailed from Victoria to England in 1901 on a 64,360-kilometer (40,000-mile)
journey. Captain John Voss and Norman Luxton sailed westward, through the South
Pacific, around the Cape of Good Hope, to Brazil and to England. Their aim was to
prove the worth of native craft and better the more famous journey by Nova Scotian
Captain Joshua Slocum who sailed alone around the world in his small sloop the
Spray from 1895 to 1898.

Somewhat contrived but enjoyable 'British' attractions include the **Royal London Wax Museum**, with a statue of Queen Victoria, of course, and a chamber of horrors. A little out of city center, at 429 Lampson Street, **Anne Hathaway's Cottage**, **Plymouth Tavern** and the **Garrick Inn** are part of an English village recreated on the **Olde England Inne** hotel grounds. The hotel is furnished with 17th-century English antiques, as is the thatched cottage. Guides dressed in period costume escort tours daily.

Architecturally, Victoria has more to offer than Vancouver, especially among the old city's cobblestone streets, quaint alleys and brick sidewalks, arcades and small heritage squares. The restored area of 1850s-era buildings includes **Bastion Square**, where James Douglas established Fort Victoria in 1843. Street names such as Trounce Alley and Market Square recall the gone, but not forgotten, British Empire.

Victoria's shops specialize in imported Royal Doulton or Wedgwood china, fine Welsh tapestry, Harris tweeds, woven woollen clothing and crafts, English toffee, teas and biscuits as well as authentic Canadiana—native art, woolens, furs and Hudson's Bay Point blankets. These distinctive blankets in a natural wool off-white background with broad green, red and black bands were traded to the Indians for furs. Now they are also made into winter coats which are popular and practical souvenirs.

The city's other imposing heritage buildings include colonial-style **Craigflower Manor**, dating back to 1856. Across from the manor, the oldest schoolhouse in Western Canada is now a museum containing numerous pioneer artifacts. Robert Dunsmuir, a Scottish coal baron, constructed the massive 42-room **Craigdarroch Castle** in 1885 as a present to his wife. His farm represented the transition of Victoria from fur-trading outpost to permanent settlement. Fireplace bricks were baked in the farm's kiln and lumber produced at the estate sawmill. Dunsmuir died before the fine building was completed. With its towers and turrets, chandeliers and stained glass, this new world anachronism is one of Canada's few castles.

Other stately homes can be viewed from scenic Marine Drive where they front the rocky shoreline giving a sense of genteel, residential Victoria. The Hudson's Bay Company set aside **Beacon Hill**, the start of the drive, as the province's first park in the 1850s.

The 14-hectare (35-acre) **Butchart Gardens**, 21 kilometers (13 miles) north of the city, are considered by those who know as among the world's best. They date back to 1904 when estate owner Jennie Butchart decided to transform part of her limestone quarry into a sunken garden. With flowering rockeries, lawns, a rose garden, Japanese garden and a formal Italian garden with authentic Florentine statuary and sculpted shrubs, this grand floral display attracts visitors from all over the world. On Saturday evenings during July and August, the gardens in this former quarry are ablaze with lights and fireworks.

Thousands of lights outline the Parliament Buildings in Victoria, BC

■ THE SOUTH

The **Old Island Highway** to the south is well worth a half-day of exploring. While there is a local bus service, it is advisable to rent a car for the drive passes coastal viewpoints and several other attractions. **Fort Victoria Museum**, towards Sooke, is a restoration of one of the two military bastions of Fort Victoria, circa 1843, originally located in Bastion Square. Nearby, in Colwood, **Fort Rodd Hill National Historic Park** is where a late 19th-century coastal artillery installation guarded the Esquimalt Royal Navy Yards. While attractive **Fisgard Lighthouse** is not as famous as Nova Scotia's Peggy's Cove, the oldest navigational aid on the BC coast (1860) is still operating. Visitors can walk through the historic building and tour the grounds year round.

Vancouver Island

Beyond Victoria's tea-cosy-and-crumpets veneer, 450-kilometer-long (280-mile) Vancouver Island is not *Harpers and Queen* elegant but *Rod and Gun* rugged. Its 31,200 square kilometers (12,000 square miles) of largely unspoiled mountains, forests and inland farms are home to logging, fishing and mining communities. A mountainous backbone divides the island into two distinct parts: the rugged west coast, cut by deep fjords, largely unsettled except for a few small fishing villages; and the gentler eastern plain of farmlands, seaside towns and many fishing streams and lakes.

GETTING THERE AND AROUND
■ BY TRAIN

The Esquimalt and Nanaimo Railway departs Victoria daily at 8.15 am for a relaxing, day-long excursion to **Courtenay** half-way up the island, returning in time for dinner. The route dates back to 1884 when the first railroad was constructed here. The journey passes spectacular coastal scenery and quaint seaside towns. Passengers can disembark en route, ride roundtrip, return by road or continue to the north end of the island. Near Courtenay there is good fishing and hiking at **Forbidden Plateau** and **Strathcona Provincial Park**.

■ BY ROAD

The Island Highway follows the more populated east coast, with numerous hotels, motels, campsites and trailer parks for overnight stops. A spur highway mid-island crosses to the wild west coast.

A popular circle tour involves taking the BC Ferries boat (which take vehicles) from Vancouver to Swartz Bay, near Victoria. From here you can drive or take a Vancouver Island Coach Lines bus 96 kilometers (60 miles) north to Nanaimo (and beyond, perhaps) and return from Nanaimo by ferry to Horseshoe Bay in West Vancouver. Sailings are daily, approximately every two hours in winter and hourly during the summer. There are line-ups during long weekends.

SIGHTS AND ATTRACTIONS

Just beyond Victoria the 16-kilometer (10-mile) **Malahat Drive** climbs steeply to the **Malahat Summit**, with a dramatic view of the Gulf Islands, the mainland and Washington State's Mount Baker, set like a gigantic ice cream cone in the distance.

Fifty kilometers (30 miles) north, slightly south of the town of Duncan, stands a local oddity, the **Glass Castle**. Carpenter George Plumb built the castle around an old railway bunkhouse in 1962 from more than 180,000 old jars and colored bottles. Nearby, in the Cowichan Valley's **BC Forest Museum**, 23300-year-old Douglas Fir trees grow 56 meters tall (185 feet), two meters (6.5 feet) across. The park has a real steam locomotive to ride and a railway handcar to operate. **Lake Cowichan's satellite earth station** runs 45-minute tours of its facilities, including a video presentation on satellite communications.

In **Cowichan Bay**, women from the local Cowichan Indian band hand-knit heavy wool sweaters in traditional raven, bear and other motifs that make excellent and practical souvenirs. Duncan handicraft shops sell the sweaters and offer knitwear as well as wood carvings and prints.

Some 20 kilometers (12 miles) north, the town of **Chemainus** is one giant canvas, with billboard-sized murals depicting the area's history, forest industry and other local themes adorning buildings, store fronts, fire hydrants, even waste bins. When the lumber mill closed down about 15 years ago, the town decided to paint murals as a tribute to their history, and to attract visitors. The internationally famous murals, done by well-known artists as well as locals, are now a major tourist attraction.

Much older are the figures prehistoric natives cut into a broad sandstone outcrop some 10,000 years ago at **Petroglyph Park** just south of Nanaimo.

■ NANAIMO

The island's second largest city, Nanaimo, was once the home of five Indian bands until coal was discovered in the 1850s and the Hudson's Bay Company laid claim to the area. When oil-fueled ships replaced coal-burners, the mines closed and now the city lives on forestry, fishing and agriculture.

Nanaimo gave the world the nutty sport of open-sea bathtub racing. The first Great Canadian Bathtub Race (now the Great International Bathtub Race) started

(following pages) Dense forests cover great areas of British Columbia

here as a 1967 centennial project. Each July the homemade tubs cross the 35-mile (56-kilometer), often choppy Georgia Strait to Vancouver in a wild armada. The first bathtubber to cross the strait and race up the beach to ring a brass bell wins. Similar races are now held in Australia, New Zealand, the US and England.

Nanaimo's symbol is the Bastion, a small fort of peeled logs standing like a chess piece overlooking the harbor. When the Hudson's Bay Company employed coal miners here in the 19th century, they built the fort to protect settlers against hostile local Indians. When Messieurs Labine and Baptiste completed it in 1853, they boasted that a naked body could be drawn over the peeled exterior logs without getting a splinter. There is no evidence that it was ever tried.

North of Nanaimo, Highway 4 spurs west to Port Alberni. In the town of **Coombs**, en route, goats graze on the rooftops. Later, the road plunges into the softly-filtered light of lofty, 800-year-old Douglas firs in **Cathedral Grove** in **Mac-Millan Provincial Park**.

■ PORT ALBERNI

Port Alberni, at the head of a deep inlet cutting halfway through the island, is a mill town (the smell gives it away) with exceptional salmon and steelhead fishing. A number of local outfits take out charters, and even amateurs are almost guaranteed a catch. Port Alberni's **Sproat Lake** is home base for two antique Martin Mars water bombers, the world's largest, with tail fins five stories high. The forest industry still fights fires with these World War II veteran Flying Tankers.

From Port Alberni the **MV** *Lady Rose*, built in Scotland in 1937, takes day excursions along the narrow, fjord-like **Barkley Sound** to the island's west coast. The stately, 100-passenger ship stops at isolated communities en route to **Bamfield** at the sound's south end one day and through the **Broken Group** of islands to **Ucluelet** on alternate days. It is the only contact many of these little places have with the rest of the world. Along the way, passengers spot birds and wildlife, seals and, often, whales.

■ THE WEST

The road from Port Alberni continues to the wild west coast of the island, to **Long Beach** and the **Pacific Rim National Park** where giant Pacific rollers crash into vast stretches of hard-packed sand beaches and sea lions bask in the summer sun.

There are comfortable lodgings as well as camping, between Tofino in the north and Ucluelet some 32 kilometers (20 miles) south. Here the historic *Canadian Princess* steamship, which once plied the Inside Passage to Alaska, is now permanently moored, operating as a resort hotel from March through September.

Some 40 to 50 grey whales, weighing up to 30 tons each, feed year-round off the island's west coast. Thousands of other whales migrate to California breeding grounds past these windswept shores in the fall, returning in the spring.

■ THE NORTH ISLAND

Back on the east coast, the Island Highway continues north to even more remote country. **Strathcona**, British Columbia's oldest provincial park (established 1911) on Highway 28 west of Campbell River, is a wildlife sanctuary with waterfalls, rivers, wilderness trails, alpine flowers and tarns.

From **Great Central Lake Head**, experienced hikers can reach Della Falls, at 440 meters (1,443 feet) North America's highest year-round falls. Camping and lodging are available in the park.

Near Campbell River, a popular sport fishing center, the **Cape Mudge Indian Village Museum** on **Quadra Island** contains masks, carvings and ceremonial objects confiscated by the Canadian government 50 years ago when potlatch dances and feasts were outlawed. The museum, built in 1979, is suggestive of a traditional Kwakiutl structure, its form inspired by the sea snail.

Farther up-island, ferries leave seven times daily from **Port McNeil** to **Alert Bay** where the **world's tallest totem pole**, 54 meters (178 feet) high, has carved figures relating stories of the Kwakiutl Indians. (The totem is an ancient form of Northwest Coast Indian art. The carved figures depicting animals and man relate their people's beliefs and legends, such as creation myths and family history.)

Farther north is **Port Hardy**, a town set amid lakes, hills and streams, and the end of the line. Nearby **Mount Cain** is a popular ski area serving the north of the island. From here, travelers must turn around and head back south, or take a ferry up the scenic **Inside Passage** to **Prince Rupert** on the northern mainland.

The Interior

The bulk of BC's population clinging to the coastal cities know the rest of the province, the vast expanses of grasslands, mountains, forests, lakes and wooded hills, simply as The Interior.

An hour's drive out of Vancouver is like a whole different country from the urbanized coast. Here among the orchards, dairy farms, market gardens and beyond to the sprawling ranches, the pace is different. Folks wear cowboy hats and baseball caps, plaid shirts and denims, and the only brands of jeans are Levis, Lee and GWG.

Most of the population and the attractions are in the southern third of the province. The truly adventurous head north, where roads run for lonely miles without a sign of human habitation and it is not unusual to see brown bears fishing in streams.

Interior towns have little theater or sophisticated entertainment, though there are some lively, foot-stompin' country-and-western music bars. Attractions are mostly outdoors—boating, swimming, riding, hiking and historical sites from the wild pioneer days. Outdoorsmen camp and canoe, fishermen cast into small mountain lakes, hooking kokanee salmon, trophy-sized rainbow or cutthroat trout, or fish rivers and streams for Dolly Vardin and steelhead trout. Throughout the province, outfitters operate fishing, whitewater rafting, hunting and photo trips (also see pages 46–55).

Those who prefer to take the great outdoors leavened with good restaurant meals, clean sheets and hot showers can drive the province's 12,800 kilometers (8,000 miles) of paved roads, visiting parks, towns and historic sites, and staying in hotels, motels, resorts or luxury lodges.

At dude and guest ranches in the Cariboo/Chilcotin, High Country, Rockies or Kootenays, weekend cowboys and cowgirls ride the range, take part in ranching activities, dig into hearty home-cooked meals then relax before open fires with a glass of wine or something stronger.

Some resorts emphasize ranch experiences, hay rides and trail rides, barbecues and country-and-western entertainment. Try the **Sundance Guest Ranch** outside of **Ashcroft** and the **Gang Ranch** northwest of **70 Mile House**. The **Hills Health and Fitness Ranch** near **100 Mile House**, provides spa and exercise facilities and pampers guests with hydrotherapy pools, saunas and massages following games of golf or tennis. The Cariboo is renowned for its dry powder snow, ideal for sleigh rides and cross country skiing.

A GRAND CIRCLE

Tourism BC divides the province into nine regions and suggests self-drive circle trips such as the Gold Nugget Route, Valley Vineyards and Gold Rush Trail. Tourism areas are the Northwest, Peace River, Cariboo, High Country, Vancouver Island, Southwest, Okanagon, Kootenays and the Rockies.

Nondrivers can cover a large chunk of territory comfortably with a train-ferry-bus circle route. The journey starts with a train to Prince George, the province's third largest city and the northern capital, and another to Prince Rupert on the northern coast. From Prince Rupert there are direct flights back to Vancouver, or better, a ferry to Vancouver Island, a bus south to Nanaimo and another ferry back to the mainland. With stops on the way, the return journey should take about one week.

BC Rail's Cariboo dayliner journey from North Vancouver to **Prince George**, some 740 kilometers (460 miles) and 13 hours away, departs each summer morning at 8 am, with fewer runs the rest of the year. Good meals are included in the Cariboo Class ticket, and snacks and drinks are sold on board.

The train follows deep **Howe Sound** inlets and the **Coast Range Mountains** to the top of a high plateau. Sometimes small planes are spotted flying in the Fraser Canyon below. Leaving the coastal forests behind, the train enters **Cariboo Chilcotin** cowboy

The Thompson River cuts through the dry hills near Kamloops, BC

country, 13,000 square kilometers (5,000 square miles) of empty rangeland plateau. Towards evening, ranchland gives way to timber country and the great beehive burners of the lumber mills before the day's journey ends in Prince George, a mill and railroad center and hub of the north. **Prince George** is more a jumping off point for travel throughout the north than a destination in itself. There are some interesting tours of the tree nursery and various modern pulp, saw and plywood mills, as well as the **Native Art Gallery** and the **Fort George Regional** and **Railway Museums** displaying pioneer artifacts.

Three times weekly VIA Rail's Skeena Liner, traveling westward from Jasper, Alberta, departs Prince George at 6.15 am, following the **Skeena** (River of the Clouds) to the coast, 14 hours and 751 kilometers (467 miles) away. The train chugs past thick rain forest, lonely northern farms and century-old totem poles in Indian settlements such as **Kitwancoo** and **Kitwanga**. Crossing high trestle bridges and passing through long tunnels, the Skeena follows a long fjord where, in one 30-kilometer (18-mile) stretch, there are 65 waterfalls, some cascading over the train.

Prince Rupert, the rail head, is a scenic Cannery Row-type ocean port with fishing boats, tugs hauling log barges and fishing sheds on stilts. It is also the point from where the return trip to Vancouver begins.

THE TOTEM CIRCLE

A similar journey by car, BC Tourism's Totem Circle route, allows more time for stopovers. The route from Vancouver follows the once-grueling Cariboo Wagon Trail several hundred kilometers through the center of the province to the gold fields where fortune hunters flocked more than 100 years ago. It is now an easy drive on paved highway, with interesting stops such as museums in **Lillooet** (Mile O of the Trail), **Williams Lake, Quesnel, Clinton, Lac La Hache** and **Wells** recounting the rowdy 1860 gold rush days.

The major appeal is in the wild countryside. These small towns have little aside from their museums, colorful history and occasionally old buildings or churches. The exception is **Williams Lake** which every year holds the country's second largest stampede (after Calgary, see page 112) in the first weekend of July.

Barkerville, some 82 kilometers (50 miles) southeast of Prince George, once claimed to be the largest town west of Chicago and north of San Francisco. The liveliest of the Cariboo boom towns, it had saloons and breweries as well as churches, newspapers and a theater. In its heyday Barkerville yielded some $50 million in gold. Gradually the ore diminished and by the late 1800s the town was practically deserted.

In the **Barkerville Provincial Historic Park**, a 'Living Museum' of more than 100 authentic buildings and displays, there is gold panning at the **El Dorado**, shows at the **Theater Royal** and iced soft drinks at the **Root Beer Saloon**, served authentic cowpoke style.

Most of the region's more than 20 provincial parks—including **Tweedsmuir**, BC's largest, with Canada's third highest waterfall—have camping facilities. Lodges, resorts, fishing camps and guest ranches provide a more civilized comfort in the wilds.

THE QUEEN CHARLOTTE ISLANDS

Some 80 kilometers (50 miles) offshore, connected by ferry or air, are the Queen Charlotte's, 'Canada's Galapagos'. These two large islands and 150 smaller islands form a moody, fog-shrouded archipelago still largely untouched by the modern world. Here are pods of grey whales, deer, Haida Indian totems and villages the Haida Indians abandoned to escape a smallpox epidemic.

Often covered in fog and overcast skies, these are also known as the misty islands. All towns are small here, the population totals only 6,000. Despite the climate, the area is attractive for its wilderness, wildlife such as the tiny Sitka blacktail deer and eagles, and marine life such as seals, porpoises and whales found in the many inlets. Attractions are the **Naikoon Provincial Park** on **Graham Island**, the **Delkatia Wildlife Sanctuary** in **Massett**, the **Queen Charlotte Islands Museum** in **Skidegate Landing** and the **abandoned Haida villages**. Permission to visit unoccupied village sites and **Haida reserves** is necessary, from either the Massett Band Council (604) 626-3337 or the Skidegate Band Council (604) 559-4496.

This remote area with limited accommodation is suited for those looking for a true outdoor experience and not geared for mass tourism. For information on guided walks, trail rides, boat and bus tours, accommodation and other information, contact the Queen Charlotte Islands Chamber of Commerce (604) 557-4661. BC Ferries has approximately five weekly sailings from Prince Rupert to Skidegate Landing on Graham Island and there is daily air service into Sandspit on Moresby Island.

PARKS

BC has five national parks (Glacier, Kootenay, Mount Revelstoke, Pacific Rim and Yoho) as well as nearly 400 provincial parks. One in ten of these is in a wilderness area—on lakes, in the high Rockies, on islands in the Pacific and in the remote north. Many parks offer programs of walks, talks and other activities related to the area's natural and human history. Among the most popular are the already mentioned Strathcona, Cathedral, Pacific Rim and Tweedsmuir, as well as Manning Park in the Cascade Mountains two-and-a-half hours from Vancouver, the Shuswap Lake system in southern BC and Kokanee Glacier Provincial Park, an undeveloped area in the Selkirk Mountains. There are also a number of historic sights. The Ministry of Environment and Parks provides more than 30 publications describing provincial parks.

THE SOUTHERN INTERIOR

Most of BC's interior attractions are within easy reach of the Trans-Canada Highway, running east to Alberta. The south central **Okanagan**, a gentle region of orchards, lakes and dry, rolling hills, calls itself the land of beaches and peaches. Fertile soil and 2,000 hours of yearly sunshine produce lush orchards of cherries, apricots, peaches, pears, apples and prunes. The area supplies the west with its fresh and processed food products, and from late June through October, roadside stands overflow with local produce.

With its extensive vineyards, this is also BC's wine-producing area. Eleven vineyards are strung along Lake Okanagan over hilltops and along shorelines. Despite oenophilist snobbery which sneers at the local product, local wines have placed well in national and international competitions since the 1960s. Most Okanagan vineyards have wine tours, tasting rooms and specialty stores. Each fall the local wineries invite the public to sample their products in their celebration of the grape at the Okanagan Wine Festival. There are fierce competitions among attending wineries, a grape stomp and plenty of tastings.

BC's equivalent of Scotland's Loch Ness Monster, a mythical serpent called Ogopogo, supposedly inhabits 160-kilometer-(100-mile) long **Lake Okanagan**, the region's largest. No link has been made with Ogopogo sightings and imbibing at the local wineries, and tourism authorities offer a reward of $1 million worth of goods to anyone confirming the creature's existence.

You can try to spot the creature from the wheelers **MV** *Fintry Queen* out of Kelowna and the **SS** *Sicamous* out of Penticton which take leisurely lake cruises on summer afternoons and evenings.

The lake's best beaches are in Kelowna, Osoyoos and Penticton. Just south of Kelowna is the **Lake Okanagan Resort**, an exclusive year-round resort on sprawling hills overlooking the lake. Golf, tennis, boating and horseback riding are available.

Near **Osoyoos** in the southern Okanagan is a desert with the dry climate and terrain of Spain, horned lizards, burrowing owls and cacti. Desert sand stretches 48 kilometers (30 miles) north to Skaha Lake and 24 kilometers (15 miles) west along the Similkameen River. In contrast, nearby **Cathedral Provincial Park** is the physical opposite, with high mountains, alpine lakes and meadows. In the **High Country** north of the Okanagan, **Sicamous** is the headquarters of a large houseboat charter fleet on **Shuswap Lake**. Even amateurs can skipper these roomy floating homes along more than 1,000 kilometers (620 miles) of placid waters and numerous remote marine parks. Three Buoys Houseboat Vacations rents luxury floating villas for four to ten persons. Call (800) 661-9558. Portside International Houseboat Charters have self-contained units (bedding and linen not supplied) for six to ten people. Rates are $400 to $800 for three days, $600 to $1,100 a week. Call (604) 836-3339.

The high spine of the Rocky Mountain Divide marks BC's eastern boundary. The Canadian Pacific Railroad first crossed this barrier in the late-1800s, completing the link in the country's transcontinental railway. **Cranbrook**, in the southeast corner of the province in the Purcell Mountains, is the main city of the eastern Kootenays and a center for tourism. Its **Railway Museum** and gallery feature reminders of early railroading days, including a restored 1929 CPR luxury train complete with walnut paneling and china and silver displays. Baggage car No. 4481 has been turned into a gallery with changing exhibits and a film room. A sleeping car, dining car and special business car with private bedrooms, bathrooms and steward's room have all been restored.

Fort Steele, 16 kilometers (10 miles) northeast of Cranbrook, was BC's first North West Mounted Police (later Royal Canadian Mounted Police) Post. In the **Provincial Heritage Park** some 40 restored structures, including the original officers' quarters, newspaper office and water tower, depict life in the fort between 1890 and 1905.

Less authentic is mock-Bavarian **Kimberley**, Canada's highest city (1,100 meters or 3,630 feet) perched in the **Purcell Mountains**, with the world's largest **cuckoo clock**, in **Der Platzl** (people place), Bavarian-style store fronts, strudel and schnitzel. Fairmont and Radium are popular year-round mineral hot springs resorts. Tourists have been attracted to **Fairmont Hot Springs Resort**, a four-season lodging and recreational center at the headwaters of the Columbia River, since 1922. Its four outdoor mineral pools with temperatures ranging from 92°F (34°C) to 108°F (42°C) allow for mid-winter outdoor parboiling. The mountain retreat has luxurious accommodation, an 18-hole golf course, tennis, horseback riding, skiing, river rafting and spa facilities.

Two national parks straddle the BC-Alberta border, high in the Rockies. The Trans-Canada Highway follows the winding **Kicking Horse River** through **Yoho National Park**, with more than 30 sawtooth peaks higher than 3,000 meters (9,000 feet) and **Takakkaw Falls**, Canada's highest uninterrupted cascade spilling 381 meters (1,257 feet) into the Yoho River. In **Kootenay National Park**'s glacial ice fields, 200 kilometers (125 miles) of hiking trails ascend the slopes for panoramic views. Park wildlife include bighorn sheep, grizzlies, wolves, coyotes and moose. The 1,650-meter-high (5,445-feet) Vermilion Pass marks the summit of the Great Divide, where waters run east to the Arctic or Hudson Bay and west to the Pacific. Here, too, is the provincial boundary. Beyond lies Alberta and the Prairies.

The Prairies

The Prairie provinces—Alberta, Saskatchewan and Manitoba—form the Canadian heartland, the great agricultural expanse that feeds the nation—and much of the world. Many of these communities are not far removed from their pioneer days, when the sod was first broken by settlers from eastern Canada, the US and Europe. Yet the Prairies are much more than their name would suggest, with great geographical and ethnic diversity. And each province has its own distinct character.

Alberta

HISTORY

To the rest of Canada, Alberta means two things: cattle and oil. This is the wild west, a frontier of cowboys, Plains Indians and roughneck oil riggers—big sky country where the wind blows free and men on horseback still ride the open plains. Despite the stereotype, it also has two of the country's most modern cities, Edmonton and Calgary.

Even Alberta's wild history is out of step with the rest of Canada's orderly development. The first European to see this area was probably a Hudson Bay trader who came in 1754. Edmonton, the provincial capital in the north, was just a fur-trading fort for much of its existence, then a rowdy supply depot for prospectors heading for the Yukon gold rush.

More than any part of Canada, southwestern Alberta had a violent, American-style, wild-west past. In the lawless 1870s, American buffalo hunters, trappers and traders from Montana sold 'firewater' to the Indians from illegal 'whiskey fort' trading posts such as Fort Whoop-up, Stand-Off, Slide-Out, Robber's Roost and Whiskey Gap.

These turbulent years led to the formation of the red-coated, paramilitary North West Mounted Police, now the Royal Canadian Mounted Police, and the eventual settlement by ranchers and farmers, miners and merchants. Albertan place names ring with the sound of the frontier: Medicine Hat, Horsethief Pass, Battle River.

SIGHTS AND ATTRACTIONS

The large (nearly 650,000 square kilometers or 250,000 square miles) and varied province has four distinct scenic regions: the southwest Rocky Mountains, rolling semiarid prairie grasslands in the southeast, central forests and plains, and a vast stretch of natural, largely unpopulated wilderness across the north. With five national and 62

Sunset over Alberta's vibrant capital, Edmonton

provincial parks, Alberta has more parkland than any other province. Beyond the cities, there are fly-in fishing camps, guest ranches, pack-horse trips into the wilderness, river rafting, covered-wagon trips, hiking into the mountains or the sub-Arctic, even bicycle touring.

■ THE ROCKY MOUNTAINS

The most popular tourist sights are in the Rockies, that majestic mountain range stretched along the BC border. Early explorers described these jagged peaks, blue ice and white snow etched against the clear sky as far as the eye could see, as 'a sea of mountains'.

Alberta's Rockies are divided into four tourist areas: the famous Jasper and Banff National Parks in the central part of the province, and the lesser known Kananaskis country and Waterton Lakes National Park to the south. All have horse riding (by the hour or overnight pack trips), whitewater river rafting on oar-powered inflatables manned by qualified guides, camping, fishing, miles of hiking trails, canoeing on mountain lakes and game viewing. Moose, bighorn sheep, mountain goat, black and grizzly bear and golden eagles are found in these parks. Tamer pursuits include scenic lake cruises, golf, tennis and soaking in hot mineral springs.

A number of sprawling, palatial lodges were built in the Rockies resorts when tourism was just being established here. Quite incongruous in the wild mountain and forest settings, they are all worth visiting.

Banff, Canada's oldest and most famous park, an-hour-and-a-half's drive west of Calgary, was founded in 1885 when sulfur hot springs were discovered deep in the Rockies. The original four hectare (10-acre) Rocky Mountain Park expanded to become the 6,640-square-kilometer (2,600-square-mile) scenic Banff National Park, which includes Lake Louise. Banff now attracts visitors from across the US, Europe and Asia—especially honeymooners.

In 1888, in an early attempt to attract tourists, the Canadian Pacific Railway built a luxury hotel in the park at the junction of the Bow and Spray rivers. Today, the **Banff Springs Hotel**, a Scottish-style castle with one of the world's most scenic golf courses, is Canada's most popular resort.

Taking the waters is still a favorite activity, and **Upper Hot Springs Pool** on Mountain Avenue is open year-round. At nearly 40°C the soothing mineral water from the **Sulphur Mountain natural springs** is comfortable even in winter. Post-pool massage is available.

Gondolas climb three Banff-Lake Louise mountains to give breathtaking, eagle-eye views of surrounding peaks and deep river valleys. The Sulphur Mountain Gondola, the first in North America built solely for sightseeing, ends at a 360-degree observation deck and a three-tiered restaurant, the highest in the Rockies.

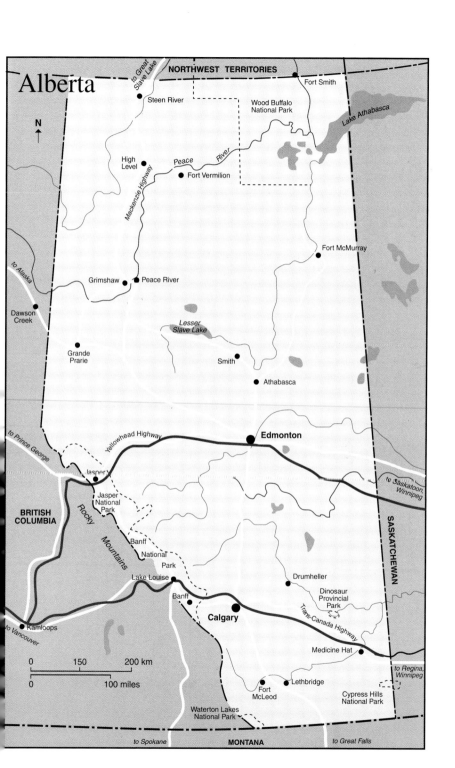

The somewhat cute and commercial alpine town of Banff sits in a dramatic setting and has its serious side in the **Banff School of Fine Arts** and the annual summer-long **festival of the arts**.

Just 56 kilometers (35 miles) and a half-hour drive northwest of Banff, little **Lake Louise** was better named originally as Emerald Lake. Queen Victoria had it renamed for her daughter, who was married to the Canadian Governor General. Louise returned the favor, changing the Saskatchewan town Pile Of Bones to Regina, her mom's formal Latin title (see page 115).

Residents claim the jewel-like lake overshadowed by **Victoria Glacier** is the world's most photographed. The 520-room **Chateau Lake Louise hotel**, built in 1905, overlooks the blue-green water like a grand, misplaced palace in the wilds.

Eleven kilometers (seven miles) from Banff, the glass-enclosed *Daughter of the Peaks* passenger boat takes two-hour scenic cruises on **Lake Minnewanka**, the only park location where motor boats are permitted.

A 230-kilometer (143-mile) 'route of the glaciers' drive, links Banff with Jasper National Park. The **Icefield Parkway** passes some of Canada's most dramatic scenery, with more than 100 glaciers, rivers and waterfalls plunging into icy lakes. It once took pack trains weeks to cross this trail which only became suitable for vehicle traffic in 1960. The route follows the continental divide, with the waters flowing to the Pacific from one side, and to the Atlantic and Hudson Bay on the other.

Evergreen forests, cut back from the highway, maximize the view and wild game often graze on these grassy tracts. It is against park rules—and is extremely foolhardy—to feed panhandling bears.

The route has scenic viewpoints, road signs explaining the terrain, wilderness trails and campsites for those who wish to linger.

The **Columbia Icefield** 145 kilometers (90 miles) north of Lake Louise is the Rocky's largest expanse of glacial ice and snow, and covers 390 square kilometers (150 square miles), including adjoining glaciers. In this awesome setting where the Athabaska Glacier creeps to less than a mile of the road, a Parks Canada interpretive center houses a scale model of the Columbia and shows an audiovisual presentation. Snowmobile tours onto the icefield depart from near the center.

Jasper, created in 1907 and now extending over 10,878 square kilometers (4,200 square miles), is the northernmost of the Rockies parks, a two-and-a-half-hour drive west of Edmonton, the provincial capital. The town and national park are on the Canadian National Railway's transcontinental line. Set in a broad valley, Jasper is less touristy and developed than Banff, though with the same spectacular scenery and wilderness pursuits. **Jasper Park Lodge** on **Lake Beauvert** is yet another railway resort in the wilderness.

(preceding pages) The rolling south Alberta foothills mark the end of the prairies

The **Jasper Tramway** climbs 2,285 meters (6,169 feet) up **Whistler Mountain** to hiking trails continuing even farther up. From this summit are sweeping views of faraway **Mount Robson** (Canada's highest Rockies peak at 3,954 meters or 12,929 feet), the **Yellowhead Pass** and the broad **Athabasca Valley**. From Jasper, a guided raft tour follows the early fur traders' canoe route along the **Athabasca River**.

One of the park's most scenic spots is **Maligne Lake and Canyon**, 40 kilometers (25 miles) from Jasper. In summer, two-hour scenic cruises operate hourly to **Spirit Island**, home of many Indian legends, on this, the world's second largest glacial lake.

■ OTHER PARKS

On the Canada-US border, **Waterton Lakes** became the world's first International Peace Park when it joined Montana's Glacier National Park in 1932. This small, 528-square-kilometer (200-square-mile) area is the only one of the Rockies parks with both alpine areas and prairie grasslands. Plains fauna include a herd of buffalo grazing in fields along the northern boundary. Waterton is quieter, less commercially developed than the larger parks.

The newest resort area, **Kananaskis**, an hour's drive southwest from Calgary, was the venue of the 1988 Calgary Olympics downhill ski events. The provincial government has designated the 4,000-square-kilometer (1,500-square-mile) area as a year-round, multi-purpose recreational area. Kananaskis terrain covers four distinct zones, from foothills to spruce and fir forests to alpine meadows and rocky, glacier-topped mountains. A former World War II prisoner-of-war camp now serves as a forestry research station.

Outside the Rockies, Alberta also has the world's largest park, Wood Buffalo, far to the north on the border with the Northwest Territories. Established in 1912 and with an area of 11,172 million hectares (17,560 square miles), it is the only breeding ground for the near-extinct whooping crane.

EDMONTON

Alberta is not all wilderness and this relatively unpopulated province (fewer than 2.5 million people) has two major cities of about 600,000 people each—with an active rivalry between them.

Edmonton, the province's centrally located capital, is a cluster of modern high-rises attractively set on the steep banks of the North Saskatchewan River.

This booming northern city began in 1795 as a fur-trading post. A century later, during the frantic 1898 Yukon gold rush, the village was fortunately on the All Canadian Route to the fields. Thousands of prospectors stocked up supplies before trekking the final 2,400 kilometers (1,500 miles) to the hoped-for riches ahead. Edmonton became a major supply depot, and local merchants made their fortunes, even if most gold seekers failed.

This aspect of the city's history is celebrated each summer with the ten-day Klondike Days, beginning about July 20. The Gay 90s costumes (brocade vests, sequined gowns and ostrich plume hats) and the music (Dixieland, honkytonk piano and banjo) may seem more Mississippi than northern Alberta, the false storefronts and marching bands more Hollywood than Canada, but for sheer enthusiasm and local participation, this rates as one of Canada's great festivals.

The establishment of bush plane routes to the north in the 1930s and the start of the Alcan Highway in the early 1940s further secured Edmonton's place as Gateway to the North. Oil discoveries in the early 1900s and in nearby Leduc in 1947 gave the city a tremendous economic boost.

■ SIGHTS AND ATTRACTIONS

This pleasant prairie metropolis with straight poplar forests has more parkland per capita than any other Canadian city. The **Capital City Recreation Park** extends 17 kilometers (10 miles) along the banks of the winding river valley dissecting the city. The 12,150-hectare (30,000-acre) park has some 30 kilometers (18 miles) of hiking and biking trails.

Overlooking the riverbank on the site of the original Fort Edmonton, the stately, domed **legislature building** is Alberta's seat of government. Built in 1912, it incorporates imported marble and carved hardwood oak and mahogany. Underground pedestrian walkways with tropical plants and modern bas relief carvings connect the various government buildings, while above are a fountain, reflecting pool, waterfalls, wide lawns and patterned floral arrangements. At night, the floodlit buildings seem to glow on the riverbank.

West of the legislature building, the aptly named **High Level Bridge** crosses the broad river. For Edmonton's 75th birthday, a man-made waterfall, 7.3 meters (24 feet) higher than Niagara Falls and pouring out 37,850 liters (10,000 gallons) of water a minute, cascaded over the bridge into the river. The unique falls still flow on special summer occasions.

Across the river, **Fort Edmonton Park** includes a re-creation of the last Hudson's Bay Company Fort. Its wooden buildings, stockade, fur press and dusty streets portray life in 1846. Outside the walls is a 'pioneer village' with theme streets portraying Edmonton in 1885, 1905 and 1920. There are free streetcar and train rides, and musical shows on holidays.

But Edmonton is also a modern, forward-looking city. The new **Space Sciences Center**, displaying innovative exhibits of near and deep space, is one of the world's most technologically advanced facilities, with hands-on displays of astronomy and physics, IMAX movies and laser light shows. The center is open from 10am to 10pm, year round.

The modern **convention center** housing the **Aviation Hall of Fame**, is like a huge, stylized glass staircase descending the riverbank. Nearby, the stately stone **Macdonald Hotel**, a historic riverfront landmark built by the Canadian National Railway in 1915, is one of the few old buildings on the skyline (see pages 218–9).

The four glass pyramids directly across the river are the **Muttart Conservatory**, a 'controlled environment incubator'. Three pyramids show vegetation from different climatic zones and the fourth shows changing displays.

The **Provincial Museum** depicts Alberta's vast flora and fauna through realistic habitat exhibits: the Badlands (a miniature Grand Canyon), the Rockies, forests, and grasslands.

Edmonton's **Chinatown Gate** symbolizes its friendship with its twin city at Harbin, China. Visiting Harbin artisans built the tall gate across 102 Avenue (now Harbin Road), with a granite base, eight red steel columns and a roof of hand-crafted, golden yellow ornamental tiles shaped like dragons.

The **West Edmonton Mall** is the city's most grandiose modern achievement. The world's largest indoor shopping and recreation complex encompasses 44 hectares (5.5 million square feet), with 800 retail stores and services, 11 department stores, 110 restaurants and 34 movie theaters. But statistics cannot tell the story. It has to be seen to be appreciated— or at least believed. There are exotic birds and animals, an indoor lake where Canada's largest fleet of real submarines (numbering three—the Royal Canadian Navy only has two) cruises by a full-scale wooden replica of Columbus's *Santa Maria*. The National Hockey League's Edmonton Oilers sometimes practise on the indoor skating rink, while thrill-seekers ride a triple loop roller coaster and the Drop of Doom. A massive **indoor water park** has water slides, a beach and a wave pool generating breakers big enough for body surfing. Within these expansive walls are kayak classes, golfing, dining, dancing and much more. It has to be seen to be appreciated—or at least believed. In the theme-roomed **Fantasyland Hotel**, beds are in the back of a pick-up truck, a Polynesian catamaran, a Victorian coach, a Roman villa. For some, it is the wave of the future. Others just find it bizarre.

CALGARY

Edmonton's young rival to the south, a sparkling cluster of glass and steel skyscrapers nestled in foothills, also looks to the future. Calgary, the city known as Cowtown, is an anomaly: a high tech, futuristic city with its heart, and style, set in its pioneer past.

In the summer of 1875, a detachment of Northwest Mounted Police, the legendary red-coated Mounties, arrived to bring law and order to the chaotic plains. Leader

Colonel James MacLeod named the camp at the juncture of the glacier-fed Bow and Elbow rivers, Fort Calgary after his birthplace in Scotland. Today, many downtown street names reflect this wild-west heritage: Crowchild Trail, Blackfoot Trail, Mission Road, Heritage Drive.

Fort Calgary remained a mere tent village until 1883, when the Canadian Pacific Railway chose the southern Kicking Horse Pass route through the Rockies. The railway brought settlers and ranchers to the lush, southern Alberta grazing lands, and the city mushroomed.

The people lived in log cabins at first but these were leveled in a devastating fire in 1886 and the city was rebuilt in more substantial beige-hued local sandstone, a few examples of which remain. Some more bad luck came in 1905 when Calgary was bypassed in favor of Edmonton as the provincial capital but any loss of income this might have meant was more than compensated by the huge Leduc oil strike in 1947.

The strike started the 'petro boom' that made modern Calgary the Canadian petroleum industry's corporate head office and financial center. During the 1950s and 60s the population doubled and oilmen from Texas and Oklahoma descended, helping to turn Calgary into the most American of Canada's cities. Some sneer it has become a Dallas in a Denver setting. Indeed, Calgary flaunts a cowboy, or at least gentleman rancher, style. Even local stockbrokers and lawyers sport hand-tooled riding boots, hefty belt buckles, stetsons, string ties and slim cut 'frontier suits'. Calgary's symbol is the white stetson (worn only by drugstore cowboys and tourists), the official civic gift to visiting VIPs and royalty.

Calgarians shocked stuffy Easterners and instituted a Canadian tradition in 1948 when their team, the Stampeders, finally made it to the Grey Cup, the Canadian Football League championships. It was still just a game then, but the boys from the banks of the Bow took their horses, chuckwagons, an Indian chief cheerleader, boots and stetsons to staid Toronto The Good.

The fans rode their horses through the Royal York Hotel lobby, cooked pancake breakfasts on city hall steps and paraded through the streets. When the Stamps won the Grey Cup, the weekend turned into a nonstop party. The pattern was set, and the annual Grey Cup week became Canada's longest, wildest spree, with Calgarians setting the pace even when their team is not represented. Calgary became the center of world sporting attention when it hosted the 1988 Winter Olympics, showing off its community spirit, organizational abilities and especially its first-class sports facilities.

■ SIGHTS AND ATTRACTIONS
Physically, the city has changed more than any other in Canada in recent decades. Throughout the 1970s' oil-fueled building boom, dozens of towering glass, steel and concrete skyscrapers sprouted on the bare prairies. Aside from a few sandstone build-

ings such as the courthouse and city hall, little has survived this progress. Yet many Calgarians insist theirs is the first 21st-century city. Typically, their northern rival Edmonton makes the same claim.

Only **Heritage Park**, southwest of town, gives a sense of pioneer life. Canada's largest living historical village depicts the pre-1915 Prairies, with more than 100 authentic exhibits brought from across Western Canada. The old two-story board buildings (a Chinese laundry, a hotel, a functioning bakery, newspaper office, candy store, shops and railway station) and operating CPR standard-gauge steam train seem like familiar Western movie sets.

The futuristic downtown core has adapted to a harsh, Prairie climate, leavened somewhat by Chinooks, balmy winter winds that can raise temperatures by 30°C in less than an hour. Miles of 'Plus-15s', enclosed walkways 4.5 meters (15 feet) off the ground, link many downtown buildings and the rapid transit system.

The **Devonian Gardens**, a one-hectare (two-and-a-half acre) enclosed mall at the top of Toronto-Dominion Square, is a lush, city-center oasis with some 1,600 sub-tropical plants, waterfalls, fountains and reflective pools crossed by wooden bridges. The public, indoor 'park' incorporates shops, snack bars and a playground.

Calgary's landmarks are new and grand, such as the 191-meter-high (628-feet) **Calgary Tower**, one of North America's tallest. A speedy elevator zips to the top in 63 seconds for a view of the prairies to the east, the Rockies to the west, and Western Canada's highest restaurant.

The unique **Olympic Saddledome** arena, with the world's largest free-span concrete roof shaped like a gigantic saddle, adds a distinctive presence to the skyline.

In 1985, a big and bold, $97 million, block-square, reflective glass and concrete **Civic Center** opened near the original, 75-year-old sandstone city hall. The distinctive 12-story atrium complete with trees in the center of the building has angled interior walls, skylights brightly illuminating offices and silver reflective mirrored windows with blue anodized aluminum framing, considered ideal for energy conservation.

Nearby, the new $75-million **Center for Performing Arts** houses restaurants, retail space and three modern theaters, including a 2,000-seat concert hall, home of the Calgary Philharmonic Orchestra.

Although Calgary supports a creditable collection of fine restaurants and theaters, much of its nightlife remains robust, honkytonk country and western, and decidedly macho. The city is louder, friendlier, more open than others in Canada, with a hint of the wild west in the streets.

OTHER PLACES
East of Calgary, the mountains and foothills give way to the flat prairie stretching across 1,000 kilometers (640 miles) and three provinces.

The Calgary Stampede

The Calgary Stampede, billed as the greatest outdoor show on earth and one of the world's top rodeos, helps define Calgarians' self-image. The riotous, ten-day rodeo is held the second week of July.

It started in 1886 as the Calgary Exhibition, a good, old-fashioned county fair. In 1912, American Guy Weadick, a vaudeville entertainer and trick roper from a Buffalo Bill Cody-type 'Wild West' show, organized the first Stampede. It has been a vital part of Calgary ever since.

The Stampede is part exhibition of ranching skills, part side show. The world's top professional cowboys compete for half a million dollars in prize money in popular rodeo sports like bareback and saddle bronc-riding, calf-roping, bull-riding, steer-wrestling, barrel-racing, wild horse-racing, wild cow-milking and Indian buffalo-riding.

Calgary cowboys invented chuckwagon racing in the 1923 Stampede. The race, billed as 'the most thrilling sport known to man', runs in heats of four teams of four-horse wagons and their outriders. At a signal, cowboys load tent poles and a box or barrel representing a cook stove onto the chuckwagon, race around a figure-eight pattern, then thunder through a circuit of the 800-meter (half-mile) track. It is a wild, and dangerous, race.

The 52-hectare (130-acre) Stampede Park attractions include Canada's largest midway, agricultural shows and competitions, and an 'authentic Indian village' where Plains Indians in full feathered ceremonial regalia compete in traditional dances.

Throughout the Stampede, city streets are busy scenes of free chuckwagon breakfasts, square dances and parties.

PIONEER
Canada
Government of Canada
Gouvernement du Canada

Drumheller, an hour and a half northeast of Calgary in Alberta's badlands, is a dinosaur graveyard littered with fossils and skeletons. The 48-kilometer (30-mile) **Dinosaur Trail** looping west of the city passes museums, parks and replicas of these giant beasts. The **Tyrrell Museum of Paleontology**, where scientific excavation and site work is still carried out, features the world's most extensive display of dinosaurs, including specimens from eggs to full-grown preserved skeletons. South of Drumheller the 6,075-hectare (15,000-acre) **Dinosaur Provincial Park** (one of only four UN World Heritage Sites in Canada) holds the bones of 30 species of the lumbering lizards that roamed the area for 65 million years.

South of Calgary, near Fort Macleod, the **'Head-Smashed-In' Buffalo Jump**, a UNESCO World Heritage site, is North America's largest, best preserved location of its kind. For nearly 6,000 years, until the 1880s, Plains Indians drove herds of bison off the cliffs to their death in an efficient form of hunting. Head-Smashed-In has a new interpretative center and guided walks.

Heading east beyond Medicine Hat, **Cypress Hills**, the highest point in mainland Canada between the Rockies and Labrador, supports unique vegetation and more than 200 bird species, as well as deer, moose, elk and beaver. Hiking trails and interpretive programs help if you want to see the wildlife. Cutting through the park is the Saskatchewan border, and beyond, more golden prairie wheatlands.

Saskatchewan

Saskatchewan is the most 'prairie' of the western provinces, with fields of golden wheat rippling in the wind, arrow-straight highways and flat tableland stretching out to the horizon, punctuated only by little clusters of villages and grain elevators. This level land has its own rewards, especially in its dramatic sunsets splashed across a seemingly endless sky.

Yet Saskatchewan, shaped like a tapered triangle, is more geographically varied than its stereotype of never-ending grasslands where only great herds of buffalo roamed. The north country is part of the Canadian Shield, an immense network of lakes, rivers, muskeg and swamp and 32.4 million hectares (80 million acres) of forest. Three of Canada's major river systems carve across the province, to empty into the Hudson Bay.

In southern Saskatchewan, though, trees disappear, and all wrinkles and contours flatten out. Brilliant orange oriole wings and rich purple lilacs liven prairie brown and rust and birds swirl around tractors kicking up dust in a field. Along the railway lines, stainless steel VIA trains point like great silver spears towards grey or russet Federal Grain elevators ahead.

HISTORY

Saskatchewan was included in the immense expanse of Rupert's Land that England's Charles II granted to the Hudson's Bay Company in 1670. Yet the first white explorer to visit here was Henry Kelsey, in 1690. Kelsey, apprenticed to the company as a boy, spent nearly 40 years at Hudson Bay and explored much of the Canadian plains. And while French fur traders set up trading posts in the 1750s, the first permanent European settlement was English explorer Samuel Hearne's Cumberland House in 1774. Later inhabitants were fur traders, missionaries, Mounties and Metis (mixed French and native people). In the late 19th century, with offers of free land and, especially, the CPR completing its tracks across the plains in 1882, thousands of 'sodbusters' from Eastern Canada, the US, Britain and Europe migrated to Saskatchewan.

The opening of the west led to a brief but turbulent period in Canada's history. Fearful of losing their land, the Metis set up a provisional government in 1885 under Louis Riel (considered madman or patriot, depending on the point of view, and still a controversial figure today).

A militia raised in Eastern Canada was rushed out on the newly created railway, and the decisive battle of Riel, or The North West Rebellion, was fought at Batoche, northwest of Saskatoon in central Saskatchewan. The militia used the Gatling Gun, testing it in battle at the request of its US manufacturer. It was the first time the machine gun was used in battle.

Meanwhile, Riel and the Metis soon ran out of ammunition and fired muskets loaded with nails, gravel and bits of barbed wire. They were easily defeated and Riel was hanged in Regina in 1885—an act which for decades had consequences for the ruling Conservative party. French-Canadians sympathized with Riel and saw his plight as part of the French-English struggle, and did not back the Conservatives federally until 1957 when John Diefenbaker led the party.

Battle sites have been preserved at the **Batoche National Historic Park**, including a bullet-pocked rectory and the church of St Antoine de Padoue, both now museums. The grave of Riel's military commander stands on a bluff overlooking the river, and the Canadian troops trenches are nearby.

Later in 1885, Chief Big Bear's Cree Indians skirmished with army scouts near Loon Lake, northwest of Saskatoon. **Steele Narrows Historic Park** marks the site of that last armed conflict on Canadian soil.

REGINA

Although Saskatchewan is larger than most European countries, just over one million people live there. Its two major cities, Regina and Saskatoon, are home to almost 200,000 people each. More than any other major western city, Regina, the capital, follows the prairie gridwork pattern of streets. Approaching by road or rail, it appears like a cardboard cutout silhouetted against the skyline.

Cree Indians once dried buffalo meat, cleaned hides, and collected the sun-bleached bones on the banks of Wascana Creek, giving the area the name Pile Of Bones. In a stroke of British nepotism, Princess Louise renamed it Regina (Latin for Queen) for her mother, Queen Victoria, though it is not known if there was a connection between the two names. Regina was made capital when Saskatchewan became a province in 1905.

■ SIGHTS AND ATTRACTIONS
The city center is the **Wascana Center**, a 930-hectare (2,300-acre) treed oasis surrounding a man-made lake that gives the flat landscape a distinct shape. In this extensive park, every tree was hand-planted onto the bald prairie. The artificial lake has canoeing, sailing and sailboarding as well as a marina with a restaurant.

Within the park, the 1912 provincial **legislative building** reflects stately English Renaissance and French Louis XVI styles. The cruciform building includes 34 varieties of marble, intricate carvings and changing displays.

In the nearby turn-of-the-century Government House ballroom, a local theater company re-enacts Louis Riel's trial. People from the audience sit as jurors.

Perhaps because of its regal appellation, Regina has curious British connections. The birch trees at **Speakers' Corner**, Wascana Park, were brought from Runnymede Meadow where King John signed the Magna Carta in 1215, and the antique gas lamps are from the original Speakers' Corner in Hyde Park, London. The red granite **Trafalgar Fountain** was one of a pair that sat in London's Trafalgar Square from 1845 to 1939, when it was brought to Regina. Its twin is in Ottawa.

Near Wascana is the **Norman Mackenzie Art Gallery** and, next door, the **Museum of Natural History** with an exterior frieze of more than 300 figures showing the growth of the province. The museum displays dioramas showing the history of man and prairie wildlife, and a life-sized, animated tyrannosaurus rex.

Although the Royal Canadian Mounted Police (RCMP) headquarters was transferred to Ottawa in the 1920s, the force's only training academy and museum remain in Regina. The **RCMP Centennial Museum** illustrates the long history of the scarlet-coated police force, still active today, from their dealings with whiskey pedlars and Indians to overseeing Klondike gold rush prospectors.

Here are photos, old uniforms, weapons, models of police forts and memorabilia such as Chief Sitting Bull's tobacco pouch and Louis Riel's crucifix. Modern displays

Golden wheat fields, in late fall, outside Regina, Saskatchewan

include drug paraphernalia seized by narcotics officers. The museum shows a sense of humor rare in a police force, with exhibits of Hollywood's image of the Mountie, including photos of Nelson Eddy and Jeanette Macdonald in the 1936 movie *Rose Marie.*

A Sergeant Majors' midday parade is a dazzling display of rows of scarlet coats, and summer brings the pomp and splendor of the sunset flag-lowering ceremony on the parade square.

SASKATOON

Further north, Saskatoon, the gentle, scenic riverine community, is known as the City of Bridges for the seven spans across South Saskatchewan River. An Ontario Methodist society founded a temperance colony here in 1882, naming it for the area's dark berries the Indians called 'misaskwatomin'. Temperance didn't take. Twenty years later the colony had only 113 sober citizens. Today, a cairn marks the first campsite, and there is still a Temperance Street. Until recently, no liquor was sold on the east side of the river that the society settled. The first liquor license went to the **University of Saskatchewan** faculty lounge.

The university's campus is one of the most appealing in the country, the buildings were made from local greystone by Italian stonemasons.

On the west side of the river, the **Western Development Museum** offers a 'living' glimpse of history, with a recreated Saskatchewan main street called 'Boomtown 1910'. Complete, authentically furnished frame buildings line North America's largest indoor museum street, including a barber shop, pharmacy, bank and old-fashioned movie hall showing silent films. Folks dressed in period costumes sell crafts in the shops, and the museum's restaurant serves buffalo stew and biscuits with crabapple jelly and saskatoon berries.

The **Ukrainian Museum** displays folk costumes, household utensils, tools and memorabilia of the settlers who flooded into the prairies after 1891 when Canada offered 100 free acres of land for each immigrant family. Some 170,000 peasants migrated to Canada, mainly the Prairies, from 1891 to 1914. The distinctive onion-domed Orthodox churches of the Ukrainians, and their music, dance and cuisine became an important part of the rural prairie scene.

In summers, both the *Northcote* and the W W *Prairie Schooner* cruise the tree-lined **South Saskatchewan River** for a view of the skyline. The majestic **Bessborough Hotel**, Saskatoon's own railway castle hotel built in the 1930s, is an imposing riverfront landmark (see page 280).

From Saskatoon, there are day tours to view migrating whooping cranes, and Blackstrap Mountain Provincial Park 32 kilometers southeast of the city, has boating and skiing on a mountain built for the 1971 Canadian Winter Games. The Wenuskewin Heritage Park north of the city incorporates sites where native Indian

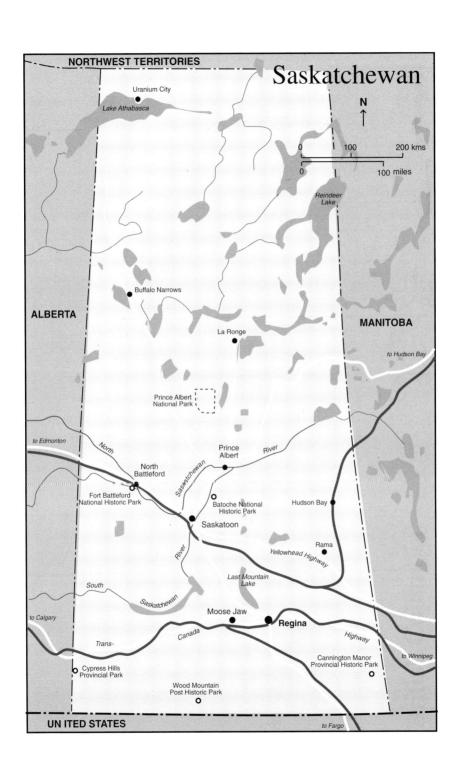

Saskatchewan

NORTHWEST TERRITORIES

N

| 0 | 100 | 200 kms |

| 0 | | 100 miles |

ALBERTA

MANITOBA

Uranium City

Lake Athabasca

Reindeer Lake

Buffalo Narrows

La Ronge

to Hudson Bay

Prince Albert National Park

to Edmonton

North

Saskatchewan

North Battleford

Prince Albert

River

Fort Battleford National Historic Park

Batoche National Historic Park

Hudson Bay

Saskatoon

River

Rama

Yellowhead Highway

South

Saskatchewan

Last Mountain Lake

to Calgary

Moose Jaw

Regina

Canada

Trans-

Highway

to Winnipeg

Cypress Hills Provincial Park

Cannington Manor Provincial Historic Park

Wood Mountain Post Historic Park

UN ITED STATES

to Fargo

Recruits drill at the Royal Canadian Mounted Police Depot, Regina, Saskatchewan

artifacts older than the Egyptian pyramids have been found. The park includes buffalo jumps, early habitation sites, audio visual programs and interpretive trails.

THE OUTDOORS

Outside the cities, Saskatchewan has plenty of attractions for outdoor lovers and adventurers. Many covered wagon train operators offer one-hour to several-day treks through areas such as the Cypress Hills and Battleford historic park. Days are marked by clopping hooves, creaking wooden wheels, the slap of leather harness and hearty chuckwagon meals around open camp fires.

Northern Saskatchewan has considerable canoeing, fishing, bird and big game hunting. **Last Mountain Lake** north of Regina is North America's first bird sanctuary, and buffalo herds roam both **Buffalo Pound Province** and **Prince Albert National Parks**. Those driving across the wheat-covered prairies tabletop will find a number of oddities, both man-made and natural. The **Rama Grotto** 260 kilometers (160 miles) east of Saskatoon, an exact replica of the famous original at Lourdes, France, was completed in 1940 by the first resident Roman Catholic priest. A miniature church stands on the site.

At **Wood Mountain Post**, Chief Sitting Bull and most of the Sioux Nation crossed the 'Medicine Line' (the Canadian-US border) from Montana after the famous Battle of the Little Bighorn in 1876. A single red-coated Mountie told the 5,000 warriors

The English Garden at Assiniboine Park, Winnipeg, Manitoba

who had massacred Custer's vaunted army that they could remain in Canada provided they obeyed the laws. The Sioux camped there in peace for years.

Cannington Manor Historic Park, 200 kilometers (125 miles) southwest of Regina, marks the spot where another misguided dream failed. Here in the late 19th century, Captain Edward Pierce attempted to establish an agricultural colony where he and his friends could live like English gentlemen. The Little England on the Prairies was to have cricket, fox-hunting and other civilized entertainments—all on the frozen, wild prairie. The privileged English lifestyle hardly suited the harsh winters, however. The original church still stands along with restored buildings and a museum in an old Victorian style home.

Manitoba

Manitoba, the keystone province because of its shape and its middle position in Canada, differs from the rest of the west in history, geography and attitude. Older, more settled, and isolated from its neighbors, it does not quite fit mould.

Its varied geography includes prairies to the west, rocky terrain covered with small lakes, rivers and bogs to the east and, to the north, the great central Lakes Winnipeg, Manitoba and Winnipegosis, networks of rivers large enough for paddle wheelers, fertile plains, huge forests and subarctic tundra.

The only Prairie province that is not landlocked, Manitoba has 780 kilometers (485 miles) of Arctic coastline on Hudson Bay. Grain is shipped to Europe from the northern seaport, Churchill, during a short nine-to-ten-week season.

HISTORY

Named for the great Indian spirit Manito, whose drum was the sound of thunder, Manitoba was first seen by a European in 1612 when English navigator Thomas Button, looking for the Northwest Passage to China, discovered the Nelson River. The Hudson's Bay Company established a trading post at Port Nelson on the shore of Hudson Bay in 1670 (the year the great company was founded, and granted almost half of Canada). French *coureur de bois*, fur traders, explorers and adventurers, explored most of the territory and establishing trading posts and settlements throughout the province, in competition with the HBC. The French surrendered title, and posts, to the British after the French and Indian War of 1763.

In 1812, Lord Selkirk founded the Selkirk settlement for evicted Scottish farmers in the central Assiniboia district, deeded to him by the Hudson's Bay Company. Problems between settlers and Metis (a mixed race of French and Indians), and the Metis' fear of losing their land, led to the first Riel Rebellion in 1870 (see page 34).

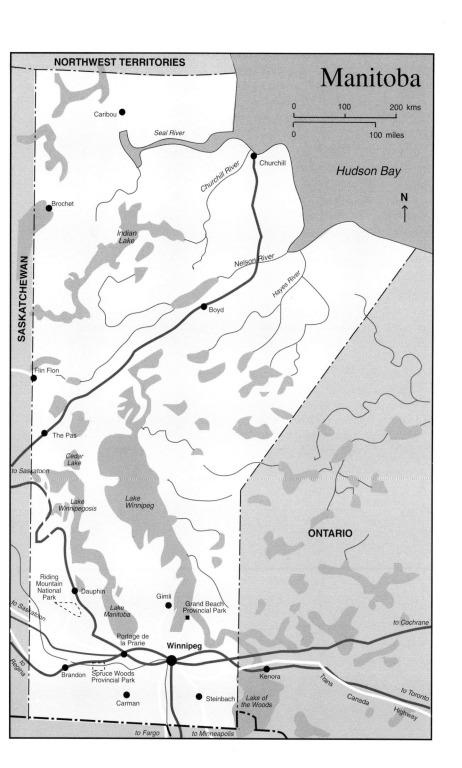

After leader Riels and his Metis supporters lost, they migrated to Saskatchewan and later staged another futile rebellion against encroaching settlers which resulted in Riel being hanged.

Increased population growth followed Manitoba's entry into the Dominion of Canada in 1870, especially after the arrival of a rail line from St Paul, Minnesota, in 1878 and the CPR in 1882.

WINNIPEG

With all east-west roads and rail lines passing through Winnipeg, the city became the prosperous transport and financial hub of western Canada. The provincial capital (and Manitoba's only large city) at the junction of the Assiniboine and Red rivers is an appealing metropolis of large trees, parks, waterways and stately buildings.

■ SIGHTS AND ATTRACTIONS

Winnipeg is noted for its historical sites and architecture, ethnic society, and its cultural life. The **Museum of Man** is rated the best man-made attraction between Toronto and the Pacific, while the **Winnipeg Art Gallery** has the world's finest collection of Inuit (Eskimo) art.

Winnipeg's skyline, especially seen from an approaching train, gives a sense of the architectural diversity here: the gleaming Golden Boy statue, perched atop the verdigrised parliament building dome; the historic Fort Garry Hotel towers; pointy church spires; and the silver-domed St Boniface College beside the Basilica. All are slowly being hedged in by tall, boxy high rises.

The modernization is of mixed success, with some pleasant additions and some less so, especially a pyramid-topped green and brick eyesore on Portage Avenue. More appealing is an extensive nearby complex with an Imax theater, an indoor waterfall that shoots three stories high on cue, an ornate clock, and an extensive shopping mall, greatly appreciated in prairie winters.

The gilded **Golden Boy** standing 69 meters (255 feet) atop the dome of the neo-classical Manitoba legislative building, was cast in a French foundry near Paris in World War I. When the factory was destroyed by bombing, the statue survived, to spend two years shuttling back and forth across the Atlantic in the hold of a troop ship. Now, the four-meter (13-foot), five-ton gold-plated bronze figure of a running boy bearing a torch and a sheaf of wheat, is the provincial symbol.

The **legislative building** is made from local Tyndall limestone, the same mottled stone used to build the federal parliament buildings in Ottawa, with fossilized fish, coral and marine life embedded right in the stone. The building incorporates Greek, British, French and Italian ornamental and structural features.

Further down Broadway, the **Fort Garry** is a classic hotel embodying the Gothic chateau style, the only example in Manitoba. The stately stone structure, built by the Grand Trunk Railway, opened in 1913.

Winnipeg's **historic center** contains Canada's best-preserved collection of turn-of-the-century commercial buildings. In the 1870s, downtown Winnipeg was a few insignificant buildings. Within a few decades, an extensive business district sprouted like spring wheat around **Portage and Main**, Canada's windiest and most famous corner. By the turn of the century, the city was the finance, wholesale and railway center of the west, and by 1910, more wheat was delivered to Winnipeg annually than to any other North American market. Banks, warehouses and supply companies sprang up, and more than 24 railway lines radiated from the city. Architecturally, Winnipeg rivalled Chicago and Minneapolis.

Fashionable restaurants, boutiques, nightclubs and shops now share the district with the stodgy original commercial firms. On summer weekends, an open air market with some 60 vendors selling fresh produce, local art and ethnic edibles thrives in the center of the district. The 20-block area is a cultural hub as well, with five theater companies, and the **Manitoba Centennial Center**, comprising the **Centennial Concert Hall**, **Planetarium** and **Museum of Man and Nature**.

■ CULTURE

Perhaps because of its isolation and its early wealth, Winnipeg developed as one of Canada's leading cultural centers. Despite its relatively small population (about 600,000), this is one of the few North American cities with all four major performing arts groups—ballet, theater, opera and symphony.

The **Royal Winnipeg Ballet** is Canada's oldest professional ballet company and the **Manitoba Theater Center**, founded in 1957, was Canada's first regional theater center, serving as a model for similar companies nationwide. **Le Cercle Molière**, the French-language group which stages productions from mid-October to mid-April, at the **Centre culturel franco-manitobain** in St Boniface, is Canada's longest continuously running theater company. **Rainbow Stage** is the most frequented Canadian theater festival.

■ AN ETHNIC MIX

Winnipeg's great ethnic diversity makes it one of Canada's most interesting cities, especially for dining. Its many and varied restaurants represent some 30 nationalities, from Asia, Europe, Latin America, and the Caribbean. Besides Chinese, Japanese and Korean, and German, Scandinavian, Ukrainian and French-Canadian cuisines, are the lesser-known Mennonite and Romanian dishes. A local Romanian specialty is Dracula chicken with, of course, lots of garlic.

The province's mix of peoples is reflected in folk festivals such as the two-week, midsummer Folklorama, one of the continent's largest ethnic gatherings. In this 'festival of nations', more than 40 pavilions scattered throughout the city offer food and entertainment from around the world. In early August, Gimli, 100 kilometers (60 miles) north of Winnipeg and the largest Icelandic settlement outside of Iceland, celebrates Islendigadagurinn. Icelanders came to Gimli in the mid-19th century and the town's name, derived from Norse mythology, means 'home of the gods'.

Also celebrated at various times during the year are a Ukrainian week, Indian Days and Pow-Wows with native dancing, Oktoberfests, La Fête de St Jean-Baptiste French cultural festival, a Highland Gathering and more. St Boniface's Festival de Voyageur in February honors the early fur traders with dances, period costumes and feasting at various 'trading post' restaurants throughout the city. (For further details of festivals, see pages 259–267).

■ ST BONIFACE
The old community of St Boniface across the Red River, the largest French-speaking community west of Quebec, retains a distinctive character. Crossing the Provencher Bridge is like going to a Quebec town.

The **St Boniface museum**, in Winnipeg's oldest building and North America's largest oak log structure, was built as a Grey Nun convent in 1846. The three-story white wood museum housing Western Canada's largest collection of Metis artifacts gives a touching sense of the simple, hard life of early prairie fur trappers, Metis and Indians.

The chapel has a hand-carved pulpit and a large, pâpier-maché statue of the Virgin Mary made by one of the original Grey Nuns from Montreal. A reproduction of an 1860s Metis buffalo hunting camp includes a full-sized replica of an all-wood Red River cart, draped with furs, and a mural of a buffalo hunt. A model of a birch-bark canoe, rifles, muskets, simple articles from the early homes, Indian beads, feather headdresses, and skins all recreate 19th-century Manitoba life.

Artefacts of the 1885 Battle of Batoche include Canadian troops' bullets and the Metis' musket balls and an exaggerated, grand painting of the battlefield. The museum displays a number of articles relating to Louis Riel, the Metis patriot and president of their brief provisional government (see page 34). **Riel House** is in a national park and his tomb is in the **St Boniface Basilica cemetery**.

Only the Romanesque facade survives of the old basilica, which burned in 1968. A modernistic church blending the old and the new has been built incorporating these ruins.

DAY TRIPS
Attractive side trips to the land of lakes beyond Winnipeg include many quiet beaches and wooded parks. Those on the southern shores of **Lake Winnipeg**, the continent's

seventh largest lake, are the largest. **Grand Beach Provincial Park**, 87 kilometers (54 miles) north of Winnipeg, where fine, powdery sand forms dunes along the shore, has one of Canada's finest freshwater beaches.

Riding Mountain National Park, 208 kilometers (129 miles) north west of the capital, where early traders and travelers changed from canoe to horseback, is a retreat of grasslands, meadows, forests and 75 small, scattered lakes. The largest, the aptly named, spring-fed **Clear Lake**, runs 30 meters (100 feet) deep. The park shelters elk, bear, deer and moose, as well as a buffalo herd grazing among the poplars.

The 16-hectare (40-acre) **Mennonite Heritage Village**, 56 kilometers (35 miles) south in **Steinbach**, is laid out in a traditional pattern with farmhouses on one side of the street, commercial buildings such as a blacksmith shop and stores on the other. A huge windmill with 20-meter (60-foot) sails turns out flour used to bake bread sold in the village. A restaurant serves Mennonite delicacies.

The **Western Canadian Aviation Museum** at **Friendship Field**, Carmen, 90 kilometers (55 miles) southeast of Winnipeg, has a collection of World War II aircraft, including Japanese Zeros, restored to flying condition.

Set in the wheatfields near the Saskatchewan-Manitoba border lies the **Carberry Desert** (now more poetically called the 'Spirit Sands'), 29 kilometers (18 miles) south of the TransCanada Highway near the Spruce Woods Provincial Park. The rolling, shifting dunes and waves of rippling hard-packed sand resemble Foreign Legion movie terrain.

NORTH TO CHURCHILL

From Winnipeg, Churchill is a two-hour flight or two-night VIA Rail trip, departing Tuesdays, Thursdays and Sundays. One of the world's great train trips arcs through Saskatchewan wheat fields, past hundreds of miles of evergreen forests, cedar bogs and muskeg.

The third day brings the 'spongy' ride to the perpetually frozen tundra, with its sparse vegetation, stunted evergreens, dwarf willows and telegraph lines strung on tripods because the poles could not be set in the hard ground. The last 250 kilometers (155 miles) to Hudson Bay and the 'Polar Bear Capital of the World' is in a straight line.

The 3,394 kilometer (2,110-mile) rail journey combines a great adventure with the comfort of first-class train travel—bedrooms or roomettes are available. This is the only transport for these northern communities, and the train frequently stops in the middle of the wilderness for a prospector or fur trapper.

Churchill, on the barren and rocky coast of Hudson Bay 1,600 kilometers (1,000 miles) by rail north of Winnipeg, was a little known northern seaport and rocket

York in 1803, *woodcut, courtesy of the National Archives of Canada*

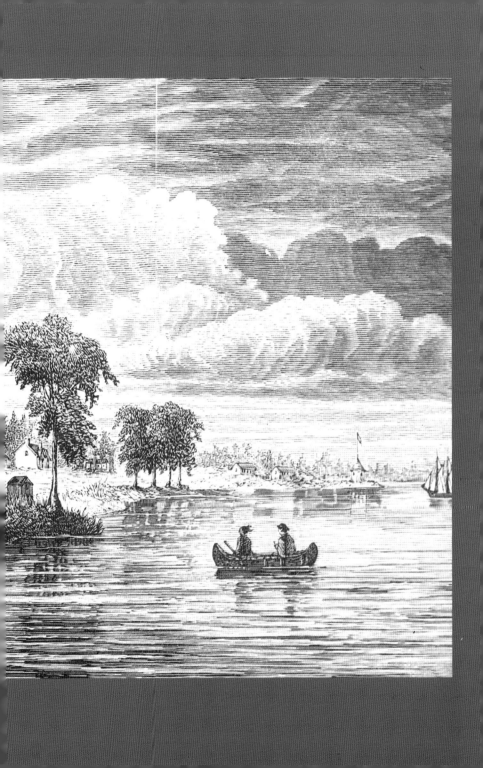

Old-Time Travel

Cruise boats have replaced the birch-bark canoes, York boats and paddle wheelers, the original means of communication along the Red and the Assiniboine rivers. In summer, five modern vessels take sightseeing and moonlight dance cruises for riverine views of Winnipeg and surroundings. The **MS** *River Rouge* carries up to 400 passengers through the heart of the city for cabaret dining and dancing. The 200-passenger **Paddlewheel Princess** and the 120 passenger **MS** *Lady Winnipeg* take scheduled day trips from the city center north to Lower Fort Garry, the only stone fur-trade fort left intact in North America. The trip allows a one-hour stop to explore the original fort.

The **Prairie Dog Central**, the oldest authentic steam train operating on a main line in North America, is a half-day journey back in time, as well as into the countryside. Every summer Sunday, the vintage train makes two-hour morning and afternoon return runs to Grosse Isle, 58 kilometers (36 miles) northwest of Winnipeg.

The hand-fired, coal-burning engine with its belching smokestack, brass-trimmed boilers and coal tender pulls six coaches, built from 1901 to 1913. Seats on these rolling museum pieces are wicker, leather or green velvet. Some cars have grained oak paneling and coal stoves for heating in winter.

The Prairie Dog, brass bell ringing, steam whistle shrieking, rolls through the suburbs into the prairie farmland, the smell of coal smoke and the squeal of metal wheels against metal tracks recalling the great railway days. During a 15-minute stop at Grosse Isle, the engine is uncoupled and recoupled, then the Prairie Dog rolls back to 'The Peg'. Volunteers from The Vintage Locomotive Society, a group of retired railway workers, lovingly operate the train.

research center until recent years. Now, it is a popular destination for adventure tourists seeking its two giant mammals, beluga whales and polar bears.

The small town of 1,200 is the world's only easily accessible community where the largest of land-dwelling carnivores can be seen in the wild. The great white bears, healthy males weighing more than 1,000 pounds, are the Lords of the Arctic. In the fall, the hungry animals prowl the coastline waiting for ice to form on Hudson Bay so they can hunt seals. Because the Churchill River freezes before the Bay, up to 150 bears wander near, or through the town from September to early November. Locally designed Tundra Buggies, customized bus chassis sitting 3.6 meters (12 feet) above ground on huge tractor tires which put little pressure on the fragile tundra, go bear-viewing near town. The lumbering bears come up to the vehicles, standing on their hind legs and leaning against them with their great, white paws.

In summer, as many as 1,000 beluga whales feed in the cold, blue waters of Hudson Bay. Attracted by the motors of open sightseeing boats, the giant sea mammals swim right alongside, diving and flashing their great flukes and calling out in the strange whines and bleats that gave them the name 'sea canaries'.

Churchill stores sell Indian and Eskimo crafts such as beaded mitts and moccasins, parkas, native prints and stone sculptures. The **Trader's Table Restaurant** serves Arctic char (a delicately flavored northern relative of the salmon) and hearty caribou stew.

Across the Churchill River from the town are the remains of **Fort Prince of Wales**, a historic park. The Hudson's Bay Company built the huge stone fort over a 40-year period in the 1700s. One of the strongest fortifications on the continent, it was called 'the preposterous fortress of the north' because it protected only the Arctic wasteland. The icy Arctic outpost was never properly manned, and when three French warships appeared in the bay in 1782, the governor, Samuel Hearne, surrendered without firing a single shot. The French sacked and burned the fort, spiked the guns and blew up parts of the wall. It was never again occupied.

Several private companies operate tours even further north from Churchill. One typical tour includes flights to Baker Lake and Rankin Inlet, in the Arctic, to see drum dances, sample Arctic food such as char and caribou, watch traditional story telling, tour an ancient Eskimo summer fishing camp and meet with community members. (See Adventure section, pages 46–55.)

(following pages) Kathleen Lake in the wild Kluane National Park in southwestern Yukon

The North

Few Canadians, let alone visitors, venture into the Great White North. It is among the harshest environments that man can survive in, with long, extremely cold winters and short but spectacular summers. Yet those who go are often caught by the magic of this strange, silent land, and fall in love with it, many returning frequently after the first revealing visit.

They are taken with the sheer immensity, the rolling, treeless tundra stretching out to the horizon, scattered emerald-like lakes and the craggy snow-clad peaks reflected in the bright summer sun. They remember fields of colorful, tiny blossoms, mosses and lichens, the sheer cliffs plunging into icy dark seas, silent icebergs larger than battleships, a sun which never sets in summer, never rises in winter, and air more clear and crisp than anything they have ever known.

While it is not for everyone, the delicate but brutal nature of this savage land leaves many visitors awestruck.

Canada's north is divided into two quite different areas, the slightly more populated and more accessible Yukon, and the Northwest Territories, itself divided into three districts, Franklin, Keewatin and Mackenzie.

Northwest Territories

The vast, sparsely populated Northwest Territories covers nearly one-third of Canada, the world's second largest country. With over 3 million hectares (1.3 million square miles) of mountains, tundra, lakes, rivers and ocean coast, its 50,000 inhabitants have plenty of space. You could fill a football stadium with all of the people living in an area larger than India. One of the world's last unspoiled areas, this is no 'If-its-Tuesday-this-must-be-Tuktoyaktuk' one-trip destination. Those adventurous enough to go north should focus on one region or activity.

The Territories include national parks (Nahanni, Wood Buffalo, Auyuittuq and, since 1986, Ellesmere Island) and four sanctuaries.

A tree line running diagonally from the Arctic coast of the Yukon in the far northwest to Churchill, Manitoba, on Hudson Bay in the southeast bisects the Northwest Territories into two distinct geographic regions. North of the line, the barren, treeless terrain is home of the Inuit, formerly known as Eskimos. (In Canada, Eskimo is considered a derogatory Indian term meaning 'eater of raw flesh'. Alaskan natives readily admit to the custom and retain the term Eskimo.) Below the line, the sub-Arctic topography of forests of mainly stunted coniferous trees is home of the Dene (northern Indians) and mixed-blood Metis.

Because of the bleakness of the terrain, sub-Arctic population densities are among the world's lowest. The Territories' population is divided roughly into 18,500 Inuit, 11,500 Dene and Metis (mixed Dene and white), and 22,000 'other'.

History

Before the 20th century, the Inuit and Dene were hunters who had lived off and traveled the land for millennia. The ancestors of the Dene, called People of the Small Knife, were thought to have occupied the Mackenzie Valley in the western sub-Arctic for at least 10,000 years, living in bands of about 25 to 30 people to hunt, fish, trap and gather wild plants.

The advent of whaling, fur-trading, religious missions and military installations by European powers changed all that. The first to arrive were the British, whose navigators were seeking a northwest route to the Orient (see page 22 and 70–71). They were also the first Europeans to show interest in the Arctic's whaling and fur-trading potential, and left their mark through such place-names as Frobisher Bay, Baffin Island, and Mackenzie River, though some of these are reverting to their native names.

The fur-trading companies were again at the forefront in exploration. Having ventured across much of the land further south, traders for the Hudson's Bay Company and North West Company looked north and began building posts in the Mackenzie Valley in the late 1700s. By the early 1900s the Hudson's Bay Company, a powerful force in the north, brought the coastal Inuit into fur trading. Life began to revolve around the trading posts and many native groups, once nomadic hunters, grew dependent upon fur sales.

When pelt prices dropped in the 1950s, the federal government began distributing welfare funds and building housing and schools. The Inuit way of life changed, with the nomadic natives moving into settlements and living together—not necessarily an improvement in their lives.

Settlements that characterize the way of life of most of the Territories' people are now unsightly affairs of mainly prefabricated houses with yards cluttered with snowmobiles and sleds, animal hides, ropes, traps, tools and drying fish. Few have running water, so in some communities once or twice a week a water truck replenishes the tanks in each home. But these dreary settlements are not what draw visitors to the north.

When to Visit

The ideal time for visiting is between mid-May and late August, when the days are long and traveling conditions over the ice are good. The summer season becomes shorter the further north you go, so most lodges south of the Arctic coast open by June 15 while those north open about one month later.

Outdoors in the Great White North

For the chance to see and touch this wildly beautiful land which has long attracted experienced outdoorsmen, you should head for the provincial parks to hike, ski and climb. Camping is also popular and a must for viewing the stunning sky show of dancing northern lights and the midnight sun. Although getting there is not easy, interest in the region has grown in recent years and fortunately there are licensed operators with special training who offer a large number of package tours covering a wide array of activities.

In the Baffin region alone, 16 operators offer more than 50 travel tours. Reputable operators include Adventure Canada, Arctic Odysseys, Canada North Outfitting, Ecosummer Canada Expeditions and Northwinds Arctic Adventures. Call the Baffin Tourism Association (819) 979–6822.

Several companies run hiking or kayaking trips on both Baffin and Ellesmere islands. For two weeks campers hike or boat all day, getting close to animals and sealife, and sleep in tents at night under the midnight sun.

The 'Top of the World Trek' crosses Ellesmere, a national park since 1986 and the world's most northerly. Each day, after an early campfire breakfast, hikers pack up their backpacks and head across the bare, open, breathtaking terrain. Long treks are broken with halts to look at the delicate flora, spot the migratory birds, snack and sip tea or coffee, take photographs in this remarkable, clear light and soak in the brief northern sun, warm in the cool air.

Other tours include snowmobile and sledge trips and dog sled excursions to view Arctic wildlife such as polar bear and musk-ox in their natural habitats. Champagne flights land on the North Pole; groups on sled or boat visit Inuit (Eskimo) settlements to meet artists and sculptors, or take wildlife excursions to photograph narwhal— whales with two-to three-meters long (six-to ten-feet) twisted ivory tusks, seals and walruses.

Hardy types camp on historic Ellesmere Island, where the musk-oxen roam, or backpack in Auyuittuq National Park, 'the land that never melts'. In this highly acclaimed mountaineering area, skiers and hikers traverse the 600-meter-thick (2,000-foot) ice of the Penney Ice Cap Glaciers.

Native people who know the wildlife and sea mammals guide hunters after bear or caribou and fishermen pursuing the gleaming Arctic char. The original kayak experts also escort tours through majestic fjords, within sight of Ellesmere Island glaciers, where bowhead whales and narwhal gather.

Further west, Yellowknife, on the Great Slave Lake, is a center for adventures such as canoeing and fishing, caribou hunting, wildlife viewing, dog sledding and viewing the eerie Northern Lights that dance across the sky, especially in the fall. Contact the Northern Frontiers Visitors Association, tel (403) 873-3131 or fax (403) 873-3654.

Icy areas like this are Canada's winter playground

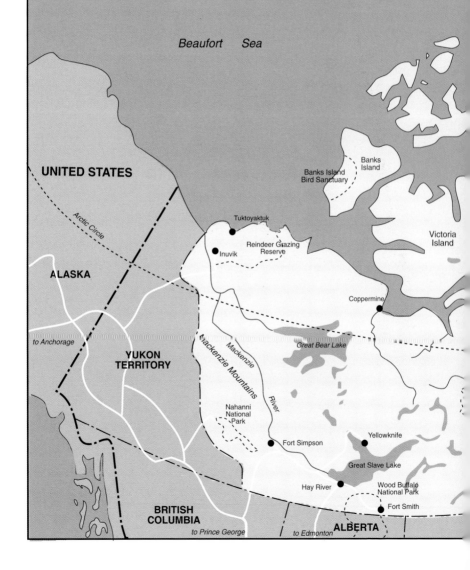

Northwest Territories

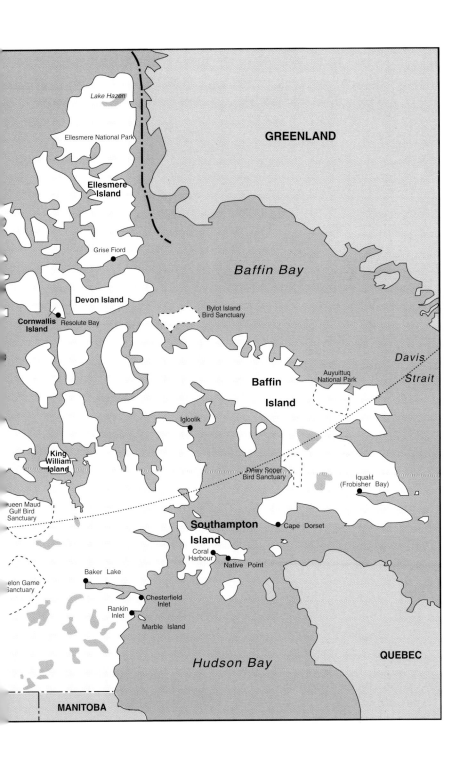

Travelers should come prepared with warm outdoor clothing and sturdy hiking boots. Sunglasses are recommended. Bring cash. Some remote settlements still do not accept credit cards or travelers' cheques.

Travel in the Northwest Territories is very expensive, and air connections can be difficult. For now, it is better for all except dedicated outdoorsmen and campers to consider one of the many package tours offered (see page 136).

Getting There and Around

The north has been an expensive and, until recent years, difficult place to travel to, but improved airstrips and navigation systems have opened much of it to tourism. There are now airlinks to Montreal, Ottawa, Winnipeg, Edmonton and Vancouver, and light aircraft on floats, skis or wheels act as truck, bus and taxi for visitors as well as residents. Meals and lodgings have improved considerably, although because of the remoteness (everything must be shipped in) prices are much higher than in the rest of Canada.

In the west, several highways penetrate the great northern expanses. The Mackenzie from Edmonton and the Liard from Fort St John and Fort Nelson, BC, run to Yellowknife, the Territories' capital on Great Slave Lake. The Dempster Highway connects from the Alaska system at Dawson City, Yukon, crossing the Arctic Circle to Inuvik, within 100 kilometers (62 miles) of the Arctic coast.

These 'all-weather gravel' roads are very hard on vehicles and require certain precautions, depending on the season, although they can be an adventure in themselves. Travelers should carry extra tires and provisions, and be prepared for a long wait in case of breakdown. Call the Arctic Hot Line (1-800-661-0788) toll-free within Canada for information. The hot line also gives hotel rates, airservice information and distances between gas stations.

The **Liard Highway**, one of the three routes into the Territories, branches from the Alaska Highway in northern BC to the **Nahanni National Park Reserve**, recognized by UNESCO as a World Heritage Site for its international significance as a unique geological area.

Here, the **Nahanni River** has carved out one of the world's eight deepest canyons, closely resembling Arizona's Grand Canyon. The valley is known throughout the north for the headless bodies of prospectors looking for a lost gold mine first discovered there early this century. No one knows what happened, but legends of the Headless Valley persist. Spend any time in a northern bar and, depending on the time of night, you will hear stories of the valley, of a lost tribe of Indians, Sasquatch (the legendary bigfoot creature), mysterious murders and fabulous lost gold mines.

The **South Nahanni River**, with its deep canyons, sulfur hot springs and abundance of wildlife, is popular with experienced canoeists. The highway continues through **Blackstone Park** camp ground to **Fort Simpson**, an old Northwest Company fur trade fort where small steam river-tugs abandoned on the riverbanks recall the days when this was a major transport point for barges going up the Mackenzie. Road transport and especially air services replaced the graceful but slow steamers and paddlewheelers which now remain as memories, and as a few sad hulls beached on lonely riverbanks.

The **Mackenzie Highway** from Edmonton goes through Fort Smith (2,500) and Hay River (3,000). Vehicles cross the Mackenzie River by ferry in the summer and drive across the ice in winter, so twice each year, during freezing and breakup, the route is cut at the river crossing.

Further north, the all-weather gravel surfaced **Dempster Highway** runs 740 kilometers (448 miles) from Dawson, center of the Yukon gold-rush country, across the Arctic Circle to Inuvik. The Dempster crosses varied tundra terrain and two mountain ranges to reach this center of oil and gas activity in the Mackenzie Delta, near the Beaufort Sea. The trip should be planned carefully, as there are few services along the way. During the summer, it is all daylight driving in the Land of the Midnight Sun.

THE MACKENZIE DISTRICT

From Yukon to the Keewatin District, and from the 60th parallel to the Arctic, the Mackenzie district includes both the relatively well-known Mackenzie Valley and the isolated coastal region.

The mainland Arctic coast is among the most remote areas of the far north, with few residents and even fewer visitors. Because the area has not been exploited by man, botanists have been able to record a remarkable 1,100 varieties of plants and flowers on these barren shores and ornithologists say there are 180 bird species, best seen at their summer home in the **Queen Maud Gulf Bird Sanctuary**.

The regional capital, **Cambridge Bay** (population 1,100), is gateway to this lonely land of musk-ox, grizzly and polar bear. Half-sunk in the harbor is Roald Amundsen's historic ship *Maud* later used by the Hudson's Bay Company. Amundsen, a remarkable Norwegian, became the first man to sail the Northwest Passage across the top of North America (1903–6 on the ship *Gjoa*. Amundsen had the *Maud* built for an unsuccessful attempt to cross the north polar basin. In 1926, Amundsen flew over the North Pole in an airship.

Local outfitters run two-week inflatable raft trips down the **Horton** or **Coppermine** rivers, and lodges provide comfortable havens in the wild. On these mixed whitewater-float trips, the long northern daylight hours provide plenty of chances to see bird and wildlife. Contact Arctic Coast Tourist Association, tel (403) 983-2224, fax (403) 983-2302.

YELLOWKNIFE

The most accessible part of the Northwest Territories is the Mackenzie Valley and the capital Yellowknife, which can be reached by road from BC or Alberta most of the year.

Yellowknife, known as YK to locals, is a thriving center of some 12,000 people and home to the municipal, territorial and federal governments. Here on the northern shore of Great Slave Lake are high-rise buildings, shopping malls, neat residential areas and typical northern shacks. Old-time miners and prospectors as well as young bureaucrats, technocrats and businessmen populate the Territories' only city, the only place where whites outnumber natives.

YK is still a small and friendly enough center so you will be on nodding acquaintance with the locals after a few days. A three-hour bus tour covers the modern city center and historic landmarks such as a cairn honoring early bush pilots and, outside town, a Bristol bomber set on a rock outcrop. In 1967, this became the first wheeled aircraft to land on the North Pole.

A tourist department pamphlet outlines a two-hour walking excursion around the **Old Town**. The **Native Arts and Cultural Center**, the two **gold mines** and the **Old Town residential** area all give an idea of what life must have been like in this remote town. **The Prince of Wales Northern Heritage Museum** (well worth a visit) displays exhibits on the town's early history and native culture. The most intriguing, and unusual, exhibit is the boat made from moose hides stretched over a wooden frame. It was erected under the guidance of the Dene elders as a replica of the boats that hunters once used to transport meat out of the mountains.

Organized attractions include boat excursions on **Great Slave Lake**, bus tours along scenic **Ingraham Trail** and underground tours of the two operating gold mines. And if you're there at the right time, Yellowknife celebrates some unusual festivals (see page 266–67).

The town has several hotels and motels (it is wise to book ahead, see page 291), souvenir shops selling etchings and soapstone carvings, and local restaurants serving northern specialties—smoked Arctic char, caribou and musk-ox. Game meats are served as roasts, steaks or burgers.

In the summer season, the best and most interesting place to eat is the **Wild Cat Café** down by the lake where the float planes land. It is set in a log cabin with benches and long tables and its menu includes game giving a taste of the true north. Walk down to the Wild Cat from town in the morning for a blueberry pancakes breakfast. In town, the **Yellowknife Inn** is good, although expensive.

Contact Northern Frontiers Visitors Association, tel (403) 873-3131 or fax (403) 873-3654.

THE FRANKLIN DISTICT

The Territories' easternmost, and largest, district includes **Baffin Island** and the **High Arctic Islands**. It has only one real 'town', Iqaluit, the region's largest community of 3,000 people set on an inlet of southern Baffin Island. Founded as Frobisher Bay trading post in 1914 by the Hudson's Bay Company, it became the site, in 1942, of the United States Air Force. They turned it over to the Canadian armed forces after it was renamed Iqaluit, the Indian word for fish camp. Later, a hospital and Royal Canadian Mounted Police headquarters were established, earning the settlement town status in 1980.

Several aircraft a day land almost in Iqaluit, which is set on a rocky, treeless shoreline. The town consists of small, portable-looking houses and a few more substantial public buildings. The **Frobisher Inn** stands like a concrete tower atop a hill, and the school is a big, white windowless block about 18 meters (60 feet) high that can accommodate the whole town in case of power failure.

Iqaluit has that vulnerable, impermanent sense of northern communities, so the sound of the aircraft coming and going that you hear even from your hotel is peculiarly comforting. Iqaluit has four suitable hotels. The Frobisher Inn is in the town's only skyscraper which also houses much of the Government, the post office, a large grocery store, the town's only swimming pool (not part of the hotel), a video rental and (a major advantage or serious drawback depending on your point of view) the Eastern Arctic's only bar, **Csaba's Cave**. Inuit carvers and artists sometimes sell their work outside the Cave on weekend evenings. The **Navigator Inn**, near the airport, is quieter. Both hotel dining rooms serve local game and fish. Local restaurant menus include Arctic char, caribou and Greenland shrimp.

The region's transportation hub is also a center for hunting caribou and polar bear, with rifle or lens. Nearby (reached by boat or snowmobile, depending on ice conditions) are ancient **Inuit sod huts** and **relics of early whalers' wooden ships**, and the 'gold mine' discovered by Sir Martin Frobisher when he arrived at the bay in 1575, believing he had finally discovered the Northwest Passage. Frobisher took ore samples back to Europe, and returned in 1577 and again in 1578 with a fleet of 15 ships. His men excavated tons of ore, which proved to be iron pyrite. Frobisher's patron was ruined, but the mariner's career continued. He later accompanied Drake to the West Indies and was knighted for heroism in the battle against the Spanish Armada (1588).

From Iqaluit, scheduled flights operate north to **Pangnirtung**, a settlement of 1,000 on a fjord off Cumberland Sound. Once rich with bowhead whales, the area was the Arctic's most important whaling center between the mid-1800s and about 1910. Today, residents still survive on marine life, fur-bearing animals, and arts and crafts.

The excellent **local artisans' cooperative** produces carvings, prints, parkas and tapestries, while a new, million-dollar visitors' center assists skiers and hikers headed

(above) The SS Klondike II, one of the last sternwheelers on the Yukon River, is now a national historic site in Whitehorse, Yukon

(left) Whitehorse's Frantic Follies vaudeville revue enlivens northern nights

for **Auyuittuq National Park** to the north. One of Canada's northernmost national parks provides ski-touring, mountaineering and downhill skiing from April to early June, and climbing, fishing and hiking from May through July.

On Baffin Island's southwest tip, **Cape Dorset** is renowned for its artists who founded the **West Baffin Eskimo Cooperative** in the mid-1950s. They produce quality soapstone carvings and lithographs and limited edition prints. Their cooperative, Cape Dorset's largest employer, welcomes visitors.

From Dorset dog sleds and small boats travel to the nearby **Dewy Soper Bird Sanctuary**, nesting grounds of the blue goose, a color phase of the snow goose, and to important archaeological **sites of early Inuit peoples**.

On North Baffin, at **Pond Inlet**, north of the Arctic Circle, the scenery is spectacular and dramatic, with sheer, icy mountains plunging into the sea and flatlands.

Pond Inlet, believed to have been an ancient Inuit campsite, nestles near the entrance to the Northwest Passage with a scenic view of the glaciated peaks of **Bylot Island** 16 kilometers (25 miles) away and the iceberg that provide the town's fresh water. British whalers slaughtered the bowheads for 20 years here in the early 19th century, hunting them to near extinction before moving on to Cumberland Sound. Whale-watching is still possible, though, and in June and July schools of single-tusk narwhal swim through the strait within sight of land.

In the spring, local families take visitors on dog-teams or snowmobiles to the char-fishing camps on the floe edge where ice meets open water. Here, they camp, fish and hunt seals under the all-day sunlight. Boats also go out to the **Bylot Island Bird Sanctuary** with its numerous migratory and year-round birds, including the snowy owl and gyrfalcon. Contact Toonoonik Sahoonik Co-op Ltd., (819) 899-8912. Pond Inlet, NWT XOA 050.

In the High Arctic, the tiny settlement of **Resolute Bay** (population 200) on **Cornwallis Island** facing the Northwest Passage was founded in 1947 as an air base and weather station. The community's weather is rated the country's worst for severity, discomfort and general gloominess. From Resolute Bay, several outfitters fly to the North Pole where, as in hot-air ballooning, the custom on landing is to celebrate with champagne. With the price tag of flying to the pole exceeding $15,000 per person, there is seldom a waiting list.

Even by the Territories' standards, the High Arctic is barren and isolated. Here, at the end of the line, **Ellesmere Island** is known for its dramatic glacier-carved mountains. A geographical oddity a relatively warm valley known as a thermal oasis—surrounds **Lake Hazen**, the largest lake north of the Arctic Circle. During the long, warm summers it is worth visiting for the profuse vegetation, 30 species of birds, Arctic hare, musk-ox and Peary caribou.

On northeast Ellesmere is **Fort Conger**, the historic camp from where US Admiral Robert Peary departed for the pole in 1909, accompanied by an assistant and four Eskimos. American explorer and surgeon Albert Cook also claimed to be the first man on the pole; but both claims are now considered false. Peary's relatively unchanged camp can be visited by charter plane.

On **Beechey Island**, three graves are ghostly reminders of Sir John Franklin's last expedition in 1845, one of the great tragedies of Arctic exploration. The simple headboards stand in a broad, bleak field of flat stones, with nothing else man-made in sight. In that cruel landscape of a frigid gravel pit, the sense of loneliness and vulnerability is frightening.

The northernmost scheduled flight is to **Grise Fjord** on the southern tip of Ellesmere, where the permanent white population numbers three. The town is a few blocks of prefabricated buildings in a spectacular setting before a huge mountain, and the only traffic is the three-wheeled all-terrain vehicle now popular in the north. Bring your own tent. Hiking here in the short season, when Arctic flowers bloom and the sun never sets, is outstanding. Nothing grows higher than your ankles, you can see to the end of the world—and spot bears for miles away. Only for experienced hikers and outdoor types. Baffin Tourism Association, tel (819) 979-6551 or fax (819) 979-1261.

THE KEEWATIN DISTRICT

Extending north of Manitoba and embracing Hudson and James bays, the eastern third of the mainland is a treeless, low-lying terrain of rock-strewn tundra and lakes known as the Barren Lands. Most communities cling to the shore where the ocean provides sustenance. The northern shore of the Arctic Ocean ranks as the country's most inaccessible inhabited region.

The aerial crossroads of Keewatin, **Rankin Inlet** (population 1,400) on the west shore of Hudson Bay, was established in 1955 as a nickel mine. The mine closed within a decade and today the area is the district's administrative and servicing center. This historic area can easily be explored on foot, boat, three-wheel all-terrain vehicle, dog sled or snowmobile. A local craft shop sells curved Inuit knives (ulus), seal hide boots (kamiks) and ivory jewelry.

Locally based outfitters organize fly-in fishing outings to **Chesterfield Inlet**, then on to interior lakes by freighter canoe. Generally flexible outfitters will organize trips of any length to suit the client.

Fifty kilometers (30 miles) away, historic **Marble Island** in Hudson Bay is a spooky reminder of the harshness of this northern land. The complete crews of ships seeking the Northwest Passage died here two centuries ago, and locals believe their ghosts still inhabit the island.

Baker Lake, the district's only inland community, is center for artists, carvers and Inuit throat-singers (women who play a game involving rhythmical noises combined with audible breathing). It is noted for the spectacular Northern Lights (aurora borealis) that shimmer in the sky in fantastic, seemingly supernatural, dancing shards of greenish light. Get someone to take you out on the frozen lake for the best view.

Baker Lake is also the terminus for several wilderness river trips and claims to be the exact geographic center of Canada. The town has a hotel and a pool table for recreation, and acts as a base for day journeys to fishing spots and to archaeological sites such as an ancient cemetery near Chesterfield Inlet, dating back thousands of years to the area's first inhabitants. Further inland, in the extensive reserve of the **Thelon Game Sanctuary**, naturalists and photographers stalk musk-ox, Barren Ground grizzly and caribou, wolves and rare birds.

Outside **Coral Harbor**, the only settlement on Hudson Bay's **Southampton Island**, are beluga whales and walrus colonies. Thirty-seven kilometers (60 miles) away by boat at **Native Point**, archaeological remains include whale-bone houses and stone graves of residents, who died out at the turn of the century.

Contact Travel Keewatin, (819) 645-2618, fax (819) 645-2320.

But The Weather Was Lovely

The windows of the room were of seal gut, and, as the days were now about two hours in length, our light inside was none of the best. We slept wrapped in fur-lined blankets and skins on a platform raised about two feet above the floor, which later we had caulked with moss and covered with straw and skins. Even then, although our room was generally warm enough, the floor was intensely cold. I once hung up some damp cloth to dry; near the rafters it steamed; within a foot of the ground it froze firmly, with long icicles hanging therefrom. The air near the floor has shown a temperature of +4° when the upper part of the room was +60° or +65° Fahr...

The effect of the intense cold on our stores in the magazine was a very interesting study; our fried apples were a mass of rock and had to be smashed up with an axe, our molasses formed a thick black paste, and no knife we had would cut a slice of ham from the bone till it was well thawed in our warmer room. Our preserved meats would, with a continuation of those times, have been preserved forever and would have made, as Kane says, excellent 'canister shot'. After purchasing grouse or hares from the Indians, they would remain, uneaten, for a month or longer period in as good condition as ever, and there was no fear of their getting too 'high' in that climate.

Our coldest day for the whole season occurred in December. On the 26th of November the thermometer fell suddenly from the comparatively moderate temperature of +2° to -18°, and continued lowering steadily—day by day—till it reached (on the 5th of December) -58° Fahr., or **ninety degrees below freezing.** *But the weather was lovely; no wind blew or snow fell during the the whole time, and we did not feel the cold as much as at many other times.*

Frederick Whymper, 1866

Yukon

The territory in Canada's far northwest, stretching from the BC border on the 60th parallel to the Beaufort Sea and squeezed between the Northwest Territories and Alaska, has powerful physical attractions despite its image as a frozen waste land. The wedge-shaped Yukon encompasses the Kluane ice-field ranges in the southwest, the raging Firth River north of the Arctic Circle, vast tracts of lodgepole pine forests, unexploited (even unexplored) mountains, lakes, glaciers and streams.

HISTORY

But more important than the many physical attractions is the historic appeal, for the Yukon is synonymous with the Klondike and the world's last great goldrush. Local license plates still recall the era: they include the outline of a prospector panning for gold. From the early 1900s, the Yukon remained somewhat isolated until World War Two when the American army and Canadian engineers constructed the Alaska Highway as an overland supply route to the US forces. Between March and October, 1942, soldiers and civilians laid 2,400 kilometers (1,500 miles) of road through virgin bush and sub-Arctic wilderness from Dawson Creek, BC, to Fairbanks, Alaska. American servicemen called it 'the road to Tokyo'. For a time, Whitehorse was a construction boomtown, its population exploding from 500 to 30,000. The road permanently changed the Yukon and today is a conduit for both development and tourism. In summer, recreational vehicles crowd the highway like migrating caribou.

GETTING THERE

Although it remains largely 'unpeopled and still', as poet Robert W Service called it, the Yukon is slightly more populated than the Northwest Territories, its 27,000 people concentrated mainly in the capital, Whitehorse. The territory is well served with roads that draw motorists throughout the summer season, particularly those in RVs (recreational vehicles), campers and four-wheel drives.

Motorists enter the Yukon along the Alaska Highway that is paved for most of its 2,414 kilometers (1,500 miles) from Dawson Creek to Fairbanks, Alaska, or the more rugged Stewart-Cassiar Highway through the heart of British Columbia. Roads continue through to Inuvik near the Arctic Ocean or on to Alaska via the Top of the World and Alaska Highways. From Haines or Skagway, Alaska, scheduled car ferries return south to Prince Rupert, Vancouver, or Seattle, Washington for those who would make a circle tour. Outdoor adventures can be as relaxing as parking the RV at a roadside campsite near a fishing stream to paddling a whitewater river to the Arctic Ocean. Wildlife biologists escort special interest groups in search of Dall sheep, caribou, grizzly and black bears. Experienced dog handlers give instruction on how to run a team, then head into the snowy wilderness on one- to five-day sled tours. Here, too, is rafting and kayaking, horseback riding, alpine trekking, hunting and fishing.

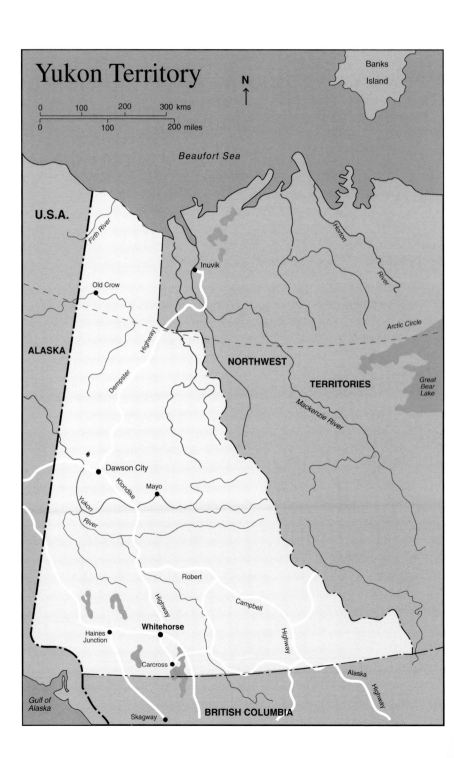

Yukon Territory

Banks
Island

N
↑

0   100   200   300 kms
0   100   200 miles

Beaufort Sea

U.S.A.

Firth River

● Inuvik

● Old Crow

Horton
River

ALASKA

Dempster
Highway

NORTHWEST

Arctic Circle

TERRITORIES

Great
Bear
Lake

Mackenzie River

● Dawson City

Klondike

Mayo ●

Yukon

River

Robert

Highway

Campbell

Highway

Haines ●
Junction

Whitehorse

Carcross ●

Alaska

Highway

Gulf of
Alaska

Skagway ●

BRITISH COLUMBIA

WHITEHORSE

Nearly 19,000 people now live in Whitehorse, once a staging ground for those gold seekers who made it through the White and Chilkoot passes. The Canadian north's largest community now serves as a busy crossroads, a regional service and tourist center. This relatively small, isolated community has a surprising number of attractions. The **Visitor Reception Center** shows informative audio-visuals such as *Faces of the Yukon* describing the Alaska and Dempster highways, Dawson City and other attractions. The **SS** *Klondike*, launched in 1937 as the largest sternwheeler on the Yukon River, carried passengers and freight between Whitehorse and Dawson City. Guided tours through this designated historic site, now restored and permanently dry-docked downtown, recall days when Whitehorse was a busy river port.

The **Yukon Historical and Museums Association** escorts free walking tours of downtown, with guides reading from diaries of the original Yukoners and relating the history of the old wood buildings. The most interesting buildings include the original **telegraph office** built in 1900 and the city's first church, the **Anglican Cathedral** built in 1900, opened as the **Old Log Church Museum** in 1962. The **Macbride Museum** displays gold rush artifacts, transportation exhibits and stuffed northern animals, with some replicas dating back to the Ice Age, such as a giant beaver as big as the black bears now roaming the forests. Outside the museum sits the **Cabin of Sam McGee**, that wily prospector whom Robert Service immortalized in his famous poem *The Cremation of Sam McGee*. Horse-drawn carriages, buses and jet helicopters take tours of the city and surroundings, while the Yukon Conservation Society escorts nature walks of **Grey Mountain**, **Miles Canyon** and **Hidden Lake**. On board the **MV** *Schwatka*, which cruises through the once-dangerous **Miles Canyon rapids** on the **Yukon River**, guides relate the history of the Klondike.

The **Northern Splendor Reindeer Farm**, 30 minutes north of town, shows videos on Northern Canada and Alaska reindeer, and conducts tours, during which guests can help feed the livestock. Back in town, they can reverse the procedure and dine on reindeer at several restaurants. Nearby **Takhini Hotspring** has hikes, horseback riding, and swimming in the natural hot springs. Bathing suits and towels are available for hire. For those with the time and the inclination to follow the trail of the gold seekers, the 18-meter (60-foot) riverboat **MV** *Anna Maria* makes six round-trips each summer between Whitehorse and Dawson City. The northbound trips are four days, southbound five. The trading vessel, designed to reflect the style and atmosphere of a turn-of-the-century Yukon River sternwheeler, has stateroom accommodation and deck passage, a dining room and a saloon complete with piano. Deck passengers camp in tents or stay in hotels at nightly stops along the river.

The 740-kilometer (460-mile) route is rich with remnants of the Klondike days—abandoned North West Mounted Police posts, Indian villages and fish camps, old dredging equipment and beached river boats. The trading vessel operates daily dinner cruises when in town. Whitehorse has a lively, if somewhat contrived, **nightlife**. There is so much of it for a small community, it seems almost frenetic. The **Frantic Follies Vaudeville Revue** evokes the spirit of the '98 gold rush with songs, cancan dancing, readings of Robert Service's poetry and humorous skits held daily from the end of May through mid-September.

Eldorado, a lively musical drama about the Klondike, features characters such as gambler Danny Drummond, innkeeper Missy Muldoon and prospector Bedrock Ben Strauss. The Frostbite Music Society presents summer concerts featuring local musicians and entertainers performing songs, skits, poetry readings and tales of the north.

Dawson City

Dawson City, 240 kilometers (150 miles) south of the Arctic Circle at the juncture of the Klondike and Yukon rivers, was once a bustling community of nearly 40,000 but deteriorated to a somewhat ramshackle collection of dirt streets, board sidewalks and old buildings. With an eye on the tourist trade, and a concern for heritage, the federal Parks Board is renovating the town to a semblance of its gold rush glory days.

The city is isolated—Whitehorse is 500 kilometers (310 miles) south and Inuvik 700 kilometers (435 miles) north on the Dempster Highway—but worth the trip for anyone interested in northern history.

The **Dawson City Museum** in the stately old **Territorial Administration Building** has extensive exhibits of native Indian and Klondike history, as well as a special treat for film buffs. It shows rare silent films that were unearthed during a construction project in 1978.

The Parks Board takes free tours through historic **Fort Herschmer**, including the RCMP barracks, churches and administration buildings. The steamer *Keno*, one of the last of more than 200 riverboats used on the Yukon up until the mid-1950s, is now a National Historic Site open for free guided tours.

Englishman Robert W Service was the Bard of the Yukon, the poet laureate of the Klondike, famous for works such as *Songs of a Sourdough* and *The Cremation of Sam McGee*. Service's 'ghost' now gives daily readings on the lawn before his old log cabin, where he wrote some of his best-loved poems. **Service's cabin** is now a historic site and besides its historic / literary interest, it gives an idea of just how basic life was for those tough sourdoughs (prospectors).

At **Jack London's cabin**, readings from the American writer of northern tales such as *White Fang* and *Call of the Wild,* are presented daily and a photo exhibit illustrates his life in the Klondike. London was a journalist who came to the Yukon seeking gold and ended up writing about this cold, unforgiving land.

Modern fortune hunters can pan for gold in several places, such as **Claim #6 Above Discovery** (free, bring your own pan and shovel), **GuggieVille** ($5.50 per pan) and **Claim 33** on Bonanza Creek Road ($5, with gold guaranteed in every pan). **Bonanza Creek** also has the largest wooden hull dredge in North America.

Other attractions related to the gold industry include a walking tour of an operating placer mine in the Klondike fields with explanations of the industry and a visit to the original discovery claims, complete with vintage mining equipment. Jet helicopters fly over the gold fields, a Top of The World flight tours the **Bonanza and Eldorado creeks** and **Moosehide Village**, and the *Yukon Lou* takes leisurely, hour-and-a-half cruises down the river from the Front Street dock.

At night the **Gaslight Follies Revue** plays at the reconstructed **Palace Grande Theater**. The circa 1900s variety show includes music, songs, dances and colorful period costumes. **Diamond Tooth Gertie's Gambling Hall**, in an old saloon, is believed to be the world's northernmost casino, and was until recently Canada's only permanent legal gambling house. There is blackjack and roulette, a licensed bar, and Gertie herself leads the floor shows, accompanied by piano and cancan dancers.

The city has made its own, unique contribution to international bibulousness—the Sourtoe Cocktail. The story is that one exceptionally cold winter, a miner froze off his toe, which he pickled in a jar of rum. A local character found the toe and invented this concoction: the toe immersed in a glass of champagne. The toe must be returned after the drink is consumed. 'I think we're on about our third toe', says a tourism official who has yet to imbibe. It takes a special sort of midnight-sun macho, or tourism bravado, to toss back a Sourtoe Cocktail, and Labatt's or Molson's beer is preferred in most Yukon bars.

ELSEWHERE

Throughout the Yukon, numerous ghost towns and abandoned Indian villages, rusted gold dredgers and abandoned river boats recall the short glory days when this was the center of world attention.

Nearby **Carcross** (population 150) has a general store dating back to 1911, the 1898 Caribou Hotel, an old steam boat, a locomotive and the nearby graves of those men who started it all—George Carmack, Taglish Charlie, and Skookum Jim.

Experienced hikers can follow the original **Chilkoot Trail** from Skagway, Alaska, to Bennett, British Columbia. The well-marked trail is a tough climb in places, and takes at least three days.

It is possible to cross the pass without the sweat. From 1898 to 1900, rail workers laid lines from Whitehorse and from Skagway. The two lines met at Carcross—after the gold rush was over. It was a major feat of engineering in that forbidding terrain. The **White Pass and Yukon Railway**—one of the world's last operating narrow-gauge railways—closed down in 1982 but now is back in service. The train runs excursions from Skagway to Whitehorse and back.

The Klondike Gold Rush

Prospector George Washington Carmack and his Indian brothers-in-law Skookum Jim and Tagish Charlie made history's greatest gold strike on August 17, 1896 in Rabbit Creek, a tributary of the Klondike River near today's Dawson City.

When news of the fabulous strike spread, some 100,000 fortune-seekers from around the world headed to the north, most by steamer up the BC coast to Skagway, Alaska. From there, they hauled their supplies over either the White or Chilkoot passes to the headwaters of the Yukon River that runs 1,000 kilometers (600 miles) to Dawson. Old photographs show long, ant-like lines of men making their way through the snow to the summit. It was a gruelling climb that many didn't make. Today, a marker along the White Pass Road indicates Dead Horse Trail across the chasm where 3,000 horses died during the rush.

Concerned that inadequately supplied prospectors might starve to death, the North West Mounted Police enforced a rule that anyone heading for the gold fields must have a year's provisions. The fortune hunters had to make the arduous climb up the mountain many times.

Most were forced to winter at Lake Bennett at the top of the pass. More than 10,000 boats and rafts were made in that clearing. Many of them broke up in the raging river, ending dreams of richness. (It is now possible to run those famous rapids—more safely in inflatable rafts.)

When they reached the gold fields, the fortune-hungry hordes quickly turned Dawson from a tent camp into a sprawling town of shacks and more substantial wood structures, many of which still remain. History took quite a different turn here from American frontier settlements. The North West Mounted Police's legendary superintendent Sam Steele with a hundred men imposed strict regulations on the boom town. Despite all the saloons and brothels, the casinos where fortunes were gambled away, there was none of the rampant lawlessness usually associated with goldrush boom towns such as Skagway, Alaska's gateway to the Yukon.

Dreams of fortunes went largely unfulfilled. The best claims were staked long before the outsiders arrived, and the gold rush petered out after just a few years, with few making their fortunes. By 1905 the population had dropped from nearly 40,000 to 5,000, and soon Dawson was almost a ghost town. Still, the 'Spirit of '98' lives on in memories, in local folklore, in the atmosphere of the remaining communities and in tangible artifacts such as abandoned mines and weathered dredges, log cabins and riverboats.

Ontario

As Canada's second largest (after Quebec) and most populous province, with more than ten million people, Ontario dominates the country's financial and political life.

Ontario is sprawls across a massive amount of varied real estate between the older eastern provinces and the west. From its borders with Quebec it stretches out over the Canadian Shield to Manitoba, and from its southernmost point (further south than the northern tip of California) it extends north to the Arctic. Ontario covers nearly 1.3 million square kilometers (a half-million square miles). Within that area are 156,700 kilometers (60,500 square miles) of fresh water or one-quarter of the world's supply, and a coastal area that includes four of the five Great Lakes. With 400,000 rivers and lakes in all, the province claims some 80 per cent of the world's trout fishing waters. Many of these are within a few hours' drive of the urbanized south end of the province.

History

In the early 17th century, the French arrived and tentatively explored Ontario, but their settlement was gradual. The Iroquois Wars, a series of conflicts between the Iroquois and the French, with their Huron and Algonquin allies, disrupted settlement. In 1649, the wars forced the abandonment of the first European settlement in present-day Ontario, the Jesuit mission Ste Marie Among the Hurons. In the late 1700s, the British established trading posts along Hudson Bay, eventually gaining control of Ontario and French Canada with the 1763 Treaty of Paris.

Large-scale settlement of Ontario did not begin until the 1780s, some 20 years after the treaty, when United Empire Loyalists who, following the American Revolution, remained loyal to Britain and the Crown and migrated north. Staunch conservative types, they gave Ontario its strait-laced character.

In 1791 the area was renamed Upper Canada and separated from Quebec, which became Lower Canada. When the US declared war on Britain in 1812, American soldiers invaded Canada through Detroit. After a series of bloody battles, Canada finally retained her territory, and in 1841 Upper and Lower Canada were united.

However, resulting conflicts between the English and French eventually led to another split and in 1867, Ontario and Quebec entered Canadian confederation as separate provinces, which they remain today.

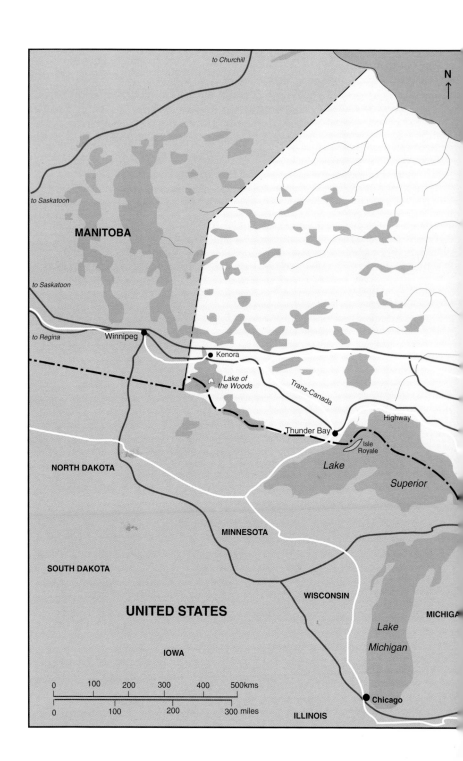

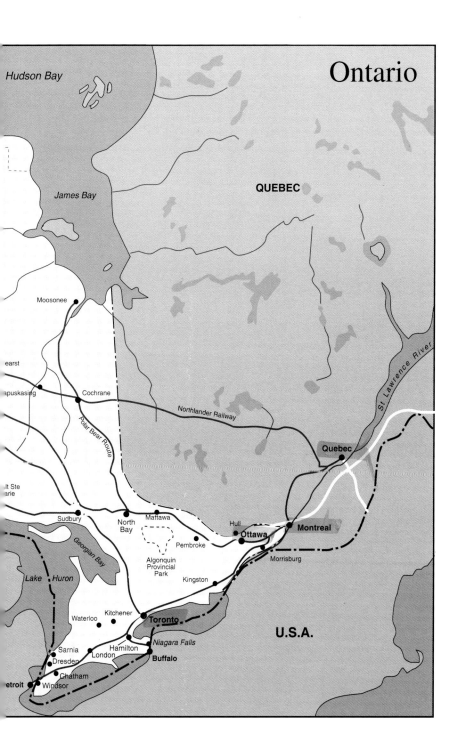

Toronto

The area which would later become Toronto—an Indian word meaning roughly 'place of meeting'—was first spotted by a European, French explorer Etienne Brule, in 1615. Brule, the first Frenchman to live among the native people, became a skilful interpreter and intermediary. He was probably the first European to see lakes Huron, Ontario and Superior and for awhile the only one. The Toronto area was not settled until 1749 when Quebecois fur traders established Fort Rouille.

Lake travel and the coming of the railway in the late 1800s led to a building boom. The 3,200-kilometer (2,000-mile)-long St Lawrence Seaway, which opened to shipping in 1961, played a major part in the city's and province's history and economic development. Grain, ore and manufactured goods are shipped via this narrow, east-west waterway to the world's far-flung ports. Now, Toronto is one of North America's fastest growing, most prosperous cities and Canada's economic center.

The country's largest city (nearly 3 million people), which has been called Muddy York, Hogtown and Toronto the Good, demands recognition. Smarting from its century-long reputation for stodginess and its dubious distinction as a puritan village, the city constantly insists that it really is a lively entertainment and cultural center.

ETHNIC TORONTO

Toronto has matured in recent years, with European, Caribbean and Asian immigrants injecting life into its true-blue conservative and loyalist veins. There is a substantial Italian community, North America's largest Portuguese population, and many Greeks, all with their own neighborhoods. With recent massive immigration, Toronto now has five 'Chinatowns' with exotic potions such as Korean ginseng and ground deer antlers, as well as steaming *wonton* (a Chinese noodle soup) and other culinary delights.

Between Dundas and College streets is **Kensington Market**, a long-standing Jewish market stocked with smoked salmon, cages of live rabbits and old men selling homemade *halvah* (a Jewish sweet). This is Toronto at its ethnic, exotic best, with Portuguese fishmongers, Kosher butchers, Chinese and West Indian greengrocers, second-hand stores, delis and restaurants from around the world. The prices are good and bartering is encouraged. Another market, the **St Lawrence Market**, founded in 1844 at 95 Front Street, sells fresh produce from Canadian farmers, butchers and fishermen.

Toronto is also enlivened by a large Caribbean population best displayed at the week-long Caribana celebration of culture and dances in mid-summer. The West Indian festival held at various places throughout the city includes a Miss Caribana

Pageant and Ball, Grand Carnival Parade, Carnival Dance and especially a Toronto Islands Festival of lively steel bands and reggae.

SIGHTS AND ATTRACTIONS
■ CITY CENTER

The city offers all of the rewards of sophisticated urban life and few of the drawbacks. This is a clean, efficient and safe metropolis that enjoys a healthy cultural and out-door lifestyle. (Hollywood filmmakers shooting here once attempted to make the streets look authentically American by scattering litter around. But while they were away for a lunch break, the city sanitation department cleaned the mess up.)

Many of the attractions are centrally located and can be visited on foot or by the excellent public transit system. Toronto's buses and subways make getting around easy, and the streetcars which trundle along Queen Street to the suburbs provide a pleasant, inexpensive view of the city's communities. Especially attractive are **the Beaches**, on Lake Ontario (reached by taking the streetcar east), with three kilometers (1.8 miles) of sand, a tree-lined wooden boardwalk, sport park and several outdoor cafes and bakeries.

Nathan Phillips Square, downtown on **Queen** and **Bay Streets**, is a good beginning for a walking tour. This popular plaza, named after a former mayor, hosts summer festivals and outdoor concerts and is perfect for people-watching. In winter, the reflecting pool transforms to a crowded skating rink.

Behind the square is the city's main symbol, the city hall completed in 1965. The distinctive, clam-shaped structure features a central white dome enclosed by curved 27 and 20-story towers, and a Henry Moore bronze sculpture (in the entrance way) called *The Archer*. Visitors can take conducted tours.

The **Old City Hall** (completed in 1899) next door is striking for its stained glass window, marble columns, reproductions of the city's old coat of arms appearing on many doorknobs—and the grotesque gargoyles carved in the stonework, caricatures of politicians of the mid 1800s.

On the other side of the new **City Hall**, the restored **Osgoode Hall**, formerly Ontario's Supreme Court, has been the headquarters of the Law Society of Upper Canada since 1832. The entrance features the original wrought-iron cow catcher gates built in 1832 to keep. out the herds grazing nearby. Inside are Corinthian columns, stained glass and intricate tile flooring.

The main entrance to **Eaton's Center**, Toronto's largest shopping mall, is at the corner of **Dundas** and **Yonge Streets**, also the city's unofficial 'speaker's corner'. The block-long, sky-lit mall, housing dozens of shops and restaurants, is especially convenient during Toronto's cold winter months. The mall is organized according to price, with the cheapest stores on the lowest of the three levels and most expensive

on the top. At either end are two of Canada's major department stores, and two subway stops, Dundas and Queen.

Yonge Street south of Bloor is Toronto's liveliest area, a neon lit avenue of bargain bookstores, record shops and rough bars as well as trendy cafes and clothing boutiques.

Farther north, the corner of Yonge and College Streets is the home of the **Maple Leaf Gardens**, where the Toronto Maple Leafs National Hockey League team hangs its hockey sticks. As well as hosting hockey games, it features entertainers from hulking wrestlers to crooning folk singers. Below College Street there are bargain bookstores and cluttered record shops.

North of here are the Gothic-style **University of Toronto** and the provincial **legislative buildings**. The University, Canada's largest (founded in 1827) is noted for its research (pablum was one of its inventions). Its graduates include Canadian prime ministers MacKenzie King and Lester Pearson and author Marshall Mcluhan. At the downtown campus, **Kings College Circle** has a variety of architecture dating from 1859. Free, hour-long walking tours are conducted weekdays from June through August. Tours are also available of the solid stone legislative buildings which officially opened in 1860.

The nearby intersection of Yonge Street, which divides downtown east and west divide, and Bloor, the north-south division. The intersection is a meeting place of street vendors, musicians and artists.

Northwest of the intersection at Avenue Road and Bloor is **Yorkville**. The former hippy haven turned into an elegant, trendy shopping area of courtyards, lanes and mews, is representative of trendy Toronto. Money is made on Bay Street, Canada's financial center, but spent in these fashionable shops and coffeehouses.

In the late 1800s, Yorkville was an independent village. By the 50s and 60s, it became an artsy, bohemian area where struggling Canadian talents such as Gordon Lightfoot and Joni Mitchell, now international stars, played crammed folk clubs. Renovated town houses have replaced crash-pads, craft shops turned into boutiques and Toronto career-types power-lunch in expensive sidewalk cafes. The old houses and galleries along **Scollard Street** and **Hazelton Avenue** are splendid Victorian restorations. Amid these sprout modern architecture such as **Hazelton Lanes, Cumberland Court and York Square**. Yorkville is the site of the annual Festival of Festivals, the world's largest public film festival.

Northwest of Yorkville, the unique, chateau-like **Casa Loma** is a local curiosity. In 1911, eccentric millionaire Sir Henry Pellatt built the expensive monument to his ego for $3 million. North America's largest castle has gold-plated bathroom fixtures, private elevators and an underground passageway leading to turreted riding stables with Spanish tile floors, mahogany stalls and porcelain troughs. Servants scurried down secret passages so Sir Henry wouldn't have to meet them.

Commuters board a bus on Toronto's busy Spadina

But extravagance, and some investment blunders, took its toll and by the 1920s Pellatt was destitute. In 1924, the city took over the huge castle and auctioned off the contents. For a time it stood empty, until the Kiwanis Club leased Casa Loma and opened it to the public in 1937. Now Pellatt's folly is open for touring every day.

South of City Hall, along **Bay Street**, dubbed 'Canada's Wall Street', towering skyscrapers create wind tunnels so strong, yellow ropes are rigged for pedestrians to cling to. Bay Street bankers parade down the thoroughfare in their three-piece pin-stripe suits—five of Canada's major financial institutions have headquarters here. The tallest is the white marble 72-story **Bank of Montreal** building, also known as First Canada Place as it was the country's first chartered bank. Most dramatic is the **Royal Bank Plaza**, a pair of gleaming triangular towers resembling great gold bricks, with their windows gilded in $250,000 worth of gold dust.

At the foot of Bay Street, **Union Station** (built in 1927), the hub of the city's transport system, is a great, imposing stone edifice with a facade of 22 tall pillars of Bedford limestone and a 27-meter high ceiling of Italian tile. Across the street is the fortress-like Royal York Hotel, one of Toronto's oldest.

Farther west are the Canadian National Exhibition grounds, site of the world's largest annual fair which runs from mid-August until Labor Day in September. It has been affectionately called the 'Ex' for nearly a century with its craft shows, hucksters, the latest model cars and midway madness, complete with the standard roller coaster and Ferris wheel. The rest of the year, visitors can tour the **Canada's Sports Hall of Fame** and the **Marine Museum of Upper Canada**, both on the exhibition grounds.

The exhibition grounds are also the entrance to **Ontario Place**, open mainly from May to October. This green oasis on Lake Ontario features concrete paths lined with bushes and trees, gardens, man-made ponds with paddle boats, restaurants and bars. An innovative **Children's Village**, where kids can climb, jump and slide, is on the eastern side of the complex next to a **Waterworld** for all ages and a free outdoor amphitheater where you can sit on the grass and listen to everything from rock to the Toronto Symphony. Ontario Place's landmark is the **Cinesphere**, a geodesic dome which houses a movie theater showing films year-round.

■ TOWERING VIEWS

Several observation points from the lakeside city provide a bird's-eye view of the surroundings. On Front Street, just west of Union Station, is the world's highest observation deck on the lofty needle of the **CN (Canadian National Railways) Tower**. At 553 meters (1,185 feet) high, the tower is also the world's tallest free-standing structure and has no exterior supports. Inside are the **CN rail and communications center**, **Sparkles nightclub**, **Top of Toronto** revolving restaurant which 'tours' the city every 72 minutes, and the observation deck. Someone once observed that the tower was built to give Torontonians a view beyond their city. Indeed, on smog-free days one can see up to 160 kilometers (100 miles), as far as the 'smoke' of Niagara Falls.

There are also observation decks in the bank buildings on Bay Street and another revolving restaurant, **the Lighthouse**, atop the **Harbour Castle Westin Hotel**. Like the CN Tower, they overlook the harbor and the Toronto Islands which can be reached from behind the Harbour Castle Hotel.

■ THE WATERFRONT
Walk-on ferries depart from behind the hotel every 20 minutes for the Toronto Islands Park opposite the downtown area. This is one of the city's favorite spots for picnicking, boating, swimming, tennis or exploring. Toronto Islands Park features an illuminated promenade called the Avenue of the Islands and a lagoon with waterfowl. In summer the islands bustle with ethnic festivals. Center Island has bicycle and boat rentals, a children's amusement park, beaches and sailing.

On the mainland, Toronto's once derelict harbor front has been revived in recent years. Now the 40-hectare (100-acre) central **Harbourfront** is a mixed residential, commercial and public area. Some 4,000 cultural, educational and entertainment events, many free, are staged here annually. There are six hectares (15 acres) of public park land, landscaped gardens, sports facilities, boat rentals, art galleries, antique markets, theaters, and, of course, bars and restaurants.

Despite its sprawling size, Toronto has good access to outdoor pursuits. Its own tall ship, the 29-meter (95-foot) schooner *Challenge*, departs three times daily in summer (weekends mid-May to September) from Queen's Quay Terminal Building for two-hour harbor tours. The *Trillium*, a unique steam-driven sidewheeler built in 1910, takes two hour harbor and islands tours twice a day, from July to the end of August, as do several other vessels.

Hospitable Toronto, unlike other cities, has more than 200 municipal parks which bid visitors to 'Please walk on the grass'. You can walk or rent a bicycle and peddle a 20-kilometer (12-mile) scenic waterfront trail.

The greatest addition to the waterfront area, which has been altered by new development, is the Skydome near the CN Tower. The world's first stadium with a fully retractable roof is home of the Blue Jays, World Series baseball champions for two consecutive years.

The Center includes a 348-room hotel with 70 rooms overlooking the playing field and seven restaurants and bars.

■ FOR CHILDREN OF ALL AGES
In the suburb of **North York**, the **Ontario Science Center** is a kind of educational funfair, a carnival of learning with an electricity demonstration that literally stands

At the Canadian National Exhibition in Toronto

(left) Highway 401 connecting Montreal and Toronto via the Thousand Lakes region; (below) Toronto at twilight; Canada's largest city lights up

Delis, sidewalk cafes and nightclubs on Toronto's fashionable Queen Street West

your hair on end, and a 'disorientation chamber'. Exhibits include a chess-playing computer, musical instruments for visitor use, simulated moon landings and some 800 hands-on scientific and technical toys.

Slightly north of Highway 401, in the suburb of **Scarborough**, the **Metro Toronto Zoo** has recreated habitits for Africa, Indo-Malaysia, Australia, Eurasia, the Americas and Polar regions, each one with its own climate-controlled pavilion.

In an innovative approach to zoo displays, the humans are restricted in their movements while the animals roam free through some 700 acres (287 hectares) of forests and pastures. The zoo, which is open daily year-round, doubles as a cross-country ski network in winter, with equipment rentals available.

■ MUSEUMS AND GALLERIES

Toronto has its share of pursuits for the culture-oriented, in particular the splendid **Royal Ontario Museum** at Bloor Street and Avenue Road. Canada's largest museum has one of North America's greatest collections of Chinese artefacts—20 rooms are dedicated to Chinese painting alone. Other displays include mummies and remnants of ancient Egypt, as well as artwork and armor from Greece and Rome, dinosaur bones, and lifelike replicas of snakes and lizards. One gallery is the three-dimensional Bat Cave, an accurate replica of Jamaica's St Clair Cave which is home to thousands of bats. A soaring, 28-meter (91-foot) totem pole from Nass River in British Columbia, has artistic and stylized carvings of birds and animals, representing the rich west coast Indian culture. A stairway circles 'The Pole of Chief Mountain'.

The **Art Gallery of Ontario** displays more than 10,000 paintings, including old masters such as Rembrandt and Renoir, new ones such as Picasso and a major collection of Canadian artists. The gallery's **Henry Moore Sculpture Center** houses the world's largest public collection of the English sculptor's work.

The **McMichael Gallery**, northwest of Toronto, specializes in Canadian art, particularly the Group of Seven. Its members were mainly landscape artists—Lawren Harris, Franklin Carmichael, A Y Jackson, Franz Johnston, Arthur Lismet, J E H Macdonald and F H Varley—who formed their own 'school' in 1920. Their favorite subjects were the forests and frozen wastelands of Canada, and the gallery is a perfect setting for viewing their work. It overlooks a forest and its wide windows are set close to the artists' interpretations of similar sights. In addition to the Group of Seven are works by Tom Thomson, the brilliant Canadian artist who was close to members of the group but drowned in the wild a few years before his friends joined forces.

There are numerous smaller galleries and museums such as **Toronto's First Post Office** at Adelaide and George streets.

You can write home as it was done in the 1830s, with fine quill pens and sealing wax provided by employees clad in period costumes. Northwest of the city, near York University, the re-creation of the past is taken a step further at **Black Creek**

Pioneer Village. Nineteenth-century Toronto is on view here with dirt roads, wooden buildings and barns. Pioneer homes are replicated and inside women in costume card and spin wool, bake bread over hot coals and make candles. The men can be seen at work in the blacksmith's shop, general store or barns, or nursing an ale at the saloon.

■ PERFORMING ARTS
With many major and smaller theaters, as well as museums and galleries, the Ontario capital proudly parades its credentials as one of Canada's leading cultural centers.

Toronto is a theater center second only to New York, and a glance at the newspaper listings will reveal the impressive number of small theaters in the city. For larger productions, see what is playing at the **Bayview Playhouse, Center Stage** or the **Factory Theater.** Or pay a visit to the **Royal Alexandra Theater,** a somewhat garish grand old theater. New major theaters include the **Princess of Wales Theater** next door to the **Royal Alex, the Pantages Theater** on Yonge Street south of Dundas, the **Elgin and Winter Garden Theaters** on Yonge Street near Queen Street, and the **North York Performing Arts Center** on Yonge Street.

The vast, modern 3,200-seat **O'Keefe Center** also presents touring shows of everything from Broadway musicals to opera. In season, you can attend performances of the **National Ballet of Canada,** the **Toronto Symphony** and the **Canadian Opera Company.**

For music lovers, **Massey Hall,** opened in 1894, is a small venue with excellent acoustics. All styles of music, from classical to rock, are presented here. The new **Roy Thomson Hall,** opened in 1982 opposite the CN Tower, is another excellent place for listening to good music as is the **outdoor amphitheater** at Ontario Place.

Major rock shows are presented at **Canada's Wonderland, Exhibition Stadium** and **Maple Leaf Gardens.**

■ TORONTO BY NIGHT
Despite recent improvements, prudish 'Tranna' as locals pronounce the name, can't quite shake its stodgy image of 'Toronto the Good' and its nightlife lacks the verve of Montreal, Quebec City or Vancouver. They still ban movies in this Boston of Canada, and there is a Temperance Street downtown.

The good burghers of Hogtown, righteously indignant of the corrupting effects of bare-breasted ladies serving Molson's draft in Yonge Street topless bars, frequently closed them all down. The city has improved, though, with some bars and taverns open on Sundays.

Toronto by night now offers everything from rock to reggae, jazz to waltzing. Fashionable Yorkville in the north midtown area is good for sidewalk cafes and bars on warm summer nights. This is a somewhat pricey area of restaurants, night clubs,

jazz bars, even discos. Perhaps the most famous spot of dozens in the area is **Heming-way's**, with a more casual and comfortable atmosphere than most.

The **Esplanade area**, including **Esplanade** and **Front Streets** between Yonge and Jarvi, a domain of gentrified accompanying restaurants and bars. Most popular spots are **Brandy's** and **Scotland Yard**, **Muddy York**, and **Down Under** (in the basement of a flat iron building) at Front and Wellington. Nearby, on **Wellington St East**, **Café des Copains** is an expensive restaurant upstairs, with a good jazz club (with cover charge) in the basement. In fact, a large number of Toronto's best clubs and bars seem to be below ground. On the edge of Yorkville, the **Duke of York** is an especially pleasant English-style pub.

Further north, **Eglinton Avenue** between Yonge Street and Mt Pleasant Road is a leading bar scene for young locals. For those with an eye to singles bars, **Earl's Tin Palace** and **Friday's** both rate highly with locals in the know. At **Yonge Street** is the **Duke of Kent**, yet another of Toronto's popular, and quite authentic, British-style pubs.

Yuk Yuk's on Bay Street, the city's most famous comedy club, is one of the country's leading venues for aspiring comics—with the predictable range of results.

Toronto has other rewards of a big city. With its post-war ethnic diversity, it is an excellent dining city. The wide range of good restaurants includes, for instance, one offering the strange combination of East European and South American food. Others serve spaghetti with jazz .

Niagara Falls

Niagara Falls, 131 kilometers (83 miles) southeast of Toronto, was established as the international Honeymoon Haven in 1804 when Napoleon Bonaparte's brother, Jerome, brought his American bride all the way from New Orleans by stagecoach to view the awesome natural wonder. Today, couples still choose to spend their first few days together within earshot of these thundering rapids at the Honeymoon Capital of the World. The **Canadian Falls**, 54 meters (178 feet) high with a crest of more than 675 meters (2,227 feet), form a curve known as **Horseshoe Falls**. The smallest cataract, but one of the prettiest, is **Bridal Veil**, separated from the American falls by **Luna Island**. The most impressive panorama of these falls comes from along the well-trimmed parklands skirting the Niagara River.

For the most dramatic close-up view of Niagara Falls, take the wet and wonderful *Maid of the Mists* boat ride in front of the **American Falls** and right into the horseshoe of the main falls. It is deafening, heart-stopping fun. Boats operate daily from mid-May to mid-October.

The turreted Castle Loma, a private castle in Toronto

Near the **Whirlpool Rapids Bridge** you can take an elevator to the river level to view exhibits of daredevils who tried to go down or cross over the falls, and stroll along the rapids of the **lower Niagara River.**

The immense **floral clock** at the generating station ten kilometers (six miles) away is one of the world's largest, with 25,000 colorful blossoms. This floral masterpiece keeps accurate time and plays the Westminster chimes every 15 minutes. There is also a **Marineland** nearby with a 4,000-seat aquatheater where dolphins and a killer whale perform, and the world's largest steel roller coaster.

Honeymooners and other visitors can take double-decker bus tours, hike to glens and observation points, ride above the falls in a helicopter—everything but go over them in a barrel. There are three observation towers, two with restaurants. From Toronto, Grey Coach Tours (416) 979-3511 and Niagara Tours (416) 868-0400 operate regular bus excursions.

Ottawa

Ottawa, Canada's capital and the province's second major city, is situated some 520 kilometers (323 miles) northeast of Toronto. To the rest of Canada, Ottawa is seen as removed, aloof, peopled by pampered politicians and bureaucrats. Yet the city has its charms.

HISTORY

Until 1857, Ottawa was just another wild, rough lumber community at the confluence of the Rideau and Ottawa rivers. It was then known as Bytown for Lieutenant Colonel John By who built the historic Rideau Canal. Then Queen Victoria, enamored of some watercolors of the area, named it the new Dominion's capital. Both the French-Canadians who were vying for Montreal and the British, who favored Toronto or Kingston, were outraged. Nonetheless, Bytown became the capital and was renamed Ottawa, Indian for 'buying and selling'.

'Westminster in the Wilderness' blossomed from its humble beginnings to a bustling capital of some 700,000 people. It is elegant, quiet, conservative and, naturally, the center for many of Canada's cultural activities.

SIGHTS AND ATTRACTIONS
■ PARLIAMENT
Ottawa's main attraction is the neo-Gothic **Parliament Buildings** perched above the Ottawa River. The **Peace Tower**, the central structure, is a good beginning for walking tours. The original Center Block was destroyed in the early 1900s by a fire in

which several women died rushing into the flames to retrieve their fur coats. The new **Center Block** was reconstructed in 1916 with a 92-meter (300-foot) tower, a limestone monolith with three-meter (ten-foot) gargoyles and a four-faced clock.

The ramrod-back, military-type guide tells visitors all about the fossilized limestone and the Irish linen ceilings. He doesn't mention that while the building was going up, sheets of copper roofing were left on the ground so workmen could urinate on them to speed up oxidation and thus ensure its rich green hue. The **Eternal Flame** in the center of the complex has reputedly flickered out several times since it was lit for Canada's centennial in 1967. Inside, a monument commemorates Canadian soldiers and an enormous Bourdon Bell strikes the hour. Tours run every 15 minutes daily with extended hours in summer. Some 7,000 people take the tour each day.

The **House of Commons** in the Center Block plays to packed houses so if you want to be among the 500 allowed into the public gallery, get there early. Aficionados of parliament say the best show is during question period, although they complain that this has deteriorated, with MPs hamming it up for the TV cameras now.

On fair summer days, a half-hour **changing of the guard** takes place at 10 am in front of the Peace Tower. All the pageantry makes for a colorful spectacle; with the brilliant red outfits and bearskin hats of the Governor General's Foot Guards, the Canadian Grenadier Guards of Montreal and the accompanying fife and drum. (The Guards ceremony once appeared threatened when feminists demanded the right to march in bearskins alongside the men.)

Statues surrounding Parliament Hill include the likeness of Sir Wilfred Laurier, Canada's first French-speaking prime minister, situated at the eastern corner of the grounds, and the one of Canada's first prime minister, Sir John A Macdonald, in the southeastern end of the Center Block.

■ CITY CENTER

Nearby, **Sparks Street Mall** is a five-block pedestrian area stretching from Elgin to Lyon streets. Fountains, artwork and sidewalk cafes characterize the area and a rock collection features samples from each of Canada's provinces.

Near the mall stands **Confederation Square** with its powerful bronze war memorial commemorating Canadian soldiers who died in World War I. To the left is Parliament Hill and to the right, the **Château Laurier**, one of the grand Canadian Pacific Railway hotels (see page 283). The imposing lodging with its grey turrets and sweeping public areas overlooks the Parliament Buildings and the Rideau River. Directly ahead, the huge locks in the Ottawa River can lift boats some 24 meters (80 feet) into the Rideau Canal. Steps down from the gorge lead to **Bytown Museum**, the city's oldest stone building, erected in 1826 which displays artifacts from the city's pioneer days.

(following pages) Tour boat Maid of the Mists takes visitors in front of the Niagara Falls

The **Rideau Canal** runs through the city and is the core of its outdoor life—as the world's longest skating rink in winter and a popular waterway for boating in summer. During frosty January and February days, serious civil servants skate to work along the frozen canal beside denim-clad collegiates gliding off to classes. Briefcases and steaming cups of coffee are oft-seen accessories carried by Ottawa's skating citizens. When warm weather arrives, bicyclists and joggers take to the ten kilometers (six miles) of paths rimming the canal and canoeists and cruises ply the waters.

Ottawa is not all bureaucracy and buildings; it has a human side, too. Farmers bring their produce (including live pigs) past the Chateau Laurier, left on William Street, to sell in the downtown **Byward Market**, as they have since 1830. Fishmongers, craftsmen and cooks share space with the farmers in this lively country atmosphere. Here is the only place to sample an Ottawa specialty, beavertails, a fried pastry topped with your choice of cinnamon and sugar, jam, cheese, ham and eggs. These crepe-like goodies are sold at market stands and at booths on the Rideau Canal during the three-week winter carnival, Winterlude, held each February.

Beyond, along **Sussex Drive**, restored Georgian and Victorian buildings house trendy boutiques, art galleries and cafes. The **Notre Dame Basilica**, built in the mid-1800s on the corner of Sussex and St Patrick, has a fine wood interior crafted by Philippe Parizeau, whose work appears in the National Library.

Canada's head of state, the Governor-General, resides in **Rideau Hall** or **Government House**, separated by a park from the prime minister's abode at 24 Sussex Drive. Rideau Hall has a cricket pitch, skating arena, grand ballroom and abundant acreage where the public can join summer tours of the woodland or formal gardens.

Harkening back to its British beginnings is Ottawa's **Old Chelsea Mall**, 1725 Bank Street. Here, McIntosh and Watts Ltd sells Wedgwood and other fine English bone china.

■ MUSEUMS AND GALLERIES

The nation's capital is well served by museums on subjects ranging from coins to boy scouts. The **National Museum of Science and Technology** has steam locomotives, horse-drawn carriages and antique automobiles as well as sections on astronomy and a working meteorological station.

The **Canadian Ski Museum** traces the development of the sport from Europe 5,000 years ago to its introduction in this country just 100 years ago. Exhibits include early twisted birch bindings and modern, high-tech racing skis, archives detailing the sport's evolution, and tributes to successful Canadian competitors.

Other worthy stops are the **Canadian War Museum**, **National Museum of Man and Natural Sciences**, **Museum of Canadian Scouting** and the **National Aviation Museum** in a new, custom designed-building.

For the culturally minded, there are the **National Arts Center**, **National Gallery of Canada**, **National Film Board Gallery**, **National Library and Public Archives of Canada**. The new **Museum of Civilization** in Hull, across the river from the Parliament Buildings, includes the world's first combined IMAX/OMNIMAX theater.

Nepean Point, high above the Ottawa River near the Alexandra Bridge and just north of where the Rideau Canal enters the river, home to the $160 **National Gallery of Canada** in May 1988. The dramatic, modern building, described as a glass cathedral rising from the limestone cliffs, is considered the showpiece of what Ottawa sees as its cultural renaissance.

■ ACROSS THE RIVER AND INTO THE BARS

The view from Nepean Point shows Ottawa's dual personality. Behind, are the majestic spires of Parliament Hill and across the river is the neon and industrial congestion of Hull, Quebec, often considered the most interesting part of the National Capital Region.

Ottawa is not known for its lively nightlife, bureaucrats being what they are, and the streets are empty at night. For nocturnal action, one must cross the river to **Hull** where the frequently bawdy bars are livelier and stay open much later. Although the oldest European settlement in the area (founded in 1800), Hull is not a particularly attractive or interesting town. However, as part of Quebec it does have a French 'foreign' feel, particularly in its restaurants and night spots.

The Province

Beyond Toronto and Ottawa, Ontario is actually two separate regions, divided by a line following the Mattawa and French rivers from Georgian Bay northeast to Mattawa. To the south, the peninsula surrounded by lakes Ontario, Erie and Huron is a crowded industrial and agricultural area. The north is a vast and largely unpopulated mining, timber and fur-trapping country of rocky terrain, lakes, rivers and forests. This is the domain of the fishermen, hunter, canoeist and camper.

SOUTHERN ONTARIO

Much of Canada's early history was played out in the fertile region of southern Ontario, where even the names speak of the British heritage: London, Kingston, Niagara-on-the-Lake, Brockville.

For all the pride in 'the world's longest undefended border', Canada and the US had their military disputes early on. A number of forts and battle sites along the border mark those bellicose days. South of Toronto, **Old Fort Erie**, first built in 1764 at the junction of Lake Erie and the Niagara River opposite Buffalo, New York, was destroyed twice by storms and once by war. The restored building contains relics and equipment of both British and American armies. Throughout the summer, guards in period uniforms perform military drills.

Nearby **Fort George** was built between 1779 and 1799, burnt by American soldiers in 1813, rebuilt in 1815, and eventually abandoned. Restored in 1939, it is now a national historic park where colorfully costumed 'soldiers' display their skills.

Fort George is close to **Niagara-on-the-Lake**, yet another Ontario nod to its British heritage. The well-preserved 19th-century village has an apothecary museum, a store that has been operating since 1835, a fudge shop, the Victorian Prince of Wales Hotel and numerous fine old residences.

The attractive town is best known for the annual **Shaw Festival** featuring productions of playwright George Bernard Shaw and his contemporaries.

West of Toronto, the **Kitchener-Waterloo area** was first settled by Germans, including many Mennonites from Pennsylvania. These origins surface during the ten-day annual Oktoberfest, North America's largest, with huge tubas accompanying lively oom-pa-pa bands, hefty beer steins overflowing with the lusty brew, singing, merriment and tables groaning under the weight of German food and strong drink. Permanent fixtures are the glockenspiel and 23-bell carillon, and a restored, 1850s-era **Pennsylvania Mennonite home**.

Further west is **Stratford on Avon**, where each summer the theaters present a festival of Shakespearean plays. On fine summer days, swans and picnickers crowd the riverbanks and theatergoers sit under lacy trees and at sidewalk cafes until the performances begin.

Among the greenery is the **Shakespearean Garden** with its flowers, plants and herbs growing along the languorous **Avon River** many of which are referred to in the bard's works. An arched, vine-covered entrance with stone walls and meandering gravel walkways leads to a brilliant mass of perennials, tulips and daffodils in spring, followed by peonies, poppies, Shasta daisies and other late-bloomers. The floral oasis was built in 1957, just off Stratford's main artery, Ontario Street. A focal point here is an old brick tower belonging to a woolen mill which occupied the site in the early 1900s. Nearby is a bust of William Shakespeare.

Another literary connection can be found in Ontario's deep south, a mile west of **Dresden**. A cabin here was the inspiration for Harriet Beecher Stowe's anti-slavery novel *Uncle Tom's Cabin*. It was built with home-made nails in 1842 by escaped slave Reverend Josiah Henson, and is now a small museum displaying Henson's rocking chair and other possessions.

The verdigrised copper-roofed House of Parliament overlooks Ottawa's Rideau Canal

EASTERN ONTARIO

The road between Toronto and Ottawa passes many places rich in Ontario's colonial and Indian history, but these can easily be missed if you take Highway 401 (the Macdonald-Cartier Freeway) which runs along the St Lawrence River. **Highway 2**, running parallel to the 401, is the better route, for the variety of places it passes through and the lovely scenery. Much of the land is undeveloped and you will pass many lakes and forests—particularly impressive in the fall when the leaves turn every shade of orange, red and yellow.

The first stop east of Toronto is **Peterborough**, where serpent-shaped mounds 600 meters (200 feet) long, seven meters (25 feet) wide and two meters (six feet) high, are believed to have been built 1,700 years ago by people who preceded today's Indians. These early inhabitants lived on the hillside overlooking Rice Lake and buried their dead beneath the mounds.

The sacred grounds are open May to mid-October and give an insight into the region's Indian heritage.

Closer to Ottawa, near **Morrisburg**, is **Upper Canada Village**, an authentic depiction of an early-1800s Ontario settlement. Many original villages had to be flooded with the construction of the St Lawrence Seaway in the early 1960s, so the best of the heritage buildings were moved here—the site of the Battle of Crysler's Farm where British troops repelled invading Americans.

The village's 35 buildings are open from mid-May to mid-October. You can take tours of the area by horse-drawn carriages or 'bateaus', or stroll past the church, general store, saloon, sawmill, blacksmith's shop and schoolmaster's cottage. Employees in period costume relate historical lore and answer queries.

Between Peterborough and Morrisburg is Kingston, one of Canada's oldest cities and home to many historical sites.

■ KINGSTON

Located at the mouth of Lake Ontario, the 300-year-old settlement of Kingston is also known as the Limestone City for its solid gray limestone structures. This ancient (by Canadian standards) town was founded in 1673 by Count Frontenac, the governor of New France. The sturdy French stronghold, **Old Fort Henry**, was in its day the principal fortress in Upper Canada.

From mid-May to mid-October, history is recreated in an impressive show of cavalry and artillery. Cannons fire muskets, as they did in the 1870s, and there is a ceremonial changing of the guard each Monday, Wednesday and Saturday evening. The pageantry, fierce explosions of cannons and the sun sinking behind the old fort evoke visions of more exciting, if less peaceful, times.

As well as its military place in history, Kingston has been a British citadel, the capital of Canada and the home of the country's first prime minister, Sir John A Macdonald. The city is rich with relics of Upper Canada colonialism and its limestone structures, such as the long-standing **Queen's University** and **Sir John A Macdonald**'s first home, are reminiscent of other former British colonies. You can take the 16-kilometer (10-mile) **Confederation Tour train** past 22 historical sites including Canada's Royal Military College.

Kingston is strategically located midway between Toronto and Montreal and at the point where the Rideau Canal meets the St Lawrence, making it a major transportation hub. Its naval spirit is reflected in the 150-year-old **Rideau Canal locks** at **Kingston Mills** and the harbor where many vessels wait to take passengers through the scenic waterways.

The building of the Rideau Canal, which ends at Ottawa, was supervised by Colonel John By who also founded the nation's capital. He saw it as an alternative to the St Lawrence River, a military route where British warships would be secure from the Americans.

It soon became a commercial waterway, though, and now is a favorite route for pleasure boats, canoes, sailboats and especially houseboats which can be rented at either Kingston or Ottawa for a leisurely tour of this historic part of Ontario. It takes about one unhurried week to travel through the 198-kilometer (123-mile) canal and its 47 locks.

NORTHERN ONTARIO

The great portion of the province is a rugged frontier of metamorphic rock several billion years old with thousands of freshwater lakes, ideal for hunters, fishermen and seekers of solitude.

Much of this wild empty northland, with place names such as Lake Abitibi, Iroquois Falls and Smooth Rock Falls, is redolent of fur trappers, Mounties and Indians and can only be reached by rail.

Traveling the great Canadian Shield east from Manitoba is like endlessly staring at the back of the Canadian blue five-dollar bill. Here in 'Sunset Country', **Kenora**—which sounded more colorful than Rat Portage, its original name—is a favorite summer retreat for Manitobans, who still feel it should be part of their province. Those driving across the country should stop at this attractive, busy town on **Lake of the Woods** for boating and fishing, and cruises through the lake's 14,500 islands. The symbol of the town is a giant, 13-meter (40-foot) replica of a muskie fish called Husky the Muskie.

Kenora is on the Trans-Canada Highway, a few miles from the Manitoba border. The nearest Ontario cities are Fort Frances, on the border with Minnesota to the south, and Thunder Bay.

The Museum of Military History at Kingston's Old Fort Henry

In 1969, twin cities Fort William and Port Arthur combined to become **Thunder Bay**, Canada's third largest port although on Lake Superior and not on the ocean. Of interest in this northern town are Centennial Park, complete with an animal farm, a reproduction of a turn-of-the-century logging camp and a logging museum.

Old Fort William is a reconstruction of the 19th century North West Company inland fur-trade headquarters. The site has craft shops and a farm, a naval encampment and an Indian camp where large cargo canoes are shown being made. Musket-firing, bread-making and dances are also demonstrated, and guides are available. Open year round.

There are guided tours to an amethyst mine 48 kilometers (30 miles) east, the Thunder Bay Museum with Indian artifacts and pioneer relics, and daily river cruises from Waterfront Park (at the foot of Red River Rd) around the harbor and to Old Fort William from mid-May to early October 5.

ONTARIO RAIL JOURNEYS

The town of Cochrane is a sportsmen's outfitting center and the start of the adventurous **Polar Bear Express** train to the wilds of Moosonee on the shores of remote James Bay. The train follows the original route of a French soldier named Chevalier de Troyes who captured the English trading post at Moose Factory, adjacent to Moosonee. The train rolls through the province's rich clay belt, past **Otter Rapids** with its gigantic Hydro power plant, and past muskeg and pine forests which gradually become smaller until finally disappearing at the tree line.

The twin towns of **Moose Factory** and **Moosonee** were established some 300 years ago by the Hudson's Bay Company for fur-trading purposes. They have retained the spirit of the wild frontier, with some buildings dating back to the early 1700s. This is as far as you can go by rail—and the nearest road is 241 kilometers (150 miles) south. From here, charter planes travel to Ontario's largest, wildest and most remote park, **Polar Bear Provincial**, with its polar and black bears, caribou, moose and waterfowl. A permit is required to enter the area.

Further west, the **Algoma Central Railway** through the scenic **Agawa Canyon** area pushes into the rugged north from **Sault Ste Marie**, affectionately nicknamed **The Soo**, on the US border. Construction of the Algoma Central and Hudson's Bay Railway into the wild terrain of forests, lakes, rivers, rushing waterfalls and craggy mountains started in 1901. In 1914 the first passenger train rolled into Hearst, the 'Moose Capital of the World', 476 kilometers (296 miles) north. This was a real pioneer run, with women and the clergy barricaded in rear coaches away from the hard-drinking lumbermen. The train remains the area's major link with the outside world, but it is more civilized now!

Beyond rugged Agawa Canyon at mile 114, the train moves into the flat lands of the **Great Clay Belt**. Steep granite cliffs drop away alongside the tracks, and Indian names such as Howling Wolf Lake, Chippewa River and Grey Owl Lake stir memories of the first settlers here. The twisting, corkscrew run crosses more than 200 bridges and trestles, but there is not a single tunnel. The railway, which owns some 345,000 hectares (850,000 acres), escorts several tours into the area. This countryside often inspired Canada's most famous artists—the Group of Seven—with its beauty.

Further south is **North Bay**, and one of the more pleasant ways to travel from there to Toronto is on the **Northlander**, a train which passes through the interior with its few houses, occasional lakes and forests before penetrating the **Muskokas lakes region** and following the eastern edge of **Lake Simcoe**. Often the only sound is the rhythmic chugging of the train along its tracks and the clinking of dishes in the dining car.

VIA Rail in Toronto has several tour packages which include spa weekends in Chatham, whale-watching on the St Lawrence and Murder Mystery Weekends.

■ MANITOULIN ISLAND

In the northeastern edge of Lake Huron, 160 kilometer-long (92 miles) Manitoulin Island is the world's largest fresh water island. Its shorelines consist of limestone outcrops from the Ice Age and meandering beaches, some sandy, others with smooth colorful pebbles. The island, which gets its name from the Ojibwa words 'Gitchi Manitou' meaning home of the Great Spirit, is rich in Indian lore. The Ojibwa Cultural Foundation sells native crafts, rare artworks such as porcupine quill boxes, and wall hangings of animal and hunting scenes.

Around the end of July and the beginning of August, the island's six Indian nations host the lively Wikwemikong Pow Wow. In this annual festival, Canada's original inhabitants in colorful native costume parade their culture with traditional dancing, tribal ceremonies, artisans at work and craft shows.

Quebec

By anything but Canadian logic, *La Belle Province* should be a separate country, not a Canadian province—a sentiment shared by many Quebecois. It is three times larger than France, has the world's second largest French-speaking city, Montreal, and has a long, unique history with distinct traditions. That it remains a province, despite this background and frequent, sometimes rancorous, debates over its status, is a credit and a benefit to both Quebec and Canada.

Quebec is Canada's largest province in area, covering nearly a fifth of the country, and has the second largest population with 6.5 million. The province is divided into three distinct regions. The Laurentian Plateau or Canadian Shield, four-fifths of the province north of the St Lawrence River, is an enormous expanse of lake-covered highlands and low, rocky hills. In the east the Appalachian Mountains extend from the rugged Gaspé Peninsula on the Atlantic south into the US. West of the Appalachians and south of the shield are the St Lawrence Lowlands which form a flat, fertile triangle. The mighty St Lawrence, a riverine highway cutting deep into central Canada, still plays a vital role as a transportation and communications route.

For the visitor, Quebec, is the most 'exotic' piece of North America north of Mexico, with more than 80 per cent of the population French-speaking. On top of this, the Quebecois have a lively sense of fun and social energy lacking in some of their staid Anglo compatriots. But to call them 'French' is quite inaccurate. *Joual*, the Quebecois' own dialect, is a slangy working-class dialect, distinct in both vocabulary and pronunciation from 'French' French.

History

France's explorations in Quebec began with Jacques Cartier charting the St Lawrence river in 1534–5. King Henry IV of France later granted a group of French merchants a fur-trading monopoly in the area. Quebec was officially founded in 1608 when Samuel de Champlain established a fur-trading post on the site of present-day Quebec City.

For the next several decades, French explorers, missionaries and fur traders penetrated the interior of the continent, mapping huge tracts of land. It was a feat of exploration rarely equalled anywhere. In 1663, the area called New France was proclaimed a royal colony.

In 1754 the nine-year French and Indian War erupted, with Britain eventually taking control of the colony. The action culminated in 1759 at the historic Battle of

the Plains of Abraham (see page 27). In the 1763 Treaty of Paris, France ceded her interests to Britain, ending an era in North American history. Some ten years later, the British passed the Quebec Act to retain the French language and institutions.

After the American Revolution, many British United Empire Loyalists fled north, and in 1791 Upper Canada (now Ontario) and Lower Canada (Quebec) were separated. Then in 1867 Quebec and Ontario joined the newly formed Dominion of Canada as separate entities. But the desire for greater independence remained strong, and reached a violent climax with the appearance of the Fédération de la Libération du Québec (FLQ) in October 1970. Separate FLQ cells kidnapped British commercial attaché James Cross and killed Quebec labor minister Pierre Laporte. The federal government declared a state of 'apprehended insurrection' and the terrorist movement fizzled out. Even in Quebec, there remains little opposition to the government's swift action. Robert Bourassa, premier of Quebec at the time of the crisis, again heads the provincial government.

The quest for independence did not die out, and in 1976, the separatist Parti Québecois peacefully won the majority in the provincial assembly. The party pledged a referendum on separatism which was held in 1980. Those for and against campaigned vigorously but the separatists lost by a 20 per cent margin. Although the Parti Quebecois was defeated in a 1985 election, separatism remains an important issue.

To reinforce the French historical and cultural dominance, the province has made French the official language. All traffic and commercial signs must be *en français* so the cities are becoming even more 'foreign'.

Montreal

With 2.8 million people, Quebec's most cosmopolitan city makes up nearly half of the province's population. Canada's second largest city after Toronto occupies an island in the junction of the St Lawrence and Ottawa rivers 52 kilometers long and up to 16 kilometers across (32 by 10 miles). Although 1,600 kilometers (1,000 miles) from the ocean, it is a major sea port.

Montrealers are a carefree, fun-loving and flamboyant lot, given to fine food and drink, music and laughter. Although compared with Paris because of its Frenchness and sophistication, Montreal has a more relaxed, lively spirit, and its own distinct charm.

The city is a patchwork of distinct *quartiers*, ethnic neighborhoods such as the Jewish quarter (where they claim to make the world's best bagels), a Chinatown, a Portuguese area, and Westmount and Outremont—exclusive English- and French-

A Quebec restaurant depicting the military garb of an earlier era

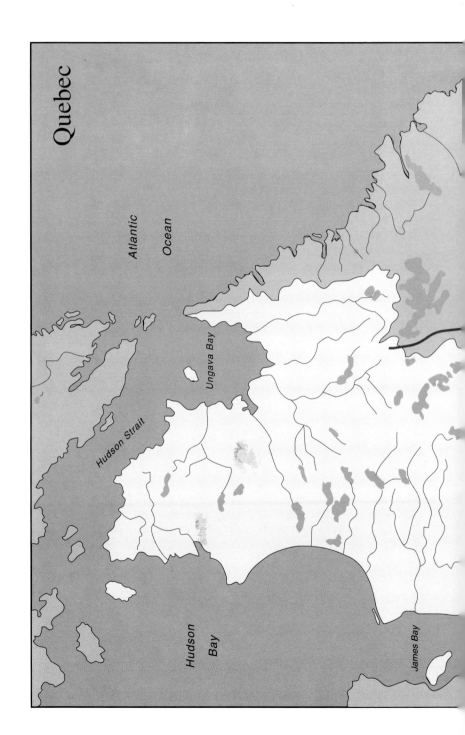

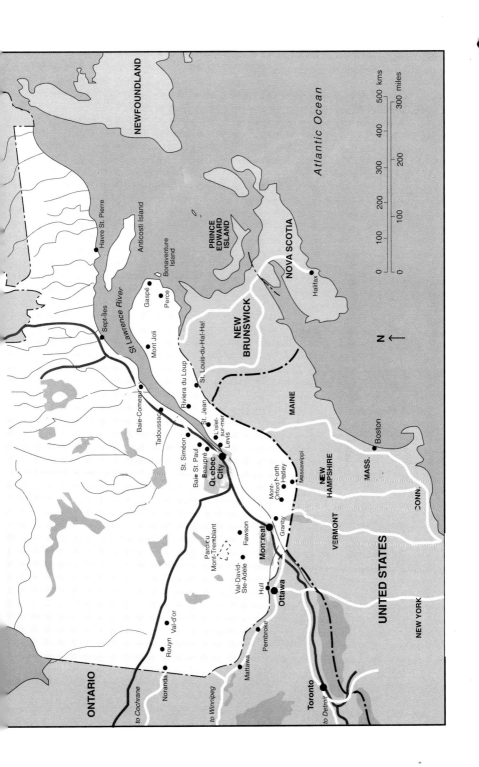

QUEBECOIS CULTURE

Quebec literature, art, music and theater, which once drew inspiration from Paris and the US, have developed along their own lines since World War I. In the heady years of the 1950s and 60s, times of great turmoil in Quebec, the culture had a powerful political and social foundation, but in recent years has looked more to pure art—and entertainment.

The literature is satirical and anti-establishment, highly introspective and often stresses sociological analysis. It developed with novelists such as Gabrielle Roy (actually a Manitoba francophone), Yves Theriault, Roger Lemelin, Ann Hebert and Marie Claire Blais. Prolific playwright Michel Tremblay's work, sometimes written in the *joual* street language, has been translated into English and moved beyond Quebec.

Theater is especially popular in Montreal, which has ten established companies with their own premises and about 100 active and innovative troupes. In the summer, more than 50 troupes present plays in Quebec resort areas. Up to 30 films are produced locally each year, as well as a number of TV productions.

The non-verbal arts—painting and music especially—are more accessible to the anglophone. From the 1940s Quebecois artists, always influenced by Paris, established their own movements—from the Automatistes, impressionists with the inevitable political overtones, to the 1950s *Les Plasticiens*, to current vogue seen elsewhere in Canada, photograph realism, and what critics, for want of a new, neat term, call a stylistic anarchy. In Quebec and Old Montreal, as in Paris, art comes out of the museums and into the streets, where painters create and sell their work. As in Paris, the quality of art varies widely.

Quebec music found its own home-grown voice in the 1950s, when Félix Leclerc sang his own folk songs of ordinary Quebecois working people. His songs focused on cultural and political alienation, survival and exploitation, and remain popular across the province.

Leclerc's success gave impetus in the 50s and 60s to the *chansonniers* who sang poetry to the accompaniment of music, appealing to a Quebecois sense of identity. The trend was accompanied by the rise of *boîtes à chanson* (song boxes), the distinctive Quebec nightclub popular with students, intellectuals, politicians and franco-bohemians. Perhaps the best known folk singer is Gilles Vigneault who emerged in the 60s and brought attention from abroad to the Quebec *chanson*. His passionate *Mon Pays* (1964) became the unofficial Quebec anthem.

In the 1970s and 80s music moved away from politics to original Quebecois rock, complete with regional pop stars such as Ginette Reno and Michel Pagliaro. *Rolling Stone* magazine, the chronicler of rock and roll, called theatrical performer Robert Charlebois 'the Dylan of Quebec'. The voice of the Quebec youth movement sang in *joual*, and Quebecois records, available across the province, still make for lively listening even for those who do not understand the language.

speaking neighborhoods respectively. For its vivacity and historical roots, many Canadians and Americans find Montreal a slice of transplanted Europe.

Montreal is easily explored on foot or by rented bicycle along some 20 designated paths, including one starting at McGill and de la Commune Streets and running along the Lachine Canal. In summer, traditional horse-drawn carriages (*calèches*) run leisurely private sightseeing tours for about $40 an hour from a number of places throughout the city. In winter, one-horse open sleighs operate in Mont Royal Park.

Summer is a time of outdoor festivals with many free shows in Montreal, especially the Jazz Festival in July and Just For Laughs, a humor festival with international comics (including some from China recently) in late July and early August.

SIGHTS AND ATTRACTIONS

■ OLD MONTREAL

The 38 hectares (95 acres) of Vieux-Montreal by the harbor, once part of a walled city, is easily the city's greatest attraction. Old Montreal has been officially designated a heritage site, and although many early buildings were demolished, enough examples of restored religious and secular architecture remain to make this one of the continent's finest old cities. You don't have to be an historian to appreciate its narrow cobblestone streets, centuries-old greystone buildings, monuments and historic sites.

The tourist information center (174 Notre Dame Street East) provides a map of a proposed three-kilometers (two-mile) walking tour which can be covered in two-and-a-half hours, though it is worth a day.

Montreal claims more churches than Rome, about 450. Grandest is the pseudo-Gothic **Notre Dame Basilica** (1829), richly decorated with artwork and stained-glass windows depicting religious scenes and the parish's early history. Especially when the Orchestra Symphonique performs classical music here once a month and during special Christmas masses, Notre Dame equals Europe's great cathedrals.

The same order of Sulpician priests still occupies the oldest surviving structure, the **St Sulpice Seminary** off Notre Dame Street, built in 1685. Peer through the iron gate to the still-functioning woodwork clock, dating to 1710 and probably the oldest of its kind on the continent. Electrical movements were installed in 1966 to replace wooden works which finally wound down half a century ago.

Throughout the years, French, English and Canadian governors lived in the **Château de Ramesay**, built in about 1705 by Governor Claude de Ramesay. In 1775, generals and envoys of the American occupation army, including Benjamin Franklin and Benedict Arnold, were headquartered here. The finely preserved stone structure is now a museum of historical artefacts, furniture and art depicting 18th-century life in New France.

A random stroll through the old city reveals historical landmarks such as part of a stone gate dating to 1610, a monument to city founder Samuel de Champlain in **Place d'Armes**, and, in **Place Royale**, an obelisk marking the foundation of the original 1642 settlement here as selected by de Champlain.

There is a thriving street life among these restored ruins, historical monuments and stately 18th- and 19th-century mansions with boutiques, *café-terrasses*, theaters and *boîte à chansons*. Tiny **St Amable Lane**, just off **Place Jacques Cartier** which looks out onto the Old Port, is an outdoor market for local artists who line their colorful canvases against the stone walls. The lane runs to **Saint Vincent**, once a Quebecois Fleet Street with six newspaper offices.

■ MONT ROYAL

Two hundred hectares (494 acres) of Mont Royal, rising in the middle of the city, have been reserved as a park with trails, benches amid the trees, and man-made **Beaver Lake** where ducks swim in summer and locals skate in winter. From atop the former volcano rising 230 meters (752 feet) above sea level, you can easily see Vermont and New Hampshire mountain ranges on cloudless days. A 30-meter (100-foot) illuminated cross, visible for miles, commemorates the original planted in 1643 after Ville-Marie was spared from a great flood.

Here, too, is Montreal's most imposing landmark, the world's biggest shrine dedicated to St Joseph that Montrealers know simply as 'The Temple'. The distinctive **St Joseph's Oratory**, its green dome like a mossy helmet visible around the city, was started in 1904 as a small chapel for Holy Cross Brother André, a simple man credited with many miracle cures. Born Alfred Bessette in 1845, the near-illiterate faith healer and religious counsellor became Quebec's most popular religious figure (to the consternation of the established church and the medical profession) before he died in 1937.

Two million pilgrims climb the 99 steps each year to see the original chapel, Brother André's tomb, and a museum containing hundreds of crutches and braces from those claiming to be cured here.

■ CITY CENTER

In the early part of the century, immigrants who got off the boat in Montreal harbor walked up Main Street and settled along the way. Now **Main Street** (officially, **St Lawrence Boulevard**) divides the city into east and west. Once, Jews were so dominant that Yiddish was the language of the district. Today the area is a miniature Europe of Greeks, Slavs, Germans and Portuguese. Because of large-scale immigration from Asia in the past 15 years, Montreal now has a large Chinatown with good, inexpensive restaurants, shops and several Hong Kong-owned hotels.

Prince Arthur, running off Main, is an earthy street of pedestrians, street enter-

(top) A road winding through Rorillon National Park, Gaspe, Quebec, (left) Quebec, Canada's most European City

tainers, musicians and low-cost ethnic restaurants. Along cross streets towards St Louis Square, the district's 12,000 Portuguese residents live in distinctive, vividly painted houses.

■ MODERN MONTREAL

Montreal seemed to sleep through the first half of this century but woke with a great burst of energy and growth physically and politically in the early 1960s, along with the rest of the province. Since then, the city has hosted Expo 67 and the 1976 Olympics, and undergone a major rebuilding so that anyone away for more than 20 years wouldn't recognize the downtown area.

Montreal now has a modern subway system called the **Metro, Olympic Park, Man and His World** (site of Expo 67), **Place des Arts**, a multi-million dollar center for music and the performing arts the impressive Canadian Center for Architecture and a 13-kilometer (seven-mile) **underground city.**

■ NOTES FROM UNDERGROUND

The city's great subterranean complex began with the 45-story **Place Ville Marie** office tower complex, completed in 1962 and connecting two major hotels—the Queen Elizabeth and Château Champlain.

The network spread under the city's streets so it now provides an escape from vehicular traffic and a pleasing refuge from harsh winters. In cold, stormy weather especially, Montrealers abandon the downtown streets for the 'weatherproof city' which allows access by the Metro to various downtown areas and to above-ground locations.

This is no gloomy neo-catacomb but a bright, cheery, climate-controlled sub-city with more than a thousand boutiques, several dozen movie houses, 130 bars and restaurants, eight major hotels, three department stores, the University of Quebec, 25 bank branches, Central and Windsor train stations and the bus terminal. The city beneath the city is so appealing that five sightseeing companies run underground tours.

Montreal's Metro is among the world's most comfortable and attractive subways. Trains glide along quickly and quietly on rubber wheels past stations designed by different architects, with stained glass windows, murals and other works of art to enliven many of them. Locals call it the world's biggest art gallery, and you'll find it fun to take a ride even if you don't have a specific destination.

■ THE ISLANDS

The subway goes to **Ile Nôtre-Dame**, or Notre Dame Island, site of the successful Expo 67. In summer the former **French Pavilion** (somewhat haughtily termed the

Palais de la Civilisation) hosts art and archaeological exhibitions such as Ramses II. Concerts are held in the extensive flower gardens.

La Balade des Iles, open-air trolley cars, operate free from parking areas to **Ste Helen's Island**, site of **La Ronde**, the city's favorite summer amusement park. There is nothing especially French about the more than 35 rides, including a super loop roller coaster and a giant water slide, but this Coney Island north is a welcome break from all that history and culture, especially for families and courting couples. The **aquarium** has a coral-reef tank, with brilliant tropical fish, and a penguin tank where the cold-weather birds can be observed above and below water. Eastern Canada's first casino, located on scenic Ile Notre-Dame, is one of the world's largest, with 65 gaming tables, 1,200 slot machines and a capacity for 5,000 gamblers. The popular **Casino de Montréal** has a gourmet dining room, regular restaurant and a snack bar.

■ OLYMPIC PARK

The 46-hectare (114-acre) Olympic Park in the east end includes the extensive, and expensive, sports facilities built for the 1976 summer games, including the controversial Olympic Stadium. The roof and tower of this somewhat unattractive seven-story sporting facility did not go up until 10 years after the original construction. A funicular goes to the top of the tower for an impressive view of the city, and tours are conducted in French and English.

The nearby **Biodome** recreates four separate eco-systems— the polar world, the Laurentian forest, St Lawrence marine system and a tropical rainforest. Even more unusual is the avant-garde insectarium displaying butterflies, scarab beetles, bees, giant stick insects and thousands more from around the world. The **Montreal Botanical Garden** has some 36,000 specimens of exotic plants in 10 inter-connected glass-roofed exhibition greenhouses as well as 30 theme gardens.

■ ON THE WATER

Jet boat tours running 15 kilometers (nine miles) up the foaming **Lachine Rapids** daily from mid-May to September add some excitement to a history lesson. The 500-horsepower, flat-bottomed boats depart from **Victoria Pier** in the Old Port for the wet and bumpy 90-minute trip upstream on the St Lawrence through the historic Lachine Rapids that stopped early explorers. Between waves of river water foaming over the open boat, there are scenic views of the Montreal skyline. Raincoats, hats and plastic footwear are provided. In summer, the more sedate *Miss Olympia* takes dinner and sunset cruises around the harbor.

■ WHEN THE SUN GOES DOWN

Montrealers really come alive after dark, creating a vibrant nightlife that can be earthy or sophisticated. In part this began during the American prohibition of the

1920s and 30s, that benighted attempt to legislate human virtue. Fun-seeking Americans from four states bordering Quebec would go north to Montreal for their excitement, attracted by legal booze (instead of bathtub gin), nightclubs with big floor shows and the lively Quebec ambience.

The night scene has since changed but it is different, not duller, with discos replacing many of the live cabarets, in keeping with the era's shift from spectator to participatory pleasures. Night owls will find lively drinking, music and dancing in ragtime jazz nightclubs, grand, Parisienne-style floor shows complete with lively, high-stepping Montmartre cancan, rooftop lounges, discos, even dark reggae bars.

While Anglos patronize the pubs, jazz bars and clubs of **Rue Crescent**, the French (especially the 18- to 25-year-olds) head for **St Denis** when the sun goes down. **Old Montreal's Street** is more up-market. Lively **St Catherine's Street** provides some of the city's more basic, no-frills, raunchy nightlife, with bars and taverns popular with Quebecois men, although some—such as the Super Sex Bar—hustle a touch too heavily for tips. The Super Sex Bar (and another popular strip club, Les Filles d'Eve) are found here. For the ladies, Supermale is, appropriately, on Peel Street .

Lively, basic reggae bars in the St Catherine area reflects the city's increasing multi-culturalism. Montreal's large Caribbean black population (particularly from Haiti and Barbados) add a distinctly non-Gallic air to Montreal, although there is not yet a specific popular area for bars and clubs. In June, the Caribbean community holds a Carifest with lively West Indian dancing and bands.

More genteel bars feature live music, particularly jazz. Eponymous **Biddle's** on Aylmer is popular, for the chicken and ribs as well as Charlie Biddle's trio. Other Anglo favorites are **Thursday's**, on Crescent, **Grumpy's or Woody's Pub** (both on Bishop), The **Old Dublin Pub** (on University) and **Winnie's** (rue Crecent).

■ DINING

With more than 5,000 eating places ranging from delis to bistros, Montreal claims to have North America's highest restaurant per capita ratio (one for every 200 people). **Crescent, Drummond, Prince Arthur** and **Mountain** streets are main restaurant centers, while central **St Catherine Street** is home of Montreal's justifiably-famous delis, such as **Don's**, or **Ben's** on nearby Maisonneuve, which serve excellent Montreal smoked meat in a tile-and-formica-type setting. Eating is a serious recreation for Montrealers who dine late, long and often.

In summer-starved Montreal, there are more than 500 outdoor cafes (known here as *terrasses*) and the major hotels present Parisian-style nights with dinner and can can shows.

A Tale Of Two Cities

There are some differences between the ladies of Quebec, and those of Montreal; those of the last place seemed to be generally handsomer than those of the former. Their behaviour likewise seemed to me to be somewhat too free at Quebec, and of a more becoming modesty at Montreal. The ladies at Quebec, especially the unmarried ones, are not very industrious. A girl of eighteen is reckoned poorly off, if she cannot enumerate at least twenty lovers. These young ladies, especially those of a higher rank, get up at seven, and dress till nine, drinking their coffee at the same time. When they are dressed, they place themselves near a window that opens into the street, take up some needlework, and sew a stitch now and then; but turn their eyes into the street most of the time. When a young fellow comes in, whither they are acquainted with him or not, they immediately lay aside their work, sit down by him, and begin to chat, laugh, joke and invent double-entendres; and this is reckoned to be very witty. In this manner they frequently pass the whole day, leaving their mothers to do all the business in the house. In Montreal, the girls are not quite so volatile, but more industrious. They are always at their needlework, or doing some necessary business in the house. They are likewise cheerful and content; and nobody can say that they want either wit, or charms. Their fault is that they think too well of themselves. However, the daughters of people of all ranks, without exception, go to market, and carry home what they have bought. They rise as soon, and go to bed as late, as any people in the house. I have been assured, that, in general, their fortunes are not considerable; which are rendered still more scarce by the number of children, and the small revenues in a house. The girls at Montreal are very much displeased that those at Quebec get their husbands sooner than they. The reason of this is, that many young gentlemen who come over from France with the ships, are captivated by the ladies of Quebec, and marry them; but as the gentlemen seldom go up to Montreal, the girls there are not often so happy as those of the former place.

Peter Kalm, 1749

Quebec City

Much smaller than Montreal, Quebec City is North America's most European city, with winding cobbled streets, ancient churches, Norman-style houses, fortifications, stone buildings, public squares and horse-drawn caleches. More than 95 per cent of the city's more than half a million inhabitants speak French, so the provincial capital is even more Gallic than Montreal. It is also a much quieter place, with townsfolk generally taking life at a more sedate pace, except during the pre-Lenten Winter festival (see page 259).

HISTORY
The 400-year-old settlement is ancient by New World standards. De Champlain founded the colony of New France in 1608 at 'Kebec', Algonquin Indian for 'place where the river narrows'. The 'Gibraltar of North America' is strategically placed over the approaches to the Great Lakes and the St Lawrence River.

After de Champlain built Fort St Louis on Cap Diamant, settlers followed. Parishes, *seigniories* and houses built with distinctive Normandy-derived architecture sprang up along the river and along the Chemin du roy, the Kings Road, from Quebec to Montreal.

British General James Wolfe laid siege to the city in 1759, shelling the town throughout the summer. Then, on the historic night of September 13, Wolfe's troops scaled the cliffs to defeat the French at the Battle of the Plains of Abraham. In 1775, during the American Revolution, American troops under General Richard Montgomery and Colonel Benedict Arnold attacked the city under the illusion that the Quebecois would eagerly join them. After the invaders were defeated, the alarmed British strengthened the fortifications, which now give Quebec its distinctive silhouette.

SIGHTS AND ATTRACTIONS
■ FROM THE RIVER
Quebec City's skyline etched against the bright moonlight, with the immense **Chateau Frontenac Hotel** looming on Cap Diamant like a Gothic movie stage set, is one of Canada's most imposing man-made sights.

Named after Comte de Frontenac, one of New France's early governors, the Chateau is the most famous and majestic of the old Canadian Pacific Railway hotels (see pages 286 and 212). The castle-like main structure was completed in 1893, and the central tower added in 1925. Franklin Roosevelt and Sir Winston Churchill stayed here as Prime Minister Mackenzie King's guests during historic conferences in 1943 and 1944. The hotel's St Laurent Bar provides sweeping views of the river and across to the town of Levis, Orleans Island, and on a clear day, Mont St Anne.

For the best view of the city, the hotel and the fortifications perched on Cap Diamant rising 104 meters (343 feet) above the river, take a harbor cruise or cross to Orleans Island. This was the first sight of North America for many ship passengers arriving from Europe in the 19th century.

■ THE FORTIFICATIONS

A public path winds five kilometers (three miles) around the 17th-century fortifications, the wall around the old city, past cannon batteries and bastions that are all part of the **National Historic Parks** system.

Near **Porte Kent**, one of four remaining gates, the **Artillery Park** on the wall's ramparts is a reception and information center. The park displays an interesting model of the entire city that members of the Royal Engineers Corps made in 1808. The ten-meter (33-foot) long, 1/300-scale model includes, the Upper and Lower Towns and most of the Plains of Abraham and was restored in 1977.

The giant, star-shaped **Citadel** at the southwestern extreme of **Vieux-Quebec**, overlooking the city, is North America's largest set of fortifications still occupied by troops. It was rebuilt between 1820 and 1832 according to plans made with the assistance of the Duke of Wellington, the English general who defeated Napoleon at Waterloo in 1815. Set 110 meters (360 feet) above the St Lawrence River, the complex encloses some 25 buildings, including the headquarters of the Royal 22nd Regiment, the famous 'Vandoos'. The guards change, with full pomp and ceremony on summer days at 10 am, and there are guided tours through the massive fortifications.

Outside the city walls, **National Battlefields Park** encompasses the **Plains of Abraham**, and the cliffs that Wolfe and his soldiers climbed that fateful night in 1759.

■ THE OLD CITY—THE UPPER TOWN

Quebec City's historic district, 'the cradle of French civilization in North America', is the only walled city on the continent to preserve its fortifications, and the first North American city placed on the UNESCO World Heritage List in recognition of its historical value. The booklet *A Walking Tour of Old Quebec*, available from the Tourism Information Center at Esplanade Park next door to the *Magasin de la Société des Alcools* (liquor store), guides visitors through the winding streets of perhaps Canada's most historic area. The compact city with buildings tucked in the winding streets dating to the 17th century is easily and best seen on foot.

The oldest, most attractive structures include the French Renaissance **Palais de Justice** (old court house), the **Kent House** where the capitulation of Quebec was probably signed in 1759, and the ancient **Ursulines Convent** founded in 1639.

The **Cathedral of the Holy Trinity**, dedicated in 1804, was the first Church of

The Montreal Museum of Fine Arts is Canada's oldest art museum

England cathedral built outside the British Isles. The interior includes solid English oak pews and doors. The **Royal Pew**, set apart in the gallery, is reserved for the British sovereign or representatives.

Near Parc Montmorency stands the **Post Office**, built in 1871 on the site of the old **Hôtel le Chien d'Or** (the Golden Dog Hotel). A plaque on the front shows a dog chewing a bone and bears a somewhat enigmatic inscription often read as a political statement. It translates as:

> I am a dog that gnaws his bone
> I crouch and gnaw it all alone
> A time will come, which is not yet
> When I'll bite him by whom I'm bit.

Dufferin Terrace, the hilltop promenade next to the Château Frontenac, looks down on the busy river, port and the Lower Town.

■ THE LOWER TOWN

An old **funicular** from Dufferin Terrace in the center of the Upper Town descends to Lower Town and Place Royale. The more energetic, or nervous, can follow the steep stairway 55 meters (180 feet) down the cliffside to **Place Royale**, the colony's first marketplace.

With people still living and working in the refurbished colonial square, it escapes the contrived feeling of a constructed 'living museum'. Residents worship alongside sightseers in the 17th-century **Notre-Dame-des-Victoires**. The original **vaults of the Maison des Vins** on the square, built in 1689, were the home of a general merchant then a hotel until the building burned down in 1970. Rebuilt in the old style, it is now a liquor store with the province's best selection of wine and a **wine museum** where the curator speaks knowledgeably and passionately about his subject. Many well-preserved old homes along **Rue Sainte Geneviève** and **Avenue LaPorte** provide rooms for tourists who prefer history to hotel conveniences.

The cruise boat **MV** *Louis-Jolliet* departs from opposite Batterie Royal park for excursions on the St Lawrence and around Ile d'Orléans. The much cheaper 15-minute ferry to Levis, departing from Rue Dalhousie and Rue du Marche-Champlain every half hour, gives the same impressive view.

Day Trips From Quebec City

Spectacular **Montmorency Falls** 20 kilometers (13 miles) east of Quebec City plummet 83 meters (274 feet), one-and-a-half times the height of Niagara. Visitors can peruse and picnic above or below the falls, approaching within 30 meters (100 feet) from a terraced lookout. Rain gear is recommended. In winter, the falls freeze into a giant ice cone called *pain de sucre* (sugar loaf).

A nearby bridge crosses to **Ile d'Orleans**, designated an historical site. Before the bridge was completed in 1935, the only access was by boat in summer and across the ice in winter. This isolation preserved an authentic rural Quebec pioneer spirit, with aging farmhouses, tiny villages and historical churches displaying an agreeable patina of quaintness. At only eight kilometers (five miles) wide and 21 miles long, the island is easily explored by car. In summer, you can drive up to roadside stands and buy local vegetables and fruit—explorer Jacques Cartier called the island Bacchus for its wild grapes—as well as crafts such as quilts. If you drive to the east you will see where salt water from the Gulf of St Lawrence, 965 kilometers (600 miles) away, reaches the island's freshwater river.

Back on the mainland, just past the falls on Highway 138, the famous **Ste Anne de Beaupre shrine** attracts more than a million visitors each year. According to legend, three Breton sailors who survived a storm built the chapel in 1658. In 1676 a stone church replaced it, and the site soon gained a reputation for miracle cures. A replica of the neo-Romanesque church, incorporating material from the original structure, now serves as a Memorial Chapel. The discarded canes and crutches attest to the power of faith.

Vive la Différence

Quebec is as French as New England is British. Over the centuries, the province has developed a different culture, cuisine, literature, music and especially language. (In France, Quebec movies are often dubbed.)

Despite a degree of snobbery over their cuisine, Quebecers are among the nation's biggest consumers of junk food—their own style. Much of the diet centers around smoked meat, hambourgeois, chips and gravy, Montreal steamies (hot dogs to anyone else) and colas. A slightly pejorative Anglo name for French Canadians is 'Pepsis'.

The lingua franca of the mass of the province, *joual*, is incomprehensible to the average Frenchman. Although perhaps not spoken by those in elite Outremont, this is Quebecois as it is used elsewhere, mainly in Montreal. Joual is disappearing even there, to the delight of linguistic purists but the dismay of those who feel Quebec is losing something of its unique, and colorful identity.

The *Anglo Guide to Survival in Quebec*, edited by Josh Freed and Jon Kalina (1983, Eden Press), although mainly an in-joke that will escape non Anglo-Quebecers, gives an amusing insight into French-English misconceptions and prejudices.

A curious example of the joual patois is in cursing, where only the sacred is profane. Sexual terms, or what we consider obscene, are quite ordinary to the French Canadian. As the book points out, *c'est tout fucké* (it is all messed up) is quite acceptable even in mixed company.

However, French-Canadian motorcycle riders or east-end Montreal truckers sound almost like altar boys with their frequent repetitions of ecclesiastic terms: *tabernak* (tabernacle), *calice* (chalice), *sacraman* (sacrament), etc. These are real fighting words.

The book cites a genuine example of pure, inspired Quebecois cussing: *Mon hostie-de-tabernacle, m'ot crisser une chalice de claque s'a guel, en sacrifice!* This literally translates to, 'My host of the altar, I shall Christ you a chalice of a smack on the muzzle, by sacrifice.' (Real meaning: You son-of-a-bitch! I'm gonna knock your fat head off.)

The Laurentians

Within sight of the St Lawrence River in many places and just an hour north of both Montreal and Quebec City, the Laurentian mountains are Quebec's most popular outdoor escape. The scenic region includes some of the country's most elegant, developed resorts as well as rustic inns and camping grounds, and good restaurants in scenic towns where ancient church spires poke at the clear blue sky.

Scattered throughout the Laurentians are a number of large game reserves, some allowing controlled hunting, and facilities for all of the standard outdoor activities such as fishing, camping, hiking and water sports. More than 30 species of wild animals inhabit the parks so hikers can see bear, deer, mink and porcupine on some of the more remote trails. Less adventurous outdoor lovers can take leisurely drives through the rugged back country with its wildlife and scenery—the mountains are most dazzling in the fall when the green maples turn a fantastic mosaic of auburn, red, gold, russet—then relax at night over fine French cuisine in an elegant little *auberge*, an old resort or an intimate *mère et père* inn.

It is during winter, however, that most people venture to the region. Although few peaks rise above 762 meters (2,500 feet), the Laurentians is above all a ski center—one of the world's most famous—with the continent's largest concentration of slopes.

One of the most popular recreation areas, **Mont Tremblant**, was created in 1894 as a year-round sports center and has continued to expand and modernize. In recent years, a computer-programmed system was bought to ensure good skiing conditions. The system reads temperature, humidity and ground conditions to lay down artificial snow from mid-November to the end of April.

In summers, Mont Tremblant's rugged peaks, deep valleys, waterfalls, glacial lakes and fishing streams attract canoers, campers, picnickers and hikers—and leisurely motorists.

Mont Tremblant village, a resort on Lac Mercier under the towering peak of the 960-meter- high (3,163-foot) mountain, is a popular park resort. Best-known lodges are the century-old log chateau **Tremblant Club**, the **Gray Rocks Inn** (1906) and the more recent (1939) **Mont Tremblant Lodge**.

Although mainly a center for outdoor activities, the Laurentians have their cultural aspects. **Villages** sprinkled throughout this peaceful mountain area evoke old New France: Ste Thérèse, Ste Janvier, Rosemére, Blainville, Ste Agathe des Monts. **Val-David**, an artists' and craftsmen's village, is the sight of an annual summer crafts fair and a center of modern, mostly French-Canadian, theater.

Ste Adèle on the shore of Lac Ronde is the unlikely combination of an artists'-writers' colony and ski resort. Nearby, **Village de Séraphin** is a recreated 19th-century

Laurentian settlement with more than 20 buildings, each based on a character from the well-known Quebec novel *Un Homme et Son Pêche (A Man and His Sin)*.

Visitors with not enough time for the Laurentians can make a day trip to the **Lanaudiere region**, a pleasant resort area of 11 rivers and countless lakes just 45 minutes northeast of Montreal. Three centuries of history are reflected in the stone buildings of these old French-Canadian communities. **The Canadiana Village** outside **Rawdon**, an authentic replica of a 19th-century village with a general store, smithy, settler's cabin, one-room school house, and ice cream parlor, has been used as a set for movies and commercials.

The Eastern Townships

The Quebecois call this area bordering the United States *Estrie*, but under either name they are a popular escape from crowded Montreal and Quebec City and only an hour's drive away. The townships cover 13,000 square kilometers (5,000 square miles) of waterways, villages, farmlands and the northern tip of the Appalachian Mountains bordering the United States.

The Abenakis, the original inhabitants, gave the area many of its distinctive names: Memphremagog, Massawippi, Magog, Megantic. Settled first by United Empire Loyalists fleeing the American Revolution, the towns form a kind of Canadian New England. Back roads wind through the bucolic rural countryside of covered bridges, white churches with tall steeples and New England-style villages with warm country inns.

The gateway from Montreal is **Granby**, an industrial town known for its many fountains, such as a 3,200-year-old Greek replica, a first century Roman waterworks, and a replica of Rome's famous Trevi Fountain. Its **car museum** displays an extensive collection of antique vehicles.

Bromont, a new town, is a major vacation center with man-made amusements such as alpine slides, health spas, golf, water slides, fitness and bike trails. The string of lights for night skiing on nearby Mont Bromont is an impressive sight from below.

Magog, founded in 1799 by British Loyalists, is named for nearby Lac Memphremagog, Abenaki Indian for 'vast expanse of water'. With its local crafts and antiques and cultural exhibitions, the town is called 'an international tourist center'. Boats cruise the lake passing private cottages and a Benedictine monastery.

A tall, castle-like bell tower rising above the trees marks the **Abbey of St-Benoit-du-Lac**, noted for its geometric-tiled cloister designed by a Benedictine monk-architect. Sitting above Lac Memphremagog and ringed with fertile farms, the abbey is

One of Canada's many highways cuts through typical forest scenery

both a curiosity for tourists and a religious retreat. Sixty Benedictine monks live here, clothed in traditional black cassocks and leather sandals. They produce all of their own food and manufacture a sparkling apple wine that is quite palatable, especially with their home-made sharp blue cheese, l'Ermitage.

The **Orford Provincial Park** on Mont Orford is one of the province's major downhill ski resorts with a lodge, nearly 20 slopes and a chair-lift ascending a 738-meter peak (2,400-foot) which provides an expansive view of the surrounding mountains.

Although they are definitely Quebec, and predominantly francophone, the townships retain strong links with the United States. **Lac-Massawippi** became an antebellum summer spot for wealthy Southerners who preferred to holiday in the north country without the company of the damned Yankees. Later, wealthy Americans fleeing the unnatural constrictions of prohibition were attracted to **North Hatley**, on the lake's north shore. Many of their spacious homes overlooking the lake are now peaceful, rustic inns or bed-and-breakfast places.

Tiny **Rock Island** (population, about 1,200), straddling the Canada-US border two hours from Montreal on Highway 55, is a truly international community. Many of the houses were built before the line was drawn so in some homes meals prepared in one country are consumed in another. A black line across the floor of the **Haskell Free Library and Opera House** (a smaller replica of the Boston Opera) marks the international border. In this historical monument which dates back to 1904, the stage is in Canada, the 200 seats in the USA.

The North Shore

East of Quebec City is a wilder, less populated land, and those settlements that do exist are centuries-old. Many were established by early European explorers; indeed, the area was one of the first in Canada seen by European eyes.

Highway 138

In the mid-1600s, France sent the Carignan-Salieres regiment to defend its colony from Indians, and allotted large plots of land bordering roads, lakes and rivers to those who stayed on. The landowners later split their farms into strips, one per son, so each property retained access to river, lake or road. Today, the unique pattern of thin, narrow farmlands inherited from the 17th century distinguishes rural Quebec.

These farms can be seen along scenic Highway 138 which travels east from Quebec City along the north shore of the St Lawrence River. The river gradually widens as it approaches the Gulf of St Lawrence and the sea, and you can smell salt in the air and taste it in the water from about Baie St Paul, 80 kilometers (50 miles) east of Quebec and 805 kilometers (500 miles) from the sea. The highway follows the river for 222 kilometers (130 miles) to Tadoussac, where a branch turns inland along the Saguenay River for the 120 kilometers (70 miles) to Chicoutimi. There are several alternate routes on the way and the better roads are less interesting.

As you leave Quebec City, Highway 138 skirts the foothills of the Laurentians to reach bucolic **Beaupre/Charlevoix**, a rustic region of fishing settlements and old farms, ancient villages and estates, 18th-century churches and riverine vistas.

Further along is **Baie St Paul** where houses more than 200 years old line the narrow streets. Local woodcarvers work in small studios tucked away on ancient streets, turning out distinctive local figures and scenes. **Saint-Joseph-de-la-Rive**, 115 kilometers (71 miles) east of Quebec City, has the only mill in North America to make parchment entirely by hand. The mill shop sells the deluxe paper, incorporating bits of birch silk, local flowers, leafs and ferns into the pulp.

Samuel de Champlain named **La Malbaie** (Bad Bay), overlooking the river, for its treacherous shore line after a low tide almost beached him on the clay flats in 1608; you might think it was named for the rotten-egg smell of sulfur deposits from the river bed at low tide. Here, the St Lawrence has widened to 24 kilometers (15 miles) of churning, salty brine. The town's historic buildings include an 1860 prison and courthouse, and a working forge where blacksmiths have welcomed visitors for more than 100 years.

At the nearby resort village of **Pointe-au-Pic**, the **Manoir Richelieu**, an ancient stone manor dramatically set 213 meters (700 feet) above the St Lawrence, has operated as an opulent hotel since the 18th century when Prime Minister Sir John A Macdonald himself summered here, along with other wealthy Canadians and Americans. The gracious Manoir, rebuilt in 1928–9 after fire destroyed the original structure, was recently extensively restored, and offers the elegant style of an earlier era.

From here, the population thins and the villages become less frequent. At the village of St Simeon, a ferry crosses the St Lawrence to the southern shore and the road splits, one way going to Tadoussac on the coast, the other inland to Chicoutimi.

TADOUSSAC

Tadoussac is Algonquin for 'breasts'—a reference to the softly-rounded surrounding hills. Cartier visited Tadoussac in 1535 and a French trader built the first European house in Canada here in 1599. When Champlain stopped by in 1603, it was already an established fort supplying ships traveling to Europe.

In the desert at the **mouth of the Saguenay** nearby, 550 wooden steps lead up the 112-meter- high (370-foot) sand dune where summertime skiers and tobogganers

slide down the sand and across the beach to the very edge of the St Lawrence.

Locals now arrange trips upriver to see the beluga whales that gather in the St Lawrence each summer. Boat cruises leave from Tadoussac or Chicoutimi for deep **Saguenay Fjord**, carved into the mountains by glaciers like those in Scandinavia, Alaska and British Columbia. Eastern North America's largest fjord, with cliff walls rising 457 meters (1,500 feet), slices a narrow tributary from the St Lawrence up to Lac St Jean. Powerful saltwater tides from the great river surge up the narrow Saguenay, carrying sharks and other ocean fish as far as 100 kilometers (60 miles) upstream. When the St Lawrence tide is ebbing, the dark Saguenay waters rush out with such power that small pleasure craft tie up at Tadoussac rather than venture into the mouth.

CHICOUTIMI

North of Tadoussac, at the farthest point of deep water navigation on the Saguenay River, is Chicoutimi, 'as far as it is deep' in the local Indians' language. Beyond here the fjord is unnavigable. This is a lively pioneer town with the attractions of good dining, drinking and other nightlife, as well as many galleries displaying local arts and crafts.

Chicoutimi is popular among visitors from the cities for a rustic nature rare in modern North America. Attractions include a ride on ann open, screened train through the Saint-Felicien Zoo where wolves, bear, moose and buffalo roam free, and the ghost town of Val Jalbert, abandoned since 1927 when the pulp and paper mill closed.

Chicoutimi's most prominent native son was a barber, Arthur Villeneuve, who began painting the walls and ceiling of his traditional Quebec house in 1957. The art world 'discovered' him and, in 1972, a one-man show at the Montreal Museum of Fine Arts confirmed the barber-painter's acceptance as an authentic 'primitive' artist. His house, with the original mural depicting local legends and street scenes, is open to the public.

BEYOND LABRADOR

Beyond Tadoussac and the fjord, the **North Shore**, a sprawling, near-empty land, stretches to Labrador. Only adventurous visitors with plenty of time and an affinity for empty spaces venture further up the road to the great, bleak north.

Until quite recently the string of North Shore villages, joined in places by short stretches of rough road, were reached only by coastal vessels. Labrador's rich iron ore deposits led to phenomenal development of the isolated region and now the fragments of road have been connected by a highway extending as far as Havre-St-Pierre. The road links ever fewer and more remote villages as the St Lawrence broadens into the Gulf. This trip into the wilderness does not have to be a dead end. Four different vehicle ferries along the way cross the St Lawrence to the south shore, and the Gaspé.

A fire engine-red lighthouse is a vivid sentinel on Quebec's remote Gaspé Peninsula

The Gaspé Peninsula

Jutting into the fertile, stormy waters of the Gulf of St Lawrence and the Baie des Chaleurs (Bay of Warmth), the Gaspé Peninsula extends some 282 kilometers (175 miles) along the great river, from the Matapedia River valley to its wild and isolated tip. This is a dramatic land of sheer, end-of-the-continent cliffs towering over wide and usually empty beaches, of little fishing villages clinging like barnacles to the coastline, and open, empty spaces.

The Micmacs (Indians of the Sea) have lived on the peninsula for more than 2,500 years. Acadians, Loyalists, Bretons, Basques, English, Irish, Scots and Jerseymen settlers arrived later, and traces of many accents are heard in the isolated villages.

Once, Gaspé could only be reached by boat and only footpaths linked its villages. Even with a paved coast highway, the Gaspé is a rustic land of small guesthouses, basic motels and campgrounds with facilities for recreational vehicles and tenters rather than luxury condos and slick, ultramodern resorts. Some Gaspé restaurants are almost like work camps, with benches and long tables covered with checkered oilcloth. Enamel plates of bread, bricks of butter and whole pies are set on each table. When you finish your meal, just help yourself to the pie—lemon meringue, apple or other fruit. None of these homey, no-frills restaurants are listed in the government guide, so you must ask the locals.

THE LOOP TOUR

A 1,600-kilometer (1,000-mile) loop tour from Quebec City skirts the Peninsula to Perce (meaning 'the pearl') on the far eastern tip, returning via the Matapedia Valley. The clockwise route is the more popular and crowded route. As you drive further on, the brightly colored yellow, green, pink and blue houses get smaller until some are almost like doll houses. Owners carve boats, anchors and other nautical shapes on the shutters and villagers sell roughly-crafted model boats, from about 15 centimeters (six inches) to 60 centimeters (two feet) long, with 'Gaspé' written on them.

The long, twisting road often hugs the coast where coastal communities and villages exist much as they did earlier in the century. Along quiet docks, nets and sails are piled ready for use and cod dries on racks. Just 97 kilometers (60 miles) from Quebec City, **St Jean-Port-Joli**, founded in 1721, is Quebec's handicraft center, a village of less than 4,000 where artisans and craftspeople work in a number of materials. Especially visible is a unique form of rough hewn wood carving. The old stone **St-Jean-Baptiste church** features an elaborate altar with late 1700s carvings, wooden railings and pews.

The **Maritime Museum** near **L'Islet-sur-Mer** outlines some of the history of the St Lawrence with models of original vessels which plied the waterway during its first days of exploration, antiquated navigational equipment, logbooks and old telescopes.

Next, **Riviere-du-Loup**, which connects with **St Simeon** across the river, is a meeting point for fishermen, hunters and campers heading to the peninsula. There are eight **waterfalls** nearby and the **Park of the Luminous Cross** which affords an excellent view of the surrounding countryside. Canada's largest colony of double-breasted cormorants, along with thousands of sea and shore birds such as black guillemots and great blue herons, nests on **Grand Pelerin**, five islands in the St Lawrence. A side road from Riviere-du-Loup leads to the village of **Saint-Louis-du-Ha! Ha!**, worth visiting for the odd name alone, as well as for the observatory and scientific interpretation center. The name is derived from an Indian word 'hexcuewaska' meaning 'something unexpected'. It is. Beyond Riviere-du-Loup, the main highway penetrates a hinterland of parks, forests and mountains to the edge of the continent, and the town of **Gaspé** near the tip of the peninsula. A monument commemorates the spot where explorer Jacques Cartier landed in 1534, erected a cross and took possession of Canada in the name of the King of France.

PERCE

Perce Rock or 'pierced rock', 81 kilometers (50 miles) beyond, is the magnificent monolith rising abruptly just off shore and the region's most famous attraction. From a distance, it looks somewhat like a great grey ship moored in the cold Atlantic. The huge rock, 90 meters (298 feet) high, 433 meters (1,420 feet) long and 91 meters (300 feet) wide, with a 15-meter (50-foot) natural arch at the eastern end, was part of the mainland until erosion separated it. The rock changes color, often dramatically, with shifting light and weather conditions. Sunrise through the arch is a particularly moving sight. At low tide, a sand bar at the foot of Mont Joli connects the mainland to the rock. The village of Perce sits between **Surprise Hill** and **Peak of Dawn**, a semi-circle surrounding two bays. Several paths from the main road lead up to **Mont Ste Anne**, where Micmac Indians held sun-worshiping ceremonies. A 11-kilometer (seven-mile) drive around the mountain provides a panoramic view of local villages and offshore islands.

Perce itself is not much of a town, although its seafood is excellent, especially the local dish, salmon pie, (like chicken pot pie). The hotel **La Normandie** in Perce is modern (read: not much character) but its restaurant is one of the best in town.

During the summer, small boats leave Perce's small beach-side dock hourly to view the rock and circle **Bonaventure Island** with its giant bird colony, including 50,000 gannets, the world's largest gathering of these great seabirds with six-foot wingspans. Seagulls, cormorants, puffins, kittiwakes and auks, nesting on 100-meter (330-foot) -high cliffs, have painted the ledges white. To the Micmac Indians, this place of screaming sea birds, sheer cliffs and swelling sea at Gaspé was the end of the world.

RAIL HOTELS

Most major Canadian cities and many older mountain resorts have a grand 'castle', a great, incongruous edifice that looks somehow transported from Europe.

These distinctive, chateau-type hotels started a century ago as a series of little, wayside dining halls along the Canadian Pacific Railway's route through the Rocky Mountains. Dining cars were too heavy for the first transcontinental passenger trains to haul up the steep grades, so in 1886 the CPR instituted several meal stops along the way, all in spectacular settings. When guest rooms were added the following year, the railway was in the hotel business.

The original wood-framed Banff Springs Hotel (1886–8), designed by CPR's Boston architect Bruce Price, was an elaborate resort in a wild and scenic setting. Sir William Van Horne, historic builder of Canada's first transcontinental railway, reasoned that 'since we can not export the scenery, we shall have to import the tourists'. Soon after, Banff Springs Hotel was converted into a majestic stone palace, and Chateau Lake Louise was built nearby to provide food and lodging to early travelers venturing west into the wilds.

From the 1890s to the late 1930s, Canadian Pacific Railways, Canadian National Railways and Grand Trunk Railways all built grand hotels in cities and resort areas across the country. Eventually, every Canadian provincial capital from Quebec City in the east to Victoria in the west had its palatial hostelry.

The grandiose architectural style that prevailed has been variously described as Loire chateau, Scotch baronial, modified French Renaissance, Edwardian and *beaux-arts classique*. Many of the sturdy, stone masonry hotels are topped by lofty, steeple-pitched verdigrised roofs with turrets and multiple ornate dormers, suggesting a romantic retreat. (The Banff Springs, traditionally a popular honeymoon spot for Canadians, Americans and Europeans, has recently been discovered by Japanese newlyweds.)

The Banff Springs and Quebec's Chateau Frontenac (1893) established the distinctive architectural style that influenced the design of railway stations, apartment blocks and even large government buildings in Ottawa.

Although some of the classics have been demolished, most of the original railway hotels still operate as grand old inns (as grand as such a young country can produce) and are often among the best in town. Railway resorts still operating include the Jasper Park Lodge in Alberta, Le Chateau Montebello in Quebec and the Algonquin in St Andrews-by-the-Sea, New Brunswick.

Quebec City's Chateau Frontenac, set dramatically on a cliff overlooking the St Lawrence, Victoria's ivy-draped Empress (1904–8) facing the harbor and Ottawa's Chateau Laurier (1908–12) are the finest examples of the intricate chateau style. Other city hotels, such as Toronto's Royal York, Winnipeg's Fort Garry, Calgary's Palliser, The Macdonald in Edmonton (reopened after many years), Saskatoon's Bessborough, Regina's Saskatchewan and the Hotel Vancouver, remain the most interesting and imposing (if not always the most modern and luxurious) in their cities.

CP Hotels now owns and operates most of these venerable grand dames of Canadian lodging. They are all worth a visit, a drink in the bar or at least a stroll through the lobby, for their historic and architectural place in Canada.

Quebec City's Chateau Frontenac is a prime example of Canada's castle hotels

The New Game in Town

From the first, Mr Smith, as a proprietor, was a wild, rapturous success. He had all the qualifications.

He weighed two hundred and eighty pounds.

He could haul two drunken men out of the bar by the scruff of the neck without the faintest anger or excitement.

He carried money enough in his trouser pockets to start a bank, and spent it on anything, bet it on anything, and gave it away in handfuls.

He was never drunk, and, as a point of chivalry to his customers, never quite sober. Anybody was free of the hotel who cared to come in. Anybody who didn't like it could go out. Drinks of all kinds cost five cents, or six for a quarter. Meals and beds were practically free. Any persons foolish enough to go to the desk and pay for them, Mr Smith charged according to the expression on their faces.

At first the loafers and the shanty men settled on the place in a shower. But that was not the 'trade' that Mr Smith wanted. He knew how to get rid of them. An army of charwomen, turned into the hotel, scrubbed it from top to bottom. A vacuum cleaner, the first seen in Mariposa, hissed and screamed in the corridors. Forty brass beds were imported from the city, not, of course, for the guests to sleep in, but to keep them out. A bar-tender with a starched coat and wicker sleeves was put behind the bar.

The loafers were put out of business. The place had become too 'high toned' for them.

To get the high class trade, Mr Smith set himself to dress the part. He wore wide coats of filmy serge, light as gossamer; chequered waistcoats with a pattern for everyday in the week; fedora hats light as autumn leaves; four-in-hand ties of saffron and myrtle green with a diamond pin the size of a hazel nut. On his fingers there were as many gems as would grace a native prince of India; across his waistcoat lay a gold watch-chain in huge square links and in his pocket a gold watch that weighed a pound and a half and marked minutes, seconds and quarter seconds.

Mr Smith became a local character. Mariposa was at his feet. All the reputable business-men drank at Mr Smith's bar, and in the little parlour behind it you might find at any time a group of the brightest intellects in the town.

Stephen Leacock, Sunshine Sketches of a Little Town, 1912

Atlantic Canada

The Maritimes (Prince Edward Island, New Brunswick and Nova Scotia) and New-foundland form a distinct region with an individual culture, cuisine, tradition and history. The area is older than most of Canada and predominantly British (except for a strong French, or Acadian, community in New Brunswick), yet distinctly North American. People in these North Atlantic provinces are more conservative and traditional than other Canadians, more in tune with an earlier time.

The British called the mainland Atlantic coast area Nova Scotia (New Scotland), but to the French, who settled Port Royal (now called Annapolis Royal) in 1605, it was *Acadie* (Acadia). For the next 150 years, Britain and France quarreled for Acadia, which included present-day New Brunswick and Prince Edward Island. French rule on the mainland ended when they ceded mainland Nova Scotia to the British in the Treaty of Utrecht in 1713.

The Acadians lived under the British in an uneasy truce until 1755 when the British began deporting those who refused to swear allegiance. Many of them eventually landed in Louisiana where, as Cajuns (a corruption of Acadian), they still survive as a separate community. Others gradually drifted back to establish new, more re-mote settlements out of the way of the British. Henry Wadsworth Longfellow's *Evangeline, A Tale of Acadia* tells of the whole dark period.

After the deportation, the British offer of free land to encourage settlers attracted New Englanders, British, Scots and Germans. Later, after the American Revolution, a major migration north of United Empire Loyalists, American colonists who remained loyal to Britain, added to the population. New Brunswick and Nova Scotia entered the Dominion of Canada when it was established in 1867, while Prince Edward Island entered confederation in 1873. Newfoundland became Canada's tenth province in 1949 after an emotional and stormy referendum.

Prince Edward Island

Canada's smallest province, rural Prince Edward Island, is like a great market garden or floating potato patch. White-sand beaches and rugged red cliffs ring ordered fields and small villages. The crescent-shaped island in the Gulf of St Lawrence is separated from mainland Nova Scotia and New Brunswick by the Northumberland Straight. PEI, as it is called, is miniscule by North American standards: 224 kilometers (140 miles) long and six to 64 kilometers (four to 40 miles) wide, with an area of 567,000

(following pages) Old ways live on in North Rustico,
A Prince Edward Island deep-sea fishing center

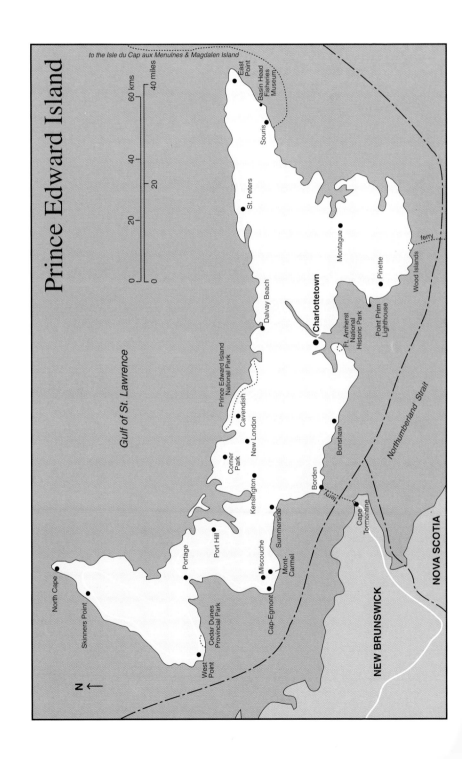

Prince Edward Island

to the Isle du Cap aux Menulnes & Magdalen Island

60 kms

40 miles

60   40   20   20   0

0

Gulf of St. Lawrence

East Point

Basin Head Fisheries Museum

Souris

St. Peters

Montague

Pinette

Dalvay Beach

Charlottetown

Ft. Amherst National Historic Park

Point Prim Lighthouse

Wood Islands

ferry

Prince Edward Island National Park

Cavendish

New London

Corner Park

Kensington

Bonshaw

Borden

Northumberland Strait

ferry

Summerside

Miscouche

Mont-Carmel

Cape Tormentine

Port Hill

Portage

Cap-Egmont

Cedar Dunes Provincial Park

West Point

North Cape

Skinners Point

NEW BRUNSWICK

NOVA SCOTIA

N ←

hectares (2,184 square miles). The capital and only city, Charlottetown, has a population of a mere 18,000.

Many attractions, both physical and historical, are packed in this tiny place the first inhabitants, the Micmac Indians, called Abegweit, 'land cradled by the waves'. The terrain ranges from gentle farmland, peaking at 152 meters (494 feet) above sea level, to wild coastline. Islanders are fond of quoting the first European visitor, Jacques Cartier, who, on discovering the island in 1534, remarked that it was 'the fairest land 'tis possible to see'.

History

The French did not settle this fairest land that they called Ile St-Jean until 1719, when Nova Scotian Acadians arrived in Port La Joie across the harbor from present-day Charlottetown. Along with much of the region, the island passed between France and Britain several times until the mid-19th century.

After France ceded the island to Britain in the Treaty of Paris in 1763, surveyors divided it into townships of 8,000 hectares (20,000 acres) which were sold to wealthy Englishmen in a great lottery in London. It remained part of Nova Scotia until becoming a separate colony in 1769.

In 1799, St John's Island, as the British called it, was renamed in honor of Edward, the Duke of Kent, commander-in-chief of Britain's forces in North America. In the 18th and 19th centuries many British settlers, mainly Scots, arrived.

Prince Edward Island considers itself the birthplace of Canada. In September 1864, representatives of Nova Scotia, New Brunswick, Ontario and Quebec met in Charlottetown's Province House to discuss union for the first time. After five days, delegates agreed on the concept of confederation. It was the first step to the eventual creation of the Dominion of Canada in 1867. When Prince Edward Island entered confederation in 1873 locals insisted it was mainland Canada that joined them.

Getting There

Access to PEI is by frequent car ferry from Caribou, Nova Scotia to Wood Island (22 kilometers or 14 miles, 75 minutes), or from Cape Tormentine, New Brunswick to Borden (14 kilometers or 9 miles, 45 minutes). Ferries also connect with Quebec's Magdalene Island, and flights by several airlines connect to mainland cities.

Charlottetown

Charlottetown, Canada's smallest capital, is a pleasant city of Victorian homes, old churches and tree-filled town squares. More than in any other major Canadian city, the atmosphere is of an earlier era.

Province House, the only remaining building associated with the historic 1864 Charlottetown Conference, has been restored. The chairs used by the Fathers of Confederation stand around the table over which they deliberated the creation of Canada. The provincial legislature still sits in this impressive 1840s Georgian structure, built from Nova Scotia sandstone. Guides escort tours daily, year-round.

Opposite Province House stands the city's most imposing (some say too imposing) modern building, the **Confederation Center of the Arts**, officially opened in 1964. Within its stark stone walls covering two city blocks are a memorial hall, museum, a major gallery of traditional and contemporary Canadian art and a theater. The center's popular summer festival features original Canadian musicals, including the popular classic *Anne of Green Gables,* the story of an orphan girl growing up in rural PEI.

Overlooking the harbor and 16.2-hectare (40-acre) Victoria Park are the regal white colonial **Government House** built in 1834, the **Lieutenant Governor's residence**, and **Beaconsfield**. This 1877 Victorian mansard-style mansion now houses the **PEI Museum and Heritage Foundation**.

The capital's most impressive churches include **St Dunstan's Basilica**, one of Canada's largest, noted for its twin Gothic spires and interior with ornate Italian carvings, and **St Peter's Anglican Cathedral** featuring murals by Canadian portrait painter Robert Harris.

Rural PEI

This compact province with its extensive road network is easily explored by car, recreational vehicle or bicycle. Three scenic drives, which correspond roughly to the three counties of Prince, Queens and Kings, cover the whole island. Each drive—190-kilometer (118-mile) Blue Heron, 288-kilometer (179-mile) Lady Slipper, and 375-kilometer (233-mile) Kings Byway—can be done in a day, but will take longer with stops and side trips.

■ LADY SLIPPER DRIVE

The island's western section is the least developed area for tourism—and so the most attractive for some. Aside from Summerside, the island's second largest community, this is a rural Acadian area of small villages and farms.

Named for the official provincial flower, this drive is a figure eight circling the coasts, with **Summerside** at the bottom. West of here the road reaches a juncture at **Miscouche**, where the **Acadian museum** displays pre-19th century artefacts. The museum flies the flag the Acadians adopted here in 1884: the French tricolor with the gold star of the Virgin, their patroness, on the blue stripe.

Following a clockwise route, the road along the south coast passes **seaside villages** such as Muddy Creek and Union Corner to Mount Carmel. Here, the **Acadian Pioneer Village**, a re-creation of log houses and other buildings circa 1800–1920, includes a

Historic Lunenburg, Nova Scotia, is a major fishing port

restaurant serving traditional fare. The menu lists *fricot au poulet*, (a hearty chicken stew), and *pâté à la rapure*, (a chicken and potato pie).

For more common PEI dining, the **Acadian Fisherman's Cooperative** at **Cap-Egmont**, five kilometers (three miles) along the coast, sells fresh lobster in late summer and early fall. Cap-Egmont people do not live in glass houses, but they do build them. On the main highway a chapel and two houses are constructed of 25,000 bottles, all different sizes and shapes and joined with mortar.

Near picturesque **Cap-Egmont Lighthouse**, the pirate Montberrie is said to have buried a vast treasure along the rocky, red shoreline, and locals talk of ghosts guarding Captain Kidd's treasure. Micmac Indian legends speak of haunted houses and a sea monster inhabiting the bays. Numerous sightings of the legendary 'burning phantom ship of Northumberland Strait' have been reported.

At **Portage**, where the land narrows, the road connects to the top loop of the figure eight in the island's extreme northwest. Continuing clockwise, the coastal road reaches **West Point** where shifting dunes of white sand line a two-kilometer (one-mile) beach at **Cedar Dunes Provincial Park**. A restored, century-old, unmanned wooden lighthouse, one of more than 60 still working on the island, has a museum, chowder kitchen and guest rooms.

North along the coast, General James Wolfe supposedly landed at **Cape Wolfe** en route to conquering Quebec City. According to Micmac Indian legend, the cape's red rocks were stained by the blood of an Indian maiden who betrayed the Thunder God.

This northern peninsula earns PEI, which grows 32 varieties of potato, its name of Spud Island. More than 12,000 hectares (30,000 acres), half the province's crop, is planted here in Prince country.

With the sea on the left, the road continues past **Skinners Pond** where the popular good-old-boy singer/songwriter Stompin' Tom Connors was raised. The road passes **Seacow Pound**, where walrus gathered before being hunted to extinction, and beyond to **North Cape**, the end of the line. Here at the island's northern tip, Gulf of St Lawrence tides meet those of Northumberland Straight. After storms, farmers and fishermen along this shore gather Irish moss, a dark purplish seaweed uprooted by waves and tide. Picking it up off the sand beaches or raking it in from the surf, they take it to drying plants with horse-drawn cart or tractor-trailers. There, carrageenan, an emulsifier, is extracted for use in toothpaste, ice cream and other food products. These wild shores provide almost half the world's Irish moss supply.

Turning south along the cape's eastern side, the road skirts the coast of windswept red sandstone cliffs that Cartier first saw. At **Jacques Cartier Provincial Park**, near **Kildare**, a monument commemorates his discovery of the island.

At **Portage**, the route continues north towards **Malpeque Bay**, where more than 10 million of the famous oysters are harvested annually. A side road leads to **Lennox**

Island Micmac Nation Reserve where a shop sells Canadian Indian arts and crafts. Back on the main road, Port Hill's Green Park Provincial Park museum displays the story of PEI's wooden shipbuilding industry. The coast road then passes tiny communities with names like Southwest Lot 16 and Central Lot 16, back to Summerside.

■ BLUE HERON DRIVE
The shortest of the three drives, named for the stately birds seen en route, covers the island's central Queen's County and part of Prince County. The drive includes the northern beaches, southern red sandstone coastal cliffs, rural interior farmlands and the capital.

From Charlottetown, Highway 1 crosses North River to run along the southern coast. At Rocky Point in Fort Amherst Historic Park, the French established Port la Joie, PEI's first white settlement, in 1720. Only Fort Amherst's earthworks, built by the British after they captured the site in 1758, remain. Nearby, a reconstructed 16th-century Micmac village shows pre-European Indian life. Displays include birchbark teepees and canoes, tools, weapons and life-size sculptures of Indians and local animals.

Borden, 54 kilometers (34 miles) from the capital, is the departure point for car ferries for the mainland, with hourly departures in summer. Cap Traverse, six kilometers (four miles) east of Borden, displays a replica of the old, five-meter (16-foot) wooden boats on runners which carried mail and passengers over ice and open water until 1917.

The route turns inland to Kensington where a military museum's displays date back to the Boer War in South Africa, in which Canadian soldiers served. Worth a side trip from Kensington are the Woodleigh Replicas in Burlington. A local family, the Johnstons, built these large-scale models of most of Britain's famous buildings such as the Tower of London, Shakespeare's birthplace and St Paul's Cathedral.

Much-loved Lucy Maud Montgomery, author of the popular novel *Anne of Green Gables* (1908), lived briefly in Park Corner on the north coast. Montgomery and her character, the red-haired, pig-tailed Anne, are possibly PEI's prime tourist attractions, drawing groups from as far away as Japan. Locals claim her novel for young girls has been translated into more languages than any other.

The Park Corner house is now a museum. Ten kilometers (six miles) further south in New London is the author's birthplace, a green-trimmed cottage containing memorabilia such as her scrapbooks. Further still, in Cavendish near the Prince Edward Island National Park, is Green Gables, the old farmhouse Montgomery immortalized. Locales from her novel, such as Anne's Babbling Brook, the Haunted Woods and Lovers' Lane, are all nearby and Montgomery, who died in 1942, is buried in Cavendish cemetery.

Although the national park is one of Canada's smallest, its 40 kilometers (26 miles) of seashore, Sahara-like dunes, excellent beaches, bluffs, salt marshes and freshwater ponds attract more than half a million visitors each summer. Stretched along the Gulf of St Lawrence, the park is noted for its pink sand, tinted by the erosion of bleached red clay, and red sandstone cliffs up to 30 meters (98 feet) high. The windy coast and sheltered bays make **Stanhope Beach** one of the country's top windsurfing spots. **Brackley Beach's** wooden walkways cross 18-meter (59-foot) sand dunes, and at **Rustico Island**, giant blue herons with two-meter (seven-foot) wing spans nest high in spruce trees.

At **Dalvay Beach**, just before the park's east exit, is the rambling, picturesque **Dalvay-by-the-Sea summer hotel** built as an estate for an American oil tycoon in 1895.

In **York**, the last attraction before the capital, the country gardens include a reconstructed 19th-century general store, smithy, one-room schoolhouse and chapel, and an antique glass museum.

■ KINGS BYWAY DRIVE

The longest island drive covers some of PEI's oldest and most interesting areas, recalling the province's pioneering days. Along the northeast coast are more sandy beaches and dramatic rust-red cliffs, old working lighthouses on craggy points jutting into the sea, fishing and farming communities.

Leaving Charlottetown in the south, Highway 2 heads to the north coast and colorfully-named **Savage Harbor**, **Cable Head**, **Beaver Point** and **Shipwreck Point**. It goes east to **North Lake**, almost the island's easternmost tip, where each summer, sport fishermen from around the world descend in pursuit of giant bluefin tuna. In 1979 a local sportsman hooked the world record, a 680-kilogram (1,496 pound) tuna. Three miles (five kilometers) south, the one-story wood frame **Elmira Railway Station** has been restored as a museum of early 20th-century train travel.

Micmac Indians long ago named this area Kespemenagek, the end of the island. The **East Point Lighthouse**, a wooden colonial structure built in 1867, marks the easternmost tip. The tall, white flashing tower is one of PEI's three remaining manned lighthouses.

A few miles along the south coast at **Basin Head**, the **Fisheries Museum** recounts the industry's history, with marine equipment such as hooks, nets, drying racks and a dory. Reconstructed fish shacks sit on the beach and an old lobster cannery on the wharf houses a small museum.

At **Souris**, car ferries depart for **Cap-aux-Meules** in Quebec's Magdalen Islands. The impressive **St Mary's Catholic church** built of island sandstone in 1901 overlooks the harbor.

The coastal town of **Montague**, further south, marks one man's failed attempt to

Country homes set in fertile fields typify the dairy region of Sussex, New Brunswick

establish a model community in Canada 250 years ago. Frenchman Jean-Pierre de Roma built wharfs, bridges, storehouses and houses here, but was plagued with bad luck. Some of his settlers abandoned him, field mice destroyed his crops and in 1745, raiding New Englanders burned the settlement. De Roma and his family hid in the forest, then escaped to Quebec. Depressions in the ground that were once cellars and a commemorative cairn are the only reminders of the dream.

At **Buffaloland Provincial Park**, inland from Albion, white-tailed deer and a buffalo herd graze in a 40-hectare (98-acre) enclosure.

Wood Islands, 51 kilometers (32 miles) before Charlottetown, is the port for car ferries to Caribou, Nova Scotia, 22 kilometers (14 miles) away. Cruises aboard a 12.2-meter (40-foot) Newfoundland schooner depart near the ferry wharf.

Farther west, **Pinnette Provincial Park** is a choice clam-digging area. At low tide, clams burrow 30 centimeters (one foot) below the surface. Diggers watch for the streams of water they eject through small holes in the sand when anyone walks by. Starfish and hermit crabs also inhabit these smooth sand beaches.

Just beyond, a 10-kilometer (16-mile) detour leads to **Point Prim Lighthouse**, the island's oldest, built in 1846 and still functioning. In nearby **Belfast**, a monument commemorating the town's first Scottish settlers stands outside **St John's church**, built in 1823. The stones at the base of the six-meter (20-foot) granite pillar came over as ships' ballast in 1803.

At **Orwell Corner historic site**, the last attraction before Charlottetown, crops and livestock are raised as they were a century ago. The crossroads restored to the late 1800s include several shingled buildings from country and town.

New Brunswick

Even in this country of contrasts, New Brunswick stands out as an anomaly. This is the only officially bilingual province in bilingual Canada. Its location, bordering Quebec and the state of Maine, surrounded on three sides by the sea and linked to Nova Scotia by the narrow, 24-kilometer- wide (15-mile) Chignecto Isthmus, has shaped its destiny.

The second largest (73,440 square kilometers or 28,347 square miles) and western-most of the Maritime provinces, New Brunswick is the crossroads of Atlantic Canada.

In 1604, French explorer Samuel de Champlain established the first white settlement here at the St Croix River. Cut off from both France and Quebec, the Acadians developed a separate culture. The influx of Loyalists from the neighboring US contributed to a conservative, British culture which is still evident.

These two groups today make up most of the bicultural province's population of

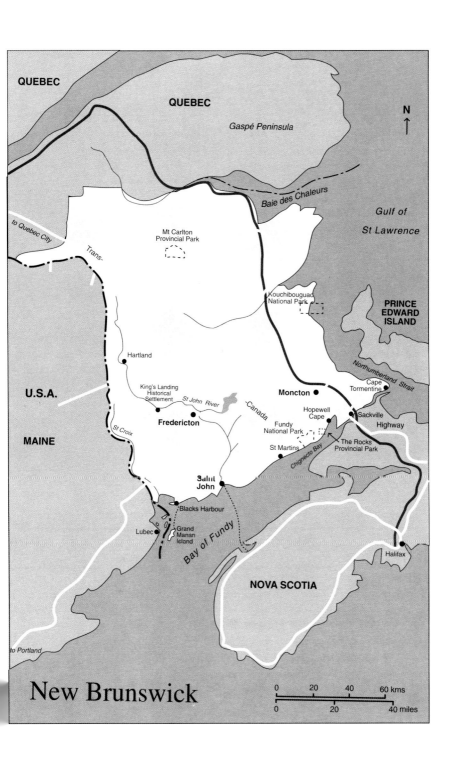

QUEBEC

QUEBEC

Gaspé Peninsula

N
↑

Baie des Chaleurs

Gulf of
St Lawrence

to Quebec City

Trans-

Mt Carlton
Provincial Park

Kouchibouguac
National Park

PRINCE
EDWARD
ISLAND

Hartland

Northumberland Strait

King's Landing
Historical
Settlement

St John River

Moncton

Cape
Tormentine

U.S.A.

Canada

Hopewell
Cape

Sackville

Fredericton

St Croix

Fundy
National Park

Highway

MAINE

St Martins

The Rocks
Provincial Park

Chignecto Bay

Saint
John

Blacks Harbour

Lubec

Grand
Manan
Island

Bay of Fundy

Halifax

NOVA SCOTIA

New Brunswick

| 0 | 20 | 40 | 60 kms |
| 0 | | 20 | 40 miles |

718,000. One-third are French-speaking Acadians while the rest are English-speaking Loyalists.

New Brunswick is geographically varied as well. More than half the province is surrounded by the sea. The 2,240 kilometers (1,400 miles) of largely unspoilt coastline encompasses the Bay of Fundy in the south, the Gulf of St Lawrence in the northeast and the Bay of Chaleur in the north. There, gentle hills lead to the Appalachian Highlands at Mount Carleton Provincial Park, while thick forests cover 85 per cent of the largely unsettled interior. Along the wild Bay of Fundy south shore, lonely lighthouses stand as sentinels on rocky cliffs. The Saint John River Valley forms a north-south stretch of gentle farmland running the length of the province to the east.

The small province has three important urban centers—Fredericton, Saint John and Moncton, all in the south.

FREDERICTON

In 1783, a group of Loyalists flocking into Canada founded a settlement on the banks of the broad Saint John River, almost in the center of the province. The Loyalists were cultured, educated people—their new community included a college, now the University of New Brunswick—so Fredericton never had the spirit of a raw, rough frontier town.

Named for British King George III's second son Frederic, Fredericton quickly developed into an elegant and gracious town. Within two years, it was made capital of the just-created province of New Brunswick because its inland site was considered less vulnerable to attack than larger Saint John, a seaport. Today, the capital city of about 44,000 retains the air of a quiet, cultured, government and university community, far removed from the crass mainstream of industry and commerce. Locals call their attractive town the City of Stately Elms for the ancient trees lining the streets.

The central **Military Compound** recalls Fredericton's martial past. Army reserve students dressed in turn-of-the-century Royal Canadian Regiment uniforms perform a **Changing of the Guard** ceremony on **Officer's Square**, the former parade ground that is now a park. Facing the square, soldiers in early 20th-century uniforms 'guard' the **York-Sunbury Historical Society Museum** in the Old Officers' Quarters, a mid-1800s three-story stone building.

A few blocks west, the refurbished **Guard House** (1827) and **Soldiers' Barracks**, a stone building with red wooden terraces, are suitably furnished with period pieces and open to the public.

In keeping with its genteel origins, Fredericton remains the province's cultural center. The renowned **Beaverbrook Art Gallery** east of the Military Compound opened in 1959 and expanded in 1983. It is Atlantic Canada's finest showcase of art with a permanent collection of canvases by Dali, Hogarth, Gainsborough and

Krieghoff. One wing contains one of Canada's most comprehensive collections of British art, the other houses an extensive representation of Canadian historical and contemporary paintings.

Further east, **Christ Church Cathedral**, consecrated in 1853, was the first new cathedral founded on British soil since the Norman Conquest of 1066. Trees and attractive frame houses surround this elegant, stone Anglican church with its slender spire. A pointed wooden ceiling known as a hammer beam roof dominates the interior. Church treasures include 'Big Ben's Little Brother' which was probably designed as a test-run for London's famous clock and a portion of the gold cloth used as decoration at William IV's coronation in 1830.

The **University of New Brunswick**, overlooking the city from a hillside setting, is one of North America's oldest. Its most interesting buildings include Canada's first astronomical observatory, now a museum, and Burden School, a restored one-room schoolhouse.

Tours and dinner cruises aboard the *Pioneer Princess III*, a replica of a paddlewheeler, depart from the wharf at the base of Regent Street downtown.

Early Saturday mornings the country comes to the city when **Boyce Farmer's Market** vendors bring in fresh produce, poultry, meat, seafood and local crafts.

Thirty-seven kilometers (23 miles) upriver from the capital, just off the Trans-Canada Highway, the **Kings Landing Historical Settlement** is a carefully-restored 19th-century Loyalist community. Most of the buildings on the sloping banks of the Saint John River were moved here when a dam project flooded the original sites.

The sprawling riverside village's 60 buildings include working grist and saw mills, a blacksmith shop and a one-room schoolhouse. More than 100 costumed 'residents' go about their daily chores while explaining pioneer life to visitors. The **Kings Head Inn**, a typical 19th-century roadhouse, serves drinks downstairs and 1800s-type fare upstairs. The **Kings Theater**, in a nearby barn, presents a variety of stage productions.

Further north, in the **Saint John River Valley**, the 'kissing bridge' spanning the Saint John River at Hartland, is the world's longest covered bridge (391 meters, 1,282 feet) still open to vehicular traffic. The first bridges in this area were built with picturesque barnlike covers to protect the timbers from rotting. They also provided some privacy for courting couples, hence the term 'kissing bridge'.

SAINT JOHN

The province's largest city (population 80,000) is an industrial center and one of the Atlantic's busiest ports. Saint John (always spelled out in full) is known as 'Fog City' for the thick mists which sometimes roll in from the cold bay. Set on a barren outcropping where the Saint John River pours into the wild Bay of Fundy (and, twice a day, vice versa), the city has a rugged, windswept charm with its hilly terrain, winding roads and dead-end streets.

The 3,000 Loyalist settlers that arrived here in a fleet of square riggers in 1783 were so patriotic they laid out **King Square** in the design of the old Union flag (the Union Jack before the cross of St Patrick was added in 1800).

Canada's oldest incorporated city (1842) has many firsts and oldests. The country's first newspaper, the *Royal Gazette and New Brunswick Advertiser*, was printed here on October 11, 1785, and Canada's first bank, the Bank of New Brunswick, opened its tellers' wickets in Saint John in 1820. The city employed North America's first paid police force in 1826, preceding London's bobbys by two years. Dr Abraham Gesner, who invented kerosene, founded Canada's first natural museum here in 1842. The **New Brunswick Museum** displays relics and models from the city's booming shipbuilding era.

The appropriately-named **Old City Market**, operating since 1867 and Canada's oldest, is open daily except Sunday, selling produce, seafood and native Indian handicrafts. Fittingly, in this shipbuilding center the interior was modelled after an inverted ship's hull.

Today, two levels of boutiques, restaurants and night spots thrive behind **Market Square's** original 19th-century facade. A major restoration has turned the once seedy waterfront into a pleasant and lively attraction.

The city's many reminders of earlier years include the **Old Loyalist House** (1810), the **Old Loyalist Courthouse** (1828) and **Fort Howe**, built in 1777–78 for defense against American privateers. **Barbours General Store**, opposite City Hall, is a clapboard building with gingerbread decoration that has been restored and stocked with goods from 1867 (Confederation year), such as pickles and peppermint sticks, smoked fish and tobacco. **Prince William Street**, with its craft stores and galleries, is one of the few to be designated a national historic site.

Despite its long history, Saint John's biggest attraction is a natural phenomenon. Because of the funnel shape of the **Bay of Fundy**, its tides are the world's highest. Twice a day, 100 billion tons of sea water flow up the shores, nearly equal to the 24-hour flow of all the world's rivers. A dry beach can be nine meters (30 feet) underwater within minutes. At its eastern extremity the tide has been measured at 16 meters (52 feet), the equivalent of a four-story building, an awesome sight and a world record, the height, that is, not the distance traveled up the beach. As the powerful tides force the Saint John River back upstream, they create the **Reversing Falls Rapids**. The effect can be measured upriver as far as Fredericton. Lookouts at **Reversing Falls Bridge** and at **Falls View Park** provide the best views.

Near Saint John, on the Bay of Fundy, the village of **St Martins' Quaco Museum** depicts the shipbuilding era. During the days of sail, as many as 126 ships were under construction here at one time. Twin covered bridges at the harbor and a picturesque lighthouse attract photographers.

MONCTON

In eastern New Brunswick, the province's second largest city, Moncton (population 55,000), is largely francophone and the unofficial capital of Acadia. Shipbuilding and railroads have made this city on the Petitcodiac river an important transportation hub.

It was named for Colonel Robert Monckton, the British commander who captured nearby Beausejour from the Acadians in 1755. The 'k' was omitted through a clerical error, and it has been misspelled ever since.

The modern **Moncton Museum**, with an incongruous facade from the old city hall incorporated into the modern building, holds mementoes of the city's past, especially as a rail center. Authentic displays from the era of steam locomotives include a big brass bell. Across the street the **Free Meeting House**, the city's oldest building (1821), is a plain New England gathering place without steeple or bell, built as a place of common worship.

The **Acadian Museum** on the **University of Moncton** campus depicts the history and culture of the Maritimes first European settlers from 1604 to the early 20th century. Nearby, the **Galerie d'Art** displays changing exhibits by Canadian, Acadian and international artists.

The **Magnetic Hill** outside Moncton is one of the province's best-known oddities. Cars driven 'downhill' to a certain point seem to coast back uphill when the engine is turned off and the brakes released—as if pulled by an unseen force. The optical illusion is a powerful tourist draw.

Boreview Park on Main Street is the best spot to observe yet another phenomenon. Right on schedule each day the **Fundy Tide** pushes a wall of water through the narrow entrance of the Petitcodiac River, filling the muddy river bottom from bank to bank. Known as the **Tidal Bore**, it has been described as Canada's most accurately named tourist attraction.

On the coast south of Moncton, in **Rocks Provincial Park**, are **Hopewell Cape's Flowerpot Rocks**, listed in *Ripley's Believe It or Not*. Powerful tides have carved these unique red sandstone pillars, each more than 30 meters (100 feet) high with trees and shrubs growing on top, into weird shapes. At high tide they are like tiny islands, at low tide like giant, mushroom-shaped 'flowerpots'. The park itself is also one of the best places to watch the rise and fall of the Fundy tides.

Highway 106 goes east to nearby **Sackville**, a pleasant university town with several attractions. Pioneer Acadians reclaimed much of the area from the sea by creating an extensive system of dams. In this crafts center, the harness shop is the only one in North America still producing handmade horse collars.

(top) Market Square complex, St John, New Brunswick,
(above) Two solitudes in Market Square

The town claims Canada's first Baptist and Methodist churches, and the first university degree granted to a woman in the British Empire was awarded by Sackville's Mount Allison University in 1875.

THE ISLES OF FUNDY

Despite the Fundy fogs and chilly weather that can descend even in summer, the three windblown islands in the western extreme of the bay are popular with both American and Canadian holidayers. Whale-watching, fishing and bird-watching are popular holiday pastimes on all three islands.

Since 1783, **Deer Island**, reached by a free, 20-minute ferry from Letete, New Brunswick, has been a fishing and lobstering center—with the world's largest lobster pond. Now it is a bucolic retreat offering outdoor activities from bird-watching to scuba diving, rock-hunting to hiking. Here, too, the Fundy tides exert their powerful forces. Just offshore, 'Old Sow', the world's second largest whirlpool, can be seen as well as heard during high tide. In summers, a private toll ferry crosses from Deer to **Campobello Island**, the favorite summer spot of the late US president Franklin Delano Roosevelt. Roosevelt's home, his 34-room 'cottage' complete with childhood photos and sketches, is maintained as a museum in the **Roosevelt International Park**, a joint Canada-US project. The island, the feudal fief of a dynasty of Welsh seamen until the late 1800s, has long been a fashionable spot for wealthy American families and a year-round, toll-free international bridge links it with Lubec, Maine.

The largest, most remote of the islands is **Grand Manan** where bird-watchers have spotted more than 275 species. The island drew rave reviews from John James Audubon, the world-renowned ornithologist, who did many of his sketches here. Seventeen walking and nature trails from 30 minutes to several hours long crisscross the island, passing lighthouses, 92-meter (300-foot) cliffs, colorful fish smokehouses and weathered wharfs stacked with wooden lobster traps and buoys.

Ferries make the two-hour crossing from Black's Harbor, New Brunswick, to Grand Manan several times a day. It is advisable to check ferry schedules and book accommodation before heading there for an overnight stay.

Nova Scotia

Nova Scotia (Latin for New Scotland) is the skirl of pipes from across a grassy glen, the crash of dark Atlantic waves against a rocky headland, the scream of gulls whirling high overhead in a bright blue sky, the splash of giant lobsters dropped into a pot of boiling sea water. This province is a charming bit of transplanted Scotland which claims more Gaelic speakers than the homeland. Many local place names reflect the heritage: Inverness, New Glasgow, Dundee, Craigmore, Campbell. Nova Scotians even claim the only heather growing wild in North America—in Halifax—from seeds British sailors shook out of their mattresses centuries ago.

But as always in Canada, there is a mingling of many cultures. The province is home to nearly 6,000 Micmac Indians, whose ancestors gave the names Antigonish (river of fish), Musquodoboit (rolling in foam), Kobelawkwemode (beaver harbor), and Necum Teuch (beach of fine sand). The French Acadian influence is seen in names such as Gaspereau Valley (ale wife), Brule (burnt land) and Bras d'Or (arm of gold).

Canada's, first permanent settlement, Annapolis Royal, was established here by the French in 1604. An Italian explorer serving France, Giovanni da Verrazzano, named the region Arcadie for an ancient Greek earthly paradise, and the name was gradually modified to Acadia. Settlers of France's first permanent North American settlement were farmers, hunters, trappers and fishermen, mainly from the Loire River region of France. (In Quebec, most of the settlers were from Normandy.) Although the British deported the Acadians to New England and to their other colonies from 1755 to 1762, they gradually returned and their numbers grew. American poet H W Longfellow's work *Evangeline* (1846) deals with the Acadians' tragic plight.

Other nations have contributed to this ethnic chowder: the Germans (Lunenburg), Portuguese (Ingonish) and Greeks (Point Aconi). More than 20 ethnic groups, many drawn to the coal and steel industries in the late 19th century, make up New Scotland. Locals say Nova Scotia is shaped like a lobster clawing its way into the Atlantic—an apt description for a province whose lifeline is the salt-water habitat of this crustacean. The lobster's 'claws' are mountainous Cape Breton Island which sits on the northern end of its 'body', the agricultural peninsula barely attached to mainland Canada by the narrow Isthmus of Chignetco. The peninsula is, in fact, more like an island and no point in the province is further than 56 kilometers (35 miles) from the sea. Long, thin Nova Scotia stretches 608 kilometers (377 miles) from Cape Breton to Cape Sable in the south and covers 55,491 square kilometers (21,420 square miles), making it slightly smaller than the Irish Republic.

In the southeast, Nova Scotia, which calls itself 'Canada's ocean playground', borders the powerful waters of the 274-kilometer (170-mile) long Bay of Fundy (see page 231), and encompasses more than 9,000 lakes. Nova Scotia is an attractive blend of extensive wilderness and historic sites.

HALIFAX

In 1749, 2,500 British settlers under Edward Cornwallis founded Chebucto to counter the French presence in Louisbourg and to exploit the rich cod fishery. It was soon renamed in honor of George Dunk, Earl of Halifax, Britain's chief lord of trade and plantations and organizer of the settlement. His eponymous community is now the provincial capital, the largest in the Atlantic provinces (population 300,000) and a communications hub.

Halifax was built on a small peninsula, and early on its rulers set out to protect it with a series of fortifications including the Citadel, British North America's mightiest fortress. For centuries, the city has been a naval and military bastion—up until World War II it was the major British naval base in the north Atlantic. This position was helped by the easy access to major sea lanes and, in the case of Halifax, a magnificent natural harbor that ranks as the second largest in the world.

A military presence and a staunch British quality remain in conservative Halifax. The armed forces is still a major local employer and grey warships of the Canadian Forces Maritime Command (Atlantic) anchor under the two massive bridges spanning the harbor between Halifax and its sister city Dartmouth.

■ SIGHTS AND ATTRACTIONS

In 1828, a major construction project began on the hilltop site of three older forts in Halifax. 28 years later the British unveiled the massive, star-shaped **Citadel Fortress** a complex system of fortifications. Despite the vast expense and energy expended, no shots were ever fired in anger from here.

The fortress is one of the best surviving examples of 19th-century fortifications and Canada's most visited historic site. In summer, there are tours of the interior, including the detention center and powder magazine and students clad as Royal Artillery and 78th Highland Regiment foot soldiers of 1869 perform colorful, complex infantry and artillery drills. Plug your ears: the soldiers fire the noon gun every day, as they have done for almost 150 years.

The hilltop site is worth a visit even when the fortress is closed. The ring road around Citadel Hill (you can drive or walk up) provides the best view of the harbor, not much changed in 200 years—except steel-hulled ships replace the tall-masted merchant and military vessels of centuries ago.

The city symbol is the giant **Old Town Clock** on the hill facing the harbor. The four-faced timepiece was a gift from Queen Victoria's punctual father, Prince Edward, Duke of Kent, who lived in Halifax for a time. The clock arrived in 1843 and has kept watch over the city ever since.

A short walk downhill leads to the well-preserved **Historic Properties** fronting the harbor next to the **Scotia Square office towers**. The dozen restored stone buildings lining **Water Street** date back to the early 1800s, a turbulent time in these waters. Despite its present air of civility, Halifax thrived on privateers who menaced the seas during the American Revolution and ran the blockade to the south during the US Civil War. The Nova Scotia schooners stored their booty in buildings like the solid stone Privateer's Warehouse until the Admiralty could auction off captured

Running To Paradise

The sound of a train whistle at night—now reincarnated as a diesel klaxon—is the key experience of North Americans, so often written about that it may have become too familiar to mean much. Yet not to me, an immigrant when I first heard it. A lonely sound. I imagined the train rushing on into the dark, past sleeping farms and fields, through forests and by lakes and across the vast prairies to the west, running westward, running to the far mountains and beyond them to an ocean on the other side of the world. It spoke rather of voyages than journeys, seafaring overland, an ocean of loneliness scattered with villages and cities like lighthouses winking from shores of sleep. The Canadian sound, suggesting the vastness and emptiness of a country still in the future, it was hinting at a destination as yet unimagined. That is the place I am restlessly faring to, riding westward, running to Paradise.

'Aida', the train sang through the steel nostrils, running westward from Toronto, myself stretched snugly in a roomette. 'Aiii-da'.

Aida wasn't opera, but a mnemonic given me by the sales manager. For I was now one of the traveling fraternity, the boys on the road: the sample cases stuffed with books and bibles out there in the porter's care attested me a salesman, a bible man. Aida was how to sell books, or boots or toothpaste or whatever. A,I,D,A. A for Attention. 'The bookseller, he sees a lot of salsmen. He's heard it all before. You got to go in there and grab his attention, okay?' Okay. And I for Interest: once you had your man's attention, you had to hold his interest. Then you came to D for Desire. The next step was awaken desire...'Let's keep this discussion on a decent level, shall we? Desire here is for the product, which in your case is books. You got to make the customer want what you're selling.' Which in my case was also bibles. After desire—then A for Action! This was what you joined for. Close the deal and make the sale. Nothing to do but write up the order and mail it...

At the Paralyser Hotel, for me the climax of the foothills, I drank late with my brother-traveler Ken Tupper. My room was by the freight yard of the railroad; we could hardly hear ourselves speak above the metallic clank and clash of the shunting trains. At three am Ken phoned the desk and made his polite enquiry. 'What time does the hotel leave for Vancouver?'

For we were impatient to get to the Coast—that by now almost mythical destination. That first time I went by train, climbing slowly till dark by the boulder-strewn Bow River and through the forested passes, looking up with awe at bare crags of the terrible mountains—those mountains that men from flat country fear and feel oppressed by, though to me, brought up in view of Mount Leinster, nostalgic and exciting— and staring, at nightfall, at the last of the sun touching faintly a distant white peak.

And I woke to a new light, the soft, changing light of British Columbia, its green grass and blue distances that threw me like a song. Running still westward to the sea, an Irish melancholy came over me, that pleasant sadness which was one of the Seven Deadly Sins of the Middle Ages. Accidia now took Aida by the hand, enfolded her in a damp and mildewy embrace, stifling her voice so that in Vancouver's Stanley Park I almost forgot her in contemplation of captive king penguins. My employers, bookmen to the backbone, roused me with a telegram: SIT NOT ON THE ORDERS OF YOUR TAKING BUT MAIL AT ONCE.

Kildare Dobbs, Landed Immigrant

ships and cargoes. Now the area is a popular center of shops, restaurants, cobbled pedestrian streets and some of the city's best pubs. In summer, the restored properties area is venue for outdoor music concerts, town crier competitions and historical feasts of the 1840s. This is no artificial, reconstructed tourist playpen, though. Haligonians use the area as their own, and thousands pass through each day heading for the ferry across the harbor to Dartmouth— the easiest way to take a quick harbor tour.

Dartmouth, called the city of lakes for the 23 waterways and seven public beaches within its boundaries, is an attractive community with hundreds of colorful flowerbeds. The small town has had an eventful history since 1750 when British troops first foraged for lumber and fuel and Micmac Indians massacred early settlers the following year. Dartmouth's many heritage sites include the original ferry terminal for Canada's oldest saltwater ferry service.

Modern ferries and terminals have replaced historic ones in Halifax where, in summer, taxis, cars, sightseeing buses, a double-decker sightseeing bus, even rickshaws crowd the streets. Even in winter, Halifax traffic is bad and parking spaces rare. The easiest way to get around is by boat and harbor tours depart from historic **Privateer's Wharf**.

Both sail and power craft are used, including a sternwheeler and the graceful *Bluenose II*, a replica of the famous fishing schooner depicted on the Canadian dime (ten cent coin). The original *Bluenose* was the pride of Nova Scotia in the 1920s and 30s, champion of the North Atlantic Fishing Fleet and winner of four international schooner races. (Bluenose is also the common name for Nova Scotians.)

You can watch the busy harbor traffic from **Point Pleasant Park**, the town's southernmost tip. Passing a few hundred meters (yards) off the park's Black Rock are tankers and container ships, reefers (refrigerator ships) and tug boats, the occasional grey-hulled destroyer, and perhaps the magnificent *Bluenose II* in full, billowing sail.

Halifax has many interesting pubs, such as **Alexander's**, set in an old foundry, the **Split Crow** and the **Peddlar's Pub**. Although this is not a place for wild revels, students from nearby universities enliven the night scene.

■ THE HALIFAX EXPLOSION
In December 1917, the French munitions ship *Mont Blanc* collided with the Belgian relief ship *Imo* in Halifax harbor narrows. It caused the world's greatest man-made explosion until the atomic bomb, flattening the entire north end of the city, killing up to 2,000 people and injuring thousands more. The sound was heard 160 kilometers (100 miles) away. Many of the victims are buried in a common grave in **Fairview Cemetery** north of town, as are 125 victims of the *Titanic* sinking. A memorial park at **Fort Needham**, a hill at the north end of Halifax, offers a view of the devastated area.

Day Trips From Halifax

Kitchen-calendar pretty Peggy's **Cove**, Canada's most photographed village, squats on giant granite boulders a leisurely 50-minute drive from downtown Halifax. The fishing village, built in 1811, is a rustic scene of bright cottages, fishing dories and North America's lone lighthouse-post office. Nearby, in a tiny provincial park, are 30-meters-long (100-foot) **stone carvings** of the hardy local fishermen and their families, the work of the late local marine artist, William de Garthe. These massive granite figures represent the local people's strong links with the sea.

The only commercial enterprise, the **Sou'wester**, sells distinctive souvenir gifts such as fishing prints, handmade model dories and Scottish memorabilia such as sporrans and plaids. More local in character are the large orange, yellow and green plywood butterflies that villagers hang outside their cottage walls. The butterfly motif dates back to an early Indian legend that if a butterfly lands on your home, its spirit will bring good luck and magic will fly your way. The pleasant coffee shop in the same building serves Solomon Gundy (pickled herrings and sour cream), fine chowder and homemade gingerbread with ice-cream. There are also 'landlubber' offerings of hamburgers and hotdogs. Despite its proximity to the capital and its international tourist status, Peggy's Cove remains relatively unsullied by commercialism. Like the province itself, it relies on tourism but resists the schlock of fast food chains, 'enchanted forests', games arcades and miniature golf courses.

Around the province

Distances are on a European scale here, and the 24,135 kilometers (15,000 miles) of road, only about half of which are paved, make Nova Scotia ideal for driving holidays. The scenery is typically Canadian, sheer cliffs, thick forests, swamps and vast empty spaces offsetting strings of quaint villages.

On the peninsula, roads wind through green rolling countryside, the fields fringed with wild lupin like purple and pink lace. Amiable rustics return from an evening's shooting bearing shotguns and .22 rifles, local youth hitchhike between villages, a custom no longer popular in most of the country, and in the harbors, honest working boats anchor alongside plaything yachts of visiting New Englanders.

Rows of mailboxes line the road like pickets, awaiting the country mailman. Roadside antique shops display dusty treasures and makeshift signs offer local paintings as well as homemade sauerkraut, smelt and lobster to cook in seawater on a beach.

There are few of the cute, contrived names found in popular tourist spots elsewhere (except the odd transgressor such as 'Pirate's Lore Beverage Room Grill' in a big, barrel-roofed hut like a country curling rink). Only a few ranch-style houses in aluminum and brick, or house trailers, jar the bucolic scene.

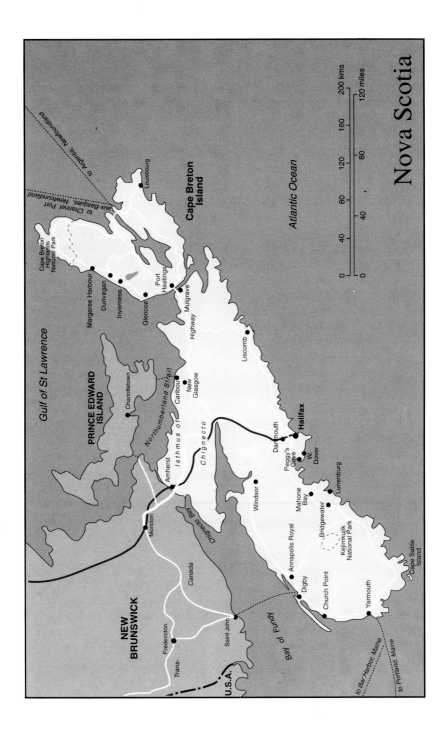

Nova Scotia

Atlantic Ocean

Cape Breton Island

Gulf of St Lawrence

PRINCE EDWARD ISLAND

NEW BRUNSWICK

U.S.A.

Bay of Fundy

Chignecto Bay

Northumberland Strait

Isthmus of Chignecto

Cape Breton Highlands National Park

Kejimkujik National Park

Cape Sable Island

to Argentia, Newfoundland

to Channel Port aux-Basques, Newfoundland

Louisbourg

Port Hastings

Mulgrave

Margaree Harbour

Dunvegan

Inverness

Glencoe

Liscomb

Charlottetown

New Glasgow

Caribou

Amherst

Moncton

Fredericton

Saint John

Trans-Canada

Windsor

Dartmouth

Halifax

Peggy's Cove

W. Dover

Mahone Bay

Lunenburg

Bridgewater

Annapolis Royal

Digby

Church Point

Yarmouth

Highway 104

to Bar Harbor, Maine

to Portland, Maine

200 kms

120 miles

0   40   80   120   160

0   40   80   120

The province sets out eight scenic driving routes, marked by a distinctive logo on roadside signs. Driving on these is at a leisurely pace; the heavy traffic sticks to the super highways. While they all have their rewards, perhaps the best are two on Cape Breton Island and a combination of the Lighthouse Route and the Evangeline Trail which circles the southern part of the peninsula from Halifax and back.

CAPE BRETON

Since 1955 the Canso Causeway has carried both road and rail traffic from the mainland to wild Cape Breton Island. The return toll on the 'Road to the Isles' is $1.50 for car, driver and passengers.

Attractions are the history, Gaelic traditions and the scenery. Alexander Graham Bell, who had a summer home here, said: 'I have travelled around the globe. I have seen the Canadian and American Rockies, the Andes and the Alps and the Highlands of Scotland, but for simple beauty Cape Breton outrivals them all'.

The bagpiper logo marks Celidh Trail along the Gulf of St Lawrence shore from **Port Hastings** half-way up the coast. (*Celidh*—say kay-lee if you want to pass as a Scotian—is Gaelic for a neighborhood party of gossip, music and dance.) The 107-kilometer (67-mile) route passes saltwater bluffs, long sandy beaches and Scottish villages until it joins the Cabot Trail at **Margaree Harbor**.

■ THE CABOT TRAIL

The Cabot Trail, a 303-kilometer (188-mile) tour encircling the wild **Cape Breton Highlands National Park**, once provided some of the country's hairiest driving—as well as its most dramatic scenery. Even now, with the broad paved highway and guard rails, most newcomers drive the loop clockwise, staying skittishly on the 'inside track'. This is true white-knuckle motoring as the road dips and turns, with many sharp switchbacks, so that drivers average only about 30 kilometers (20 miles) an hour for long stretches. The trail traverses terrain even more rugged than the Scottish Highlands, barren and craggy with bare hills and glens and the loch-like **Bras d'Or** lake.

Although the route could be completed in a day, it would mean rushing past the gorgeous scenery and bypassing some of the sights along the way. At **St Anne's** on the eastern past of the island, for instance, the province's Scottish heritage thrives at the local Gaelic College, the only one of its kind on the continent. Here, summer courses are given on piping, highland dancing and the Gaelic language. Tourists are welcome.

St Anne's was the home of a famous giant. Angus MacAskill, the 2.3 meters (7 feet, 9 inches) tall, 193 kilograms (425 pounds) 'gentle giant of Nova Scotia', died in Cape Breton in 1863. The **Giant MacAskill Highland Pioneers Museum** features a life-size model of Angus, photographs, sketches, his hat, coat, vest and cane, and his bed and chair.

Somewhat off the Cabot Trail is Cape Breton's major attraction: a reconstruction of the massive **Louisbourg Fortress**. The French built it between 1719 and 1745 to defend their colonies and to act as a base for the cod fisheries. Despite the huge expense to the French, it fell to combined British and New England forces several times until the British finally demolished it in 1760.

With an eye on tourism, the government has rebuilt the fort and populated it with costumed guides. Today, the fortress is a National Historic Park and Canada's largest heritage structure. Besides visiting the barracks, chapel and governor's apartment, visitors can sample 18th-century food at the **Hôtel de la Marine** and at **L'Épée Royale**. Dishes include hearty meat pies, chicken *fricot* (stew) and traditional roasted meats. On a more modest note, the bakery sells soldiers' bread, a dense and heavy brown variety that is basic but filling. The fortress is located a half-hour's drive from **Sydney**, the largest community on the east coast.

■ THE LIGHTHOUSE ROUTE

The south-shore Lighthouse Route from Halifax to Yarmouth encompasses the best of maritime Nova Scotia, with fishing villages, a coastline ranging from great cliffs to gentle beaches, and plenty of yarns and legends about pirates and ghost ship stories.

The west coast road dips and rolls past Peggy's Cove to **West Dover, McGrath's Cove** and **Shad Harbor**, tiny coves sheltering fishing villages where houses and fishing shacks stand on spindly stilts. Beyond is the rural Nova Scotia of forests, small farms, rocky bays, high-bowed fishing boats and lobster pots.

The coast-hugging highway winds past picturesque villages with distinctive churches topped by truncated or intact needlelike spires, and white clapboard houses with steep shingle roofs to shed heavy winter snows. In winter, schoolboys play hockey on makeshift rinks on the frozen ponds and rivers while adults fish through the ice by the warm, inviting flicker of lamps in Maritime versions of the works of Prairie painter William Kurelek.

In **Mahone Bay**, a small town further along the road, a lively bit of local history took place. During the War of 1812, a British man-of-war chased American privateer *The Young Teazer* into this bay. *The Teazer's* first mate, a British deserter, fearing capture and the noose, threw a torch into the powder magazine, blowing up himself and his ship. Now, with a sharp eye, good timing, and an active imagination, you may see *The Teazer* sail into the bay at dusk, glow red and fiery in a soundless explosion, then sink into the leaden waves. Or so the locals claim.

In 1753, the British settled nearly 1,500 German-speaking 'foreign Protestants' in **Lunenburg** to counter the presence of the French Catholics. Lunenburg's German-

Swiss settlers built an attractive town of distinctive wooden houses in a Lunenburg-Gothic of turrets and steeples, pointy roofs and bay windows. Ships' chandlers, seamen's union halls and blacksmith shops line the harbor of Canada's most important fishing port. Only a kebab shop intrudes on the maritime atmosphere.

This was home port of the *Bluenose,* the legendary schooner familiar to any Canadian child who has squeezed a precious dime (ten cent coin) on which it has appeared since 1937. In 1963, the same shipyards built the *Bluenose II,* an exact replica which makes day cruises in Halifax harbor. Local shipwrights also built the ship used in the Marlon Brando movie version of *Mutiny on the Bounty.* The **Lunenburg Fisheries Museum** is housed in three ships, including a prohibition-era rum runner and the last Lunenburg schooners to fish the Grand Banks with dories.

Past Lunenburg, the road turns inland briefly to **Bridgewater** which straddles the **La Have River,** the 'Rhine of Nova Scotia'. The local farming community is site of the colorful **South Shore International Exhibition Ox Pull** each July, where farmers bring their animals to be judged and compete in the Ox Pull, a battle of strength and speed in which teams haul heavy loads across fields.

From here, the Lighthouse Route continues to Yarmouth and **Cap Sable Island** where Eric the Red was an early visitor, according to some historians and local tourism promoters. The Vikings certainly came this way hundreds of years before any other Europeans, although the greatest evidence of their presence is in L'Anse aux Meadows, Newfoundland (see page 249).

Another road goes inland to **Kejimkujik National Park** and the **Annapolis Valley,** joining the Evangeline Trail along the Bay of Fundy shore from Yarmouth back to Halifax. Both are rewarding and the only recommended way of deciding between them is by the flip of a coin, preferably a *Bluenose* dime.

YARMOUTH

Nova Scotia's southernmost town is its closest link with the US state of Maine, and from here there are ferry crossings to Bar Harbor (six and a half hours) and Portland (11 hours). Once a major port, Yarmouth now is a peaceful fishing town. Its quiet streets are ideal for a leisurely stroll, and you can set off from here for a day of bicycling in the countryside. Its sea-faring heritage is preserved in the Yarmouth **County Historical Society Museum** set in a granite building that was once a church. The main exhibits are an extensive collection of sailing ship paintings and a runic stone believed to have been left behind by Norse explorers.

■ THE EVANGELINE TRAIL

Beyond Yarmouth, the Evangeline Trail follows the Bay of Fundy coast facing New Brunswick to Digby, Windsor and the fertile Annapolis Valley. At **Church Point,**

The Bluenose II *is still a working ship*

about an hour from Yarmouth, the 56-meter spire (185-foot) of **St Mary's** tops North America's largest wooden church. Because of high winds rocking the church, 36 metric tons (40 tons) of rock ballast have been placed in the steeple.

In **Digby**, midpoint on the coastal trail, the **Trinity Anglican Church**, the only church in Canada built by shipwrights, and designed like an upside-down hull with laminated arches, braces and iron fasteners.

Digby has one of the world's largest scallop fleets. When in port, it provides the perfect, photogenic foreground to a rosy sunset. Scallops are sold fresh at the wharf or served in local restaurants. The town also prides itself on its smoked herring fillets, known as Digby chicken. Beyond Digby, the roads run through the lush, pastoral **Annapolis Valley**, a picturesque farm land of fruit orchards leading back to the bright city lights of Halifax.

Newfoundland

Even in disparate and regionally-varied Canada, Newfoundland, the youngest province (joining confederation March 31, 1949), stands out for its unique culture. Newfoundlanders, or Newfies as they are known affectionately in Canada, form a distinct

The Bluenose II, *a re-creation of Canada's most famous sailing ship, at Privateer's Wharf, Halifax*

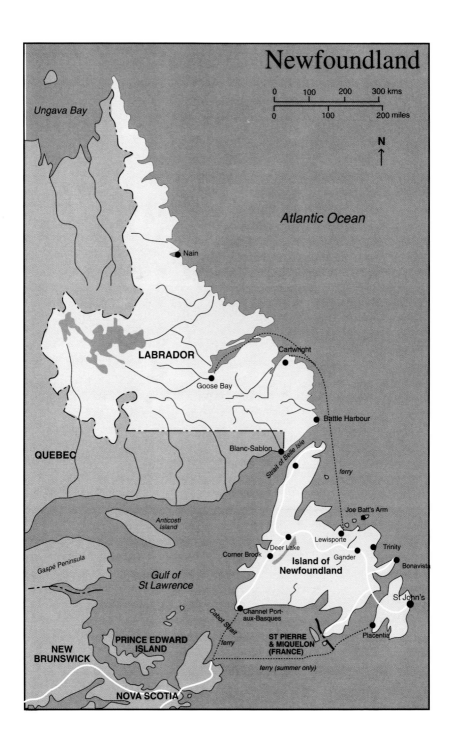

society with their own dialect, food, music and character born of a separate history and the evolvement of an island community removed from the mainland.

HISTORY

Viking explorers from Iceland and Greenland who visited Labrador and settled briefly on the north part of the island in the tenth century were the first Europeans to see North America. By the 15th century, Basque, Spanish, English, French and Portuguese fishermen were coming to the rich Grand Banks southeast of Newfoundland for the sea harvest. British merchants established seasonal colonies here to support the fishery, often in secret from the government. When Sir Humphrey Gilbert claimed the land for England in 1583—thus starting the British Empire—some 30,000 fishermen from half a dozen European nations were already fishing these waters. In an attempt to retain control of its overseas fishing domain, Britain outlawed any permanent residence in Newfoundland. The first illegal settlers were those who jumped ship and hid away in secluded coves. Despite harsh measures to discourage colonization, including house burnings, lashings and even hangings, thousands of tiny settlements grew in the coves and inlets along the 9,600 kilometers (5,965 miles) of coastline.

From 1634, under the Rule of the Fishing Admirals, the first captain into a Newfoundland port each spring became governor for the season, with near dictatorial powers. These despots took harsh measures to assure that no one should stay permanently in Newfoundland. Britain passed, then repealed, the anticolonization laws several times, but could not stop the tide of settlers attracted by the lucrative Grand Banks fish trade.

In the 17th century, the French claimed Newfoundland and set up a colony at Placentia. The island passed between British and French rule several times until the 1763 Treaty of Paris awarded Newfoundland and Labrador to Britain. Representative government was introduced in 1832, followed by parliamentary government in 1855. Voters rejected joining Canada in 1869 and subsequent attempts for union were thwarted.

Responsible government ended in 1933 when Newfoundland needed Britain's help to repay enormous debts. It returned to colonial status under a government commission. Finally, in 1949, Newfoundland voted by a narrow margin (52 per cent) to become Canada's tenth province in a bitterly fought campaign that is still not forgotten. Newfoundland and Quebec quarreled over possession of Labrador until 1927 when the British Privy Council awarded the area to Newfoundland—still a sore point with the Quebecois.

GEOGRAPHY

The combined area of Newfoundland and Labrador is more than three times the size of the other Atlantic provinces put together. Most of the 404,517 square kilometers (156,185 square miles) is uninhabited wilderness, rich in minerals and other resources.

The triangular island of Newfoundland covers just over one-quarter of the total area (111,390 square kilometers, or 43,000 square miles). This is largely uninhabited forest, lakes, moors, bogland, and mountains dropping steeply to the sea, and most of the population of 533,000 clings to the craggy, indented shoreline of sheltered coves, fjords and bays. The people live largely off the sea, in particular the off-shore Grand Banks. 'King Cod', the major industry, has suffered in recent years because of decreased fish stocks, and Newfoundland remains Canada's poorest province.

Across the narrow Strait of Belle Isle is massive, empty Labrador. There are only 35,000 people in its 293,127 square kilometers (113,147 square miles) who live mainly in scattered mining towns, visited only by the occasional hunter or fisherman.

GETTING THERE

Newfoundland is not yet discovered by overseas tourists although it attracts visitors from across eastern Canada and the US. Most who do fly in to St John's, but there are two sea routes and an overland route. Marine Atlantic operates a year-round vehicle and passenger ferry service between North Sydney, Nova Scotia, and Port aux Basques on the island's southwestern tip, on the far side of the island from St John's. In summer there is also a service between North Sydney and Argentia, the southeastern tip just 131 kilometers (81 miles) from the capital. Most travel between Newfoundland and Labrador is by air, but during the summer there is a ferry service between Lewisport and Goose Bay, Labrador.

Port aux Basques, CN (Canadian National) Marine's terminal and overland the major access point to the island, is a stark, sombre place, and truly a wild land, as a highway sign not far out of town indicates: 'Dangerous winds up to 120 miles per hour known to occur next 10 miles (16 kilometers)'. It adds that the winds have overturned cars and blown trains off the rails.

The fully-paved Trans Canada Highway crosses the island from Port aux Basques to St John's, 910 kilometers (565 miles) of mostly wilderness driving. Terra Transport operates a trans-island bus service.

For rates and schedules write: Marine Atlantic, PO Box 250, North Sydney, Nova Scotia B2A 3M3, and Terra Transport, Roadcruiser Sales Office, Station Building, St. John's, Newfoundland.

Accommodations along the way are not luxurious, but there are many 'hospitality homes'. The local version of bed-and-breakfast is so named because of the friendly family atmosphere, especially in the 'outports', the isolated coastal villages. Prices range from about $35 to $45 a night with a big breakfast included.

GROS MORNE NATIONAL PARK

Gros Morne National Park is 1,805 square kilometers (697 square miles) of spectacular mountain and fjord scenery that locals compare favorably to Alberta's Lake Louise. It is located 72 kilometers (45 miles) north of the lumbering community of Deer Lake where the Trans Canada turns east and Highway 430 continues the journey up to the Great Northern Peninsula.

The park's unique geographical formations include flat-topped mountains with little vegetation, desolate boulder-strewn tableland, sheer cliffs, bogs and sand dunes. Vegetation ranges from seaweed on the shore to tundra-like mosses and lichens on the plateau and wind-stunted balsam, fir and white spruce, known as tuckamores, along the coast. Its fjords are North America's most spectacular and were gouged out by glaciers in the last ice age.

The most striking fjord is freshwater Western Brook Pond, surrounded by towering 600-meter (2,000-foot) cliffs. Boats take two- to three-hour tours of the 'Pond' (summers only) and can be reached by a one-hour hike over a boardwalk trail from the Western Brook Pond Trail parking lot on the highway. The surrounding park has hiking trails, wildlife and birdlife, a visitor center and camp grounds with motels, guest homes, stores and restaurants in adjacent communities.

VIKING LAND

Highway 430 follows the coast for 400 kilometers (248 miles) of wilderness along the Viking Trail. This is no casual afternoon drive. At the very tip of the northern peninsula, about 25 kilometers (15 miles) off the highway, the L'Anse aux Meadows National Historic Park was the first such site placed on UNESCO's World Heritage list. Here among the low, gentle hills and meadows once lived a Norse community, the earliest known attempt at European settlement in North America. Archaeologists speculate that it may have been the entry point to explorer Leif Eriksson's Vinland. Radiocarbon dating of artefacts date the Norse settlement to about AD 1000.

The first white child in North America was born here, Snorri, son of Thorfinn Karlsefni. A boardwalk passing the remains of eight Norse buildings leads to full-scale replicas of three sod buildings that visitors can walk through. The visitors' center has many of the original artifacts, a film about the site and a model illustrating how it looked during the time of the Norse settlement.

THE EAST COAST

Where the Trans Canada Highway reaches the island's east coast, Route 230—the Cabot Highway—leaves the main road for the Bonavista Peninsula. The drive through fishing communities leads to the cape where explorer John Cabot first sighted North America in 1497. Trinity, set in a hilly peninsula, is one of Newfoundland's oldest communities, probably dating from about 1558. Many historic and public

THE EUROPEAN CONNECTION

Jutting far into the Atlantic, Newfoundland is the closest part of North America to Europe. St John's, the capital on the southwestern Avalon Peninsula, is closer to Ireland than to Winnipeg, the center of the continent. This location gives it a strategic importance for transportation and communications.

On windswept Signal Hill in St John's on December 12, 1901, Guglielmo Marconi received the first transoceanic wireless signal transmitted from Cornwall, England. The first successful transatlantic telegraph cable landed at Heart's Content, just north of St John's, in 1866. The original cable office is now a museum.

St John's has played a leading role in the history of flight. In June 1919, British aviators John Alcock and Lieutenant Arthur Whitten Brown took off from Lester's Field, St John's, on the first successful transatlantic flight. In 16 hours, they crossed the Atlantic to Cliffden, Ireland. Signal Hill was the last North American landmark American aviator Charles Lindbergh saw on his historic flight to Europe. For a brief period from 1936 to the war, Pan American Clipper flying boats flew to Europe from Botwood Sea Base north of St John's.

buildings have been preserved and locals still live in the colorful Newfoundland 'box' houses. The highway continues to the cape's end and another fishing community, **Bonavista**.

The northern peninsula is also a popular center for whale- watching and iceberg-spotting. Along this '**Iceberg Alley**', as many as 100 'growlers', jagged chunks of ice up to 91 meters high (300 feet) and glowing blue and turquoise like great diamonds, float by from Greenland during the summer months.

THE SOUTH

Throughout the summer, CN Marine operates an 18-hour overnight car ferry from Sydney, Nova Scotia, to Argentia Newfoundland. In season, many visitors arrive by one ferry service (either to Argentia or Port Aux Basques), cross the island and depart by the other.

The main attraction at Argentia is great 'game watching'. In nearby **Placentia Bay**, humpback whales play in such numbers that it is considered by some to be the whale-watching capital of the world.

After Argentia is a 131-kilometer drive (81-mile) to St John's which first passes an expanse of barren, arctic-like terrain of marshland, low brush and stunted trees at the southern tip of the Avalon Peninsula. The road skirts **Avalon Wilderness Area**, where some of the 5,000 woodland Caribou which live off the region's lichen graze by the road. Towards St John's are two, provincial parks worth a stop; **Father Duffy's Well** (named for a wandering priest), and **Butter Pot** (after the shape of a granite mountain).

St John's

The province's capital and largest city, with 150,000 people, is North America's closest point to Europe; indeed, it is physically similar to Oslo, Norway. It is set on a deep inlet surrounded by steep slopes, and narrow streets climb up from the harbor, the heart of the city. Although St John's is one of the continent's oldest cities, it doesn't show its age because of a devastating fire in 1892 which leveled almost the entire community. A few old buildings, tall with peaked roofs and London-like chimney-pots, remain downtown as reminders of the original city. More common are brightly-colored homes with mansard roofs, typical of the early 1900s. The city has the atmosphere of a robust port yet also boasts North America's only unarmed police force.

Sights and Attractions

■ SACRED ST JOHN'S

The city's two prominent churches both honor the same saint. The twin towers of the Romanesque Roman Catholic **Basilica of St John the Baptist** are the most prominent feature of the city skyline, built in the shape of a cross. The church was the largest in North America when completed in 1850, and holds 2,000 worshippers. The Gothic Anglican **Cathedral of St John the Baptist** claims to be the continent's best example of ecclesiastical Gothic architecture and is certainly worth a visit.

■ THE COLONIAL BUILDING

In typically colorful Newfoundland style, the province's first parliament sat in a tavern, that of Mrs. Mary Travers, which was the only 'suitable' building in St John's in 1833. Later governments used the more staid court house then an orphan asylum from 1850 to 1860 when the government got its own Colonial Building. The legislative building, built of white limestone imported from Ireland, had an exciting history. Disgruntled rioters upset at their rulers, ransacked the place at least three times.

The Colonial Building now stores government archives. Although there are no guides, if you ask politely someone there might show you the interior, including the council chamber, unique to the parliamentary system. This was the only house in the British Empire to break the tradition of the ruling party sitting to the right of the speaker. The stove was built into the wall on his left, so government members sat on that side to keep warm. The more important the member, the closer his seat to the stove.

(following pages) Brigus, a scenic outpost on Conception Bay, Newfoundland, known as 'the rock'

■ SIGNAL HILL

A short drive, or long, windy walk up Duckworth Street and Signal Hill Road leads to historic Signal Hill, where the British defeated the French in the last battle for North America in 1762. It was once used as a lookout for ships approaching the narrow entrance to the harbor. Flags were flown from here to announce the arrival of ships to port, giving Signal Hill its name. The 183-meter (600-foot) summit is now a national historic park that offers the best view of the harbor.

At the top is the squat, fort-like **Cabot Tower**, built between 1898 and 1900 to commemorate the 400th anniversary of Cabot's discovery of Newfoundland and Queen Victoria's Diamond Jubilee. A stairway leads to the top of the tower where, buffeted by stiff breezes, visitors get an even better view of town and surrounding countryside. Nearby is the old hospital where Marconi set up a receiving station for the first historic transatlantic wireless signal. A visitor center half-way down has a good museum depicting early Newfoundland, Cabot, 'King Cod' and the fishing industry, the wars with the French and World War II. From here, a walking trail leads to **Gibbet Hill** near **Deadman's Pond**, site of the old gallows where bodies of hanged criminals, wrapped in chains, were left dangling for up to ten days as a lesson to potential felons.

■ CITY CENTER

Water Street, called 'the oldest street in North America', is the commercial center, with some businesses dating back to 1700. At city-center **Harborside Park**, a large plastic plaque declares: 'The British Empire began here over 400 years ago August 5, 1583. Landing on this site, Sir Humphrey Gilbert claimed Newfoundland for Elizabeth I. It was the beginning of the world's greatest empire', A considerably more attractive bronze plaque across the street says much the same thing.

A few blocks away, on **Temperance Street**, is a sight not listed by the tourist office. Four identical stone houses were erected here by the builder of Cabot Tower on Signal Hill who offered them as a dowry, one for each of his daughters. 'They were ugly as sin', say locals, who delight in pointing out the houses.

■ NEWFIE NIGHTS

St John's is not a great restaurant city. Locals do not dine out much, and there is not a large enough tourist base to support many quality restaurants. Despite this, there are some good choices, particularly for seafood.

However, Newfies do drink out and the small city has Atlantic Canada's best nightlife. **George Street** is the liveliest section of any east coast city, crowded with cars and cheerful young pub crawlers frequenting places such as the **Capricorn**, the **Sundance** with a western decor and music, **Green Sleeves**, loud and crowded with live rock bands, and the smaller **Rob Roy**, an earthy Scottish pub with singers of local folk favorites.

Cabbies boast that there are 110 pubs between the Radisson Plaza and the Hotel Newfoundland, 'and that's not counting all the other pubs around town'.

Besides beer, the Newfie drink is Screech, a dark, overproof Jamaican rum sold only here and taken usually with coke, sometimes with water, or straight. Screech is so named because it made American soldiers do just that when they tried it while stationed here in World War II.

Those so inclined can get 'Screeched' at **Trapper John's**, a crowded, jumbled pub with log cabin decor, a wood stove, animal and snake skins adorning the walls, old rifles and kerosene lamps, kitchen utensils and tools hanging from the ceiling.

At the Screech-in ceremony, the Screecher stands up straight before the bar, accepts the Screech, drinks a shot straight and kisses a stuffed puffin's backside. The bartender knights the Screecher three times with a sword and puts a raccoon skin hat on his head. There is no charge for this honor, which comes complete with a signed certificate.

THE OUTSKIRTS

The countryside beyond St John's gets rustic very quickly. It is pleasant driving along the twisting, roller-coaster rural roads with little traffic and little activity. Squid hang on clothes-lines to dry, fishermen unload fish and work on nets, and it is all quite unspoiled. Some of the local architecture, especially along the southern shore, was transplanted from Ireland. The typical outport house is an elongated, straight salt-box, two storys high with a central stairwell and built 'with a hammer, a saw and a plumb bob'.

Many homes have no front steps because Newfies never use the front door but enter in back through the kitchen, the center of daily life.

■ PETTY HARBOR

About 35 kilometers (20 miles) south of St John's is Petty Harbor, Newfoundland's equivalent to Nova Scotia's Peggy's Cove without the tour buses. This delightful village was the setting for such films as *Orca* and *A Whale for the Killing,* and evokes a sense of simpler times. Fishermen in plaid shirts and rubber boots work on their skiffs, sea gulls swarm around the fish plants like flies over a piece of meat, houses perch on cliff-sides, and the brisk air smells of salt brine and seaweed.

■ BAY BULLS

Further south along the coast, this seaside town is a major center for viewing off-shore birds and for whale-watching. Several small companies and local fishermen

Newfies

The province is Canada's least ethnically-mixed area. More than 98 per cent of the people speak English; most of them were born in the province, and they are stoutly British. Ninety per cent of the people live along the coast, either in the major towns or in the 'outports', many with no land connection to the rest of the province. Many locals still refer to Newfoundland as 'my country', and consider Canada almost a separate nation. They are quick to correct a stranger's pronunciation. 'What's that you say, B'y? New-found-land? It's New-fund-land, B'y, Newfundland, the accent on land. You Canadians.'

Newfoundlanders have English-speaking Canada's most distinct accents. In St John's, it has a strong Irish quality, while in the north it is the Devon or Dorset dialect of three centuries ago. People here also have a poetic turn of phrase, particularly when describing their harsh environment. 'Silver thaw' is sleet or frozen rain; 'lolly' is soft ice forming in the harbor. Other local words include 'gumbeens', cubes of chewing tobacco, 'ballyrag', to abuse, and 'yaffle', an armful of dried fish, hence the Newfie saying: 'He is one fish short of a yaffle', not all there.

As if to assert its separateness, Newfoundland keeps its time zone half an hour out of sync with others. A Canadian joke runs: 'The world is coming to an end at midnight, 12.30 in Newfoundland'. Newfies also celebrate several distinctive festivals held in spring and summer.

NEWFIE NAMES

Travelers to Newfoundland will be struck by the imaginative place names. Many are old British, or corruptions of French, Portuguese or Basque. The most colorful are the descriptive names, such as Come by Chance, Stinking Cove, Grey's Nose, Joe Batt's Arm, Cow Head, Bumblebee Bight, Deadman's Cove, Confusion Bay and Jipujikuei Kuespem (Little River Pond) Provincial Park. Park names that could only be found in Newfoundland include Blow Me Down and Dildo Run.

THE NEWFOUNDLAND SOUND

Newfoundland has developed its own style of folk music, with a lively Irish lilt, and there's nary a Newfie that won't sing *Squid Jigging Ground,* the rousing *Kelligrew's Soirée* or 57 verses of the jaunty *I'se the B'y That Builds the Boat,* almost the province's theme song.

> I'se the b'y that builds the boat
> And I'se the b'y that sails her
> I'se the b'y that catches the fish
> And takes 'em home to Lizer.
> Sods and rinds to cover yer flake
> Cake and tea for supper,
> Cod fish in the spring o' the year
> Fried in maggoty butter.

Popular Newfoundland singers and groups include Kelly Russel, Feller, Jim Payne, Rufus, Figi Duff (named for a steamed or boiled pudding with raisins and dried fruit) and Buddy Wasisname and the other Feller, who sing the popular *Gotta Get Me a Moose, Boy*. O'Brien's Music Store at 278 Water Street claims to be the world's largest collection of Newfoundland music.

take visitors on small boats to the **Bird Islands**, sanctuaries for thousands of seabirds such as gannets, kittiwakes and razorbills. The boats anchor near the rocky islands, which include North America's largest puffin colony, as birds come swooping and diving all around in a noisy, frenzied scene. Although the boats can go in close for a good look, landing is forbidden. On the return trip, you might see humpback, minke, fin, and pothead whales which often breach nearby.

■ THE ENDCAPE
Cape Spear Park, about 17 kilometers (10 miles) from St John's, is a wild, windswept point with the dark Atlantic Ocean crashing at the foot of the cliffs. The weather changes in minutes, blue skies disappearing when a chilly fog rolls in and the fog horn bellows like a mournful banshee.

Soldiers stationed here described the place as 'cold, clammy, foggy and miserable'. A modern, functioning lighthouse and the original, now a **museum**, sit atop the granite hill. The three windows are in fact only two. Because glass is not a good insulator, builders only installed two and painted the third in so the building would look symmetrical.

An enthusiastic park warden urges visitors to inspect the huge World War II gun emplacements and underground bunkers.

A walkway leads to the easternmost point of North America where a plain plaque marks the spot: Latitude 47 31' 17' N, Longitude 52 37' 24 W.

It is the end of Canada.

Festivals

Every nation, culture and religion celebrates its unique festivals and holidays. Canada's mixed collection of peoples have brought their celebrations with them, and the nation has developed an assortment of its own, including old time fiddling shows in the Maritimes, Indian powwows in Ontario, rodeos and beard-growing contests on the Prairies, salmon bakes in BC and dog-sled races in the north.

Especially in the summer months, thousands of festivities and community parties are celebrated nationwide.

The biggest of these is **Canada Day** on July 1, when the whole country is alight with fireworks in honor of Canada's founding in 1867. It is very much an outdoor festival of picnics, barbecues and street parties.

Old Time Fairs

North America's unique, old time county fairs have developed into grand agricultural exhibitions with midways, rides, grandstands, air shows and entertainment. The biggest include Winnipeg's **Red River Exhibition**, Vancouver's **Pacific National Exhibition** and Toronto's **Canadian National Exhibition**, Canada's oldest and the world's largest such show.

Some of these, such as Edmonton's **Klondike Days** (see page 108) and Regina's **Buffalo Days** (with its Pile-O-Bones Day), also recall the pioneer past. Cities are decorated as frontier towns, local folk don turn-of-the-century costumes and old-time music resounds in streets and bars.

Ethnic Festivals

Multi-cultural Canadians celebrate a United Nations of ethnic festivals: Chinese dance with dragons in BC, red-booted Cossacks kick their heels up in Dauphin, Manitoba's **National Ukrainian Festival**, and many major cities rope off streets for Greek and Italian days. In Steinbach, Manitoba, Mennonites recall their early times with **Pioneer Days**, and Quebec towns celebrate **St Jean Baptiste Day** on June 24 with parades, bonfires and fireworks. Manitoba's 100-year-old **Islendingadagurinn** (Icelander's Day) in Gimli attracts Icelandic Canadians and Americans in bullet helmets with protruding horns, to honor the motherland with traditional music, poetry and food.

Double Trouble

The sulfrous stench from the E. B. Eddy plant was still singing in the streets of Ottawa when Joshua first arrived there, woozy from a transatlantic flight, to join Senator Hornby for lunch. No time was wasted on an exchange of pleasantries.

'As you know, I am opposed to this marriage,' the senator said.

'Aha.'

'I would like to see them go to proper schools.'

'Pauline and I will be the judge of what's proper.'

'The Hornbys have been educated at Bishop's for generations.'

'You're forgetting something, Senator. Our children will be called Shapiro.'

'Where were you educated?'

'Do you mind if I have another?'

'Please do.'

'Make it a double.'

'Certainly.'

'I was educated at Fletcher's Field High, and from there I went on to do a stint at The Boys' Farm in Shawbridge.'

'Why?'

'I got caught stealing a car.'

'No university?' he asked without flinching.

'I'm afraid not.'

'But you're a writer.'

'Of sorts.'

'Where's your family from?'

'The shtetl.'

'Ah,' he said, 'the Pale of Settlement.'

'Your parents alive?'

'Mn hm.'

'What do they think of this marriage?'

'My mother has never given a damn what I do, and so far as my father's concerned, anything that makes me happy is fine by him.'

'What does your father do?'

'If you don't mind, Senator, I think I'll have just one more.'

'A double?'

'Yes, please.'

'My father was a prizefighter. He once went eight rounds with Sammy Angott.'

'And was this Mr Angott a pugilist of some note?'

'Indeed he was.'

'And what did your father do upon his retirement?'

'Oh, many things, Senator. A good many things. A little something in the restaurant and nightclub line. Some bill-collecting. I ought to tell you that he has a prison record.'

The waiter arrived with Joshua's drink.

'Oh, on second thoughts, Desmond, I think I'll join my guest. The same for me, please.'

'But this is a double, Senator.'

'I'm quite aware of that, Desmond.'

'Yes, sir.'

Mordecai Richler, Joshua Then And Now

The **Six Nations Indian Pageant** on the native Indian reserve near Brantford, Ontario, salutes Canada's original peoples with dances, traditional foods and displays of native moccasins, beadwork and leatherwork. The all-Indian pageant is staged in a forest 'theater'. Across the country, and in the far north, native Indians stage smaller powwows with war-canoe races, singing and drumming, dancing competitions, colorful costumes, bannock-baking and barbecues.

Canada's German community stages mini-beer fests each fall. Kitchener-Waterloo's **Oktoberfest**, the world's largest outside Munich, is a week of leiderhosen, oompah-pah bands, sausages and suds. The local German clubs offer complimentary memberships so visitors can tuck into the beer and wurst, and link arms to sing 'Ein prosit, ein prosit, gemutlichkeit' to the brass bands.

The taste is rum, not beer, and the bands are steel, not brass, at **Caribana**, a colorful festival of West Indian music, art and culture held at Toronto Island Park. Caribbean people celebrate with parades, piquant native foods, limbo dancing and especially the rippling sounds of steel bands, calypso and pounding reggae.

Maritime **Caelidh** are redolent of haggis and resonant with the wail of pipes and beat of drums. These Scottish affairs feature Highland dancing, Gaelic language and song and traditional sports such as tossing the caber and tossing back the Bell's.

Each year, Halifax, Nova Scotia, holds an international **Town Criers' Championship**, with criers from Canada, the US, Britain, the Bahamas and Bermuda dressed in colorful waistcoats and frilly shirts competing for the Chuddy Chalker Trophy.

Multi-ethnic festivals such as the **Drummondville Folklore** in Quebec, the **Mosaic in Regina**, **Caravan** in Toronto and **Heritage Days** in Edmonton, Alberta celebrate cultural diversity with food, music and crafts. Winnipeg's **Folkorama**, the world's largest multi-cultural festival, is like a world fair, with more than 40 pavilions in ice rinks, hotel ballrooms, community halls and school gymnasiums. Activities range from craft demonstrations, such as the carving of Dutch shoes, to sipping Israeli aperitifs and munching Viennese pastries. Exotic fare covers the spectrum from moussaka to perogies, tempura to shish kebabs. Professional entertainers include Lebanese belly dancers, Hungarian Gypsy violinists, Irish harpists and Japanese drummers.

During Quebec's **pre-Lenten winter festival** the city displays more energy than would be expected of only half a million people. For more than a week the streets of the Old City are active, with every tavern, **boîte à chanson** and restaurant packed with young, fun-loving Quebecois.

Food Celebrations

Maritimers dedicate many summer festivals to seafood. In Nova Scotia, the **Parrsboro Beach Clam Festival** features demonstrations of various ways to prepare the honored crustacean, shelling competitions and clam-eating contests. **Lobster fests** in Pictou, Nova Scotia, and Shediac, New Brunswick, celebrate the shellfish with parades, entertainment and giant lobster feasts. Matane, in Quebec's Gaspe, honors the tasty crustacean in the **Annual Shrimp Fest**, where eating is the dominant activity. At the **Orwell Corner Strawberry Festival** in Prince Edward Island, fiddlers play Way Down East music in the community hall and village maidens hand out root beer and bowls of vanilla ice cream topped with fresh strawberries. On the Prairies, Altona has its **Sunflower Festival**, and Morden a **Corn and Apple Festival** with free corn on the cob and apple cider.

Seaside Races

With luck, a traveler in Newfoundland may happen on one of the many festivals held throughout the spring and summer there. The most famous is the **St John's Regatta** held the first Wednesday in August at Quidi Vidi Lake. The rowing competitions are North America's oldest organized sporting event, running since 1826. While the focus of the fair is the dory races across the lake, other activities indicate just how much Newfoundland still lives near, and off, the sea.

A typical day starts with a free fish breakfast followed by an open house at the Northwest Atlantic Fisheries Center. The morning's **Fish Filleting Contest** is followed by a **Kiss the Cod Competition** and then the main event, the **Hangashore Dory Race**. Lunch time there is a **Best Fish and Chips Competition**, then a **Cod Tongue Eating Competition** followed by a **Lobster Race**. Smaller but similar festivals are held throughout the province.

Rodeos

Rodeos, the foremost of festivals based on a livelihood, are held in all four western provinces from early spring until late fall. In dusty corrals, cowboys show off their skills in bareback, saddle bronc and bull riding, calf roping and steer wrestling. Music is stompin' hoedown and blue grass, and the fresh scent of new mown hay, horses and hot dogs fills the air.

CANADIAN SPORTS

For a normally mild-mannered, law-abiding and peace-loving people, Canadians have given the world some of its roughest sports—hockey and the North American style of football, known abroad as gridiron.

Hockey, that uniquely Canadian sport, was invented on Christmas Day 1885 in Kingston, Ontario, when members of the Royal Canadian Rifles army regiment took their field hockey sticks and a lacrosse ball onto the frozen lake.

Hockey can be mayhem on ice, as 'simians on skates' slash and stab each other with ashwood spears. (There is even a spearing penalty.) The National Hockey League is rife with major fights, and even kids' junior leagues can be violent. 'I went to a fight and a hockey game broke out' goes a national joke. A Canadian writer once bemoaned the game that boosts the country's reputation as 'hewers of ankles and drawers of haemoglobin'.

Scrappiness, the ability to stand and fight, is highly respected on the skating rinks across the country. 'If you can't beat 'em in the alleys, you can't beat 'em on the ice', pot-bellied, cigar-chomping coaches tell their young players.

Yet played properly, hockey is poetry on skates, a fast, graceful and extremely entertaining sport. In winter, it is played in every small town from Port Alberni, British Columbia, to Come By Chance, Newfoundland. To really understand the Canadian psyche, catch a game on TV, or better still in the arena found in any Canadian town, small or large.

Canada adapted their football (now known as the North American version of football) from the British game of rugby. In 1874, a team from McGill University in Montreal visited Cambridge, Massachusetts for a game of football. When it was discovered that Harvard played the kicking game (soccer), they played two games under each set of rules. The game of football, and the oval ball, was introduced to the US. The Americans learned fast, beating McGill in that first game. Ivy League (eastern US) universities took to the new sport, adapted most of the modern rules, and have been better at the game than Canadians ever since. Today, the stars in the Canadian Football League are American college players who can't make the National Football League in the US. Yet the Canadian version can be a superior, more entertaining game for the spectator.

Canadian football is more wide open, with larger fields and deeper end zones, allowing more scope for exciting touchdown passes. Fewer downs, limitations on players' movements and annoying time-outs mean a faster flow of play and a more exciting and unpredictable game. Pro teams in Vancouver, Calgary, Edmonton, Regina, Winnipeg, Hamilton, Ottawa, Toronto and several new American teams play from about August to the national championship, the Grey Cup, in late November.

Halifax high schoolers play made-in Canada football

Lacrosse is another sport first played in Canada and consists of a hard rubber ball about the size of a baseball thrown between players using large, curved sticks with a pocket of netting or webbing.

A Canadian, Dr James Naismith, also invented the more gentlemanly basketball in 1891 while an instructor at a YMCA training school in Springfield, Massachusetts. Looking for a vigorous form of indoor entertainment, the clergyman devised the game of throwing soccer balls into wooden peach baskets. Although it is now international, Americans have always dominated the game. Even with this ball game, it can get rough under those hoops.

Calgary's Stampede (see page 112) is perhaps the world's most famous rodeo, with the top professional cowboys competing for hefty purses. Free chuckwagon breakfasts are served downtown, square dances held on city streets and Indians of five nations in full feathered ceremonial regalia join the opening parade. The rodeo features Calgary's unique sport, dangerous and exciting chuckwagon races, in heats of four four-horse wagons with outriders.

Loggers Contests

True men of the woods gather with axe and saw in BC logging communities such as Sooke, Duncan, Squamish, and Vernon. In a flurry of sawdust and chain-saw fumes, loggers compete in Underhand Chop, Spring Board Chop and Peavy Log Rolling. In Log Birling, losing really is as easy as falling off a log. In the Axe Throwing competition, sharp-eyed loggers lob short, double-bladed axes into targets six meters (20 feet) away, while Obstacle Pole Bucking contestants step carefully out to the end of wet, slippery logs to cut off the tip with a power saw.

The Unusual

Oddball festivals flourish in this supposedly sombre, conservative country. The funniest is probably Montreal's **Just For Laughs Festival** which draws stand-up comics from around the world. Manitoba's unusual events include a **Turtle Derby at Boissevain,** the **Canadian National Frog Jumping Championships** at St. Pierre-Joly's Frog Follies and Miami's Mule Daze, the **Canadian National Annual Mule Derby.** In the zany **Nanaimo-to-Vancouver International Bathtub Race,** part of Vancouver's Sea Festival, hundreds of fiberglass 'tubs' attempt to cross the choppy, 35-mile (56-kilometer), Georgia Strait from Nanaimo, on Vancouver Island, to Vancouver (also see page 68).

Northern Festivals

Yukon and Northwest Territories carnivals take advantage of the short summer with indigenous sports such as greased-pole climbing, blanket toss games, one-foot-high-kick, ear-pull and harpoon-throwing as well as distinctive music featuring top throat singers, drum-dancers and fiddlers. The **Good Women Contest** events include muskrat-and seal-skinning, bannock-making, tea boiling, squaw-wrestling, sewing and other 'bush' skills.

Major Yukon festivals include **Kiki Bird Days, Ice Worm Squirm** and the **Klondike International Outhouse Race**. More traditional is **Yellowknife's Annual Midnight Golf Tournament** saluting 24 hours of sunlight. Players teeing off at midnight must look out for bothersome ravens who steal the golf balls. The game is the culmination of summer solstice celebrations called **Raven Mad Daze**, and is held the closest Friday to June 21. **Caribou Carnival** (March 31–April 2) is Yellowknife's biggest event, and celebrates the coming of the warm weather. **Folk on the Rocks**, is held for three days in mid-July, and draws folk musicians from across Canada and the US.

Anywhere in Canada, on a summer's day, there is likely to be some sort of festivity or community event happening nearby. They are worth taking in, to grasp the spirit of this diverse and exciting country.

Canadian Cuisine

When Canada won the 16th annual World Culinary Olympics in Frankfurt, West Germany, in October 1984, most natives were pleased but not surprised. Raised on mom's cooking in the cities, towns and farms across the country, they knew Canada had the world's finest food. It was just a matter of time for the rest of the world to recognize the fact.

The five-member Team led by Vancouver's Henri Dane took top honors in the international competition, while more than 40 Canadian chefs participating collected 40 gold medals overall. (In 1976, Canada was placed second behind Switzerland.) While most of the chefs were European or European-trained, the win showed the level that the culinary arts had reached in Canada.

Interest in food in the New World dates back to its early days. North America's first social club was the Ordre de Bon Temps (the Order of Good Cheer), a dining club that Samuel de Champlain formed in 1605 in the new colony of Port Royal (in what is now Nova Scotia). The aim of the club, fashioned loosely on a European order of chivalry, was to maintain the French settlers' spirits and to pass the time through the long, New World winter. Each gentleman took turns acting as host, providing fresh game and, as chief steward of the day, leading a ceremonial procession to the table.

Dining out has become an important Canadian national pastime in recent years, at least in the big cities. A visitor has merely to refer to the dining out section in any popular city magazine to see dozens of choices available in all types of dining and price ranges, from fast food to ethnic to the hautest cuisine.

Unfortunately for the traveler, most of the good restaurants, bistros and cafes are found in the cities and larger towns, although smaller communities can prove welcome exceptions.

Small town diners, hotel coffee shops and roadside cafés generally dish up prefrozen french fries with fast-fried steaks or chops garnished with a sprig of parsley and a slice of orange. Most small towns, especially in the west, have a Chinese café serving a Number Two Special with egg rolls and fortune cookies. You may be safest with a bacon and tomato sandwich or cheeseburger while in rural Canada.

The old trick of dining where the truckers stop doesn't work along Canada's highways, either. And never eat in a place that advertises 'Canadian and Chinese Food'; you'll get the worst of both!

Yet this is a destination that should attract the wandering gourmet for a number of reasons. A rich agricultural country, it has the finest ingredients, including many

Granville Street is a lively part of the Halifax Historic Properties

regional specialties. Europeans who first landed in the New World discovered unique foods used by the native Indians: game such as venison, elk and buffalo, various types of fish, corn and wild rice and a variety of local fruits such as blueberries, chokecherries, loganberries and Saskatoons.

The great ethnic social stew that makes up Canada has contributed many cuisines which can make for exciting dining. As with all aspects of the country's culture, the Canadian table borrows and blends ideas from all over the world. The regions also contribute specialties, and the variety of dishes would make any gourmand hard-pressed to identify a 'definitive Canadian cuisine'.

The truly distinctive dishes have evolved in the older parts of the country, notably Quebec and the Atlantic provinces.

Newfoundland dishes are amongst the most unusual. Cod tongues are somewhat like a scallop, with gelatin covering a nugget of meat. Aficionados say the smaller ones are best. They are served au gratin or in cod cakes, but most often baked or fried until crisp, and sometimes served with french fries in fish and chips shops.

Fish and brewis (say broos), another local dish, is harder to find in a restaurant. (In Newfoundland, 'fish' always means cod.) Brewis is ships' hard biscuit soaked overnight to soften it, then boiled with the cod. The dish is served with scrunchions—salt pork (fatback) cut in cubes and fried so it is crisp and slightly salty, delicious to anyone who likes good bacon. Newfoundlanders love them.

Bakeapples (small reddish berries made into jam), rabbit soup, seal soup, boiled moose, rhubarb wine and flipper pie made from the flippers of the young harp seals are also Newfie specialties usually encountered in homes rather than restaurants. The Colonial Inn in St John's sometimes has flipper pie on the menu, and they are available frozen at Bigoods grocery just outside the city. (Contact the tourist office for the address.) This one, as they say kindly, is an acquired taste.

In the early summer, keep an eye out for a phenomenon unique to Newfoundland: the caplin scull. Millions of small fish called caplin (pronounced cape-lin) swarm close to shore and even roll onto the beaches to spawn. Locals catch the little silvery fish with nets, buckets and bare hands. They cook them fresh, smoke or pickle them, or nail them to rickety picket fences to dry by the thousands, creating the appearance of 'fish forests'. Caplin scull lasts for two to three weeks from about mid-June, and can be witnessed from early evening until sunset.

In the Maritimes, Acadian specialties include rappie pie, made with grated potatoes and salt pork (and sometimes meat or chicken). Grunt is a filling, delicious dessert of rhubarb, strawberries, apples and especially blueberries. The fruit is first stewed, then dumplings are added.

New Brunswick delicacies include fiddlehead, young shoots of ostrich ferns available fresh in May and June. They are served as a steamed or boiled vegetable with butter, or cold in salads. Dulse, an edible seaweed, is a popular snack. Salmon Pie, the local version of Shepherd's Pie, is a unique Gaspé dish.

Dining in Nova Scotia can be an adventurous discovery, with unusual fare such as Solomon gundy (raw herring marinated in spiced vinegar), Lunenburg pudding (a German type of sausage), and the delightfully named finnan haddie (smoked haddock, a British dish). Marakins is a Cape Breton Island spiced sausage made in fall or winter, and scrapple a Dutch-inspired dish made from scraps of butchered hogs fried crisply. Desserts include fat archies (ginger or molasses cookies with dates) and forach, a rich Scottish-type dessert of oatmeal, whipping cream and sugar.

Quebec cuisine derives from that of the French settlers who came from Normandy more than 300 years ago, and relies on local ingredients—pork, maple syrup, game and game birds. It is hearty fare, perhaps somewhat bland to those who prefer spicy foods. Even the French love of garlic is lacking here.

Delicious and substantial pea soup is almost a national dish. Hearty onion and cabbage soups are popular in the countryside as well. The most famous traditional meal is *tourtière*, a meat and potato pie usually made with pork, though veal and chicken are also used. A truly authentic *tourtière* is based on partridge, venison or rabbit. *Cretons*, a pâté of minced pork cooked with spices, is a popular spread (available commercially) that is more piquant than most Quebec food.

Montreal is known across the continent for its smoked meats, and a beef sandwich (look for *sandwich de boeuf fumé*) on dark or rye bread with hot mustard and dill pickle makes an excellent lunch. Delicious Montreal-style chicken, grilled on a spit with a crispy brown outer skin, has fortunately spread to other parts of the country.

The Quebecois have a sweet tooth, satisfied by unique desserts based on maple syrup including *tarte au sucre* (sugar pie), a concoction of maple sugar, brown sugar, eggs, butter and chopped nuts.

Western Canada has no identifiable, distinct cuisine of its own, although as the youngest part of Canada, it remains close to its rich ethnic roots— notably Ukrainian, German and Scandinavian. Wild rice from the marshlands of Manitoba and Saskatchewan is popular among both gourmets and health food types. The distinct, almost nutty flavor goes well with game and the many game birds found in these provinces which straddle the major north-south wildfowl migratory routes.

Lake Winnipeg goldeye is a small, delicate fish (usually less than a pound) smoked over hardwood logs, then colored a golden red with food dye. It goes well with champagne. In the early 1890s, a young Englishman discovered the art of preparing goldeye by chance when he left his catch too long in his makeshift smoke house.

Across the Prairies, and in parts of the rest of Canada, game is coming back to both fine restaurants and fast-food stands. Elk and venison appear on some menus, and buffalo burgers (leaner, tastier, slightly more expensive than beef) are served in a very few places. Salmon, the basis of the West Coast Indian diet, appears on the menus in most BC restaurants, along with other local seafood and shellfish. The solid, full-flavored fish is at its simplest and tastiest as thick, pink steaks grilled at outdoor barbecues. During the province's many summer festivals, service clubs and Indian tribes grill and sell salmon in the local park or on the beach. With the mingled background aromas of salt water and burning charcoal, and the whisper of waves washing the stony shore, a juicy, barbecued salmon steak is the taste of outdoor Canada at its best.

(above) Mennonite specialities in Alberta, from produce grown on communal farms,
(right) From Gananoque, sightseeing aircraft fly over the Thousand Islands in the St Lawrence

Hotels

Accommodation in Canada ranges from basic but clean countryside motels to luxurious hotels and resorts, especially in Montreal, Quebec City, Toronto, Vancouver and environs. There are excellent local guides for hotels and restaurants available in most of the big cities or from the provincial tourist departments (see Useful Addresses page 292). In most cases it is a good idea to book ahead during the peak season, from early June to the end of September, and over Christmas.

In remote areas, accommodation can be rustic, pricey and often booked up, so check before you venture out. The top hotels in each major city are listed below.

British Columbia

Victoria

Captain's Palace, 309 Belleville Street, Victoria, BC V8V 1X2, tel (604) 388–9191.
This delightful little hotel overlooking the Inner Harbor is actually part of three large old houses. Genteel Victorian atmosphere.

Chateau Victoria, 740 Burdett Avenue, Victoria, BC V8W 1B2, tel (604) 382–4221, toll free 1–800–663–5891.
Centrally located luxury hotel with a rooftop restaurant offering harbor views and an excellent menu.

Empress Hotel, 721 Government Street, Victoria, BC V8W 1W5, tel (604) 384–8111, toll free US 1–800–828–7447, Canada 1–800–268–9411.
The stately, ivy-covered hotel facing the harbor is one of the finest examples of Canadian chateau architecture. A recent $45 million face-lift preserves the turn-of-the-century character while bringing the old hotel into the modern age.

Holland House Inn, 595 Michigan Street, Victoria, BC V8V 1S7, tel (604) 384–6644.
Small, intimate and attractive, with bright cheery bedrooms and a homey atmosphere.

Oak Bay Beach Hotel, 1175 Beach Dr, Victoria, BC V8S 2N2, tel (604) 598–4556.
An English, Tudor-style building set on the sea. A good pub, antique furnishings, and well worth the short taxi ride to town.

VANCOUVER

Barclay Hotel, 1348 Robson Street, Vancouver, BC V6E 1C5, Tel (604) 688–8850.
The typical West End apartment block is now a quiet, cozy heritage hotel, a rarity in Vancouver.

Four Seasons, 791 W Georgia Street, Vancouver, BC V6C 2T4, tel (604) 689–9333, toll free 1–800–268–6282.
Centrally located and connected to the Pacific Center shopping complex, this is one of the city's larger luxury hotels. The hotel includes indoor-outdoor pools, gym and a pleasant garden lounge.

Hotel Georgia, 801 W Georgia Street, Vancouver, BC V6C 1P7, (604) 682–5566.
The brown brick hotel is reasonably-priced and comfortable, while the basement George V pub is a pleasant lunch venue—provided you can tolerate the British-style pub food.

Hotel Vancouver, 900 W Georgia Street, Vancouver, BC V6C 2W6, tel (604) 684–3131.
The last of the great railway hotels built in 1939, with a distinctive, steeply-pitched, verdigrised roof and spacious rooms. It provides the young city with an old-world elegance.

The Hyatt Regency, 655 Burrard Street, Vancouver, BC V6C 2R7, tel (604) 687–6543
Vancouver's largest hotel, is centrally located, with good views from most rooms, many of which have balconies. Window seats from its popular seafood restaurant Fish & Co also have views of the inlet and the mountains.

Le Meridien, 845 Burrard Street, Vancouver, BC V6Z 2K6, tel (604) 682–5511.
A French-style hotel elegantly furnished in marble and antiques features one of the city's top restaurants (Le Club) and a fine bar in polished wood panelling somewhat akin to a British gentlemen's club.

Pacific Palisades, 1277 Robson Street, Vancouver, BC V6E 1C4, tel (604) 688–0461.
A former apartment block with studio, executive or penthouse suites, most with great views. All have kitchenettes with coffee maker, mini-bar, microwave oven and sink.

(following pages) Snow blankets southern Ontario for several months each winter

Pan Pacific, 300–999 Canada Place, Vancouver, BC V6C 3B5, tel (604) 662–8111.
Part of the cruise ship and convention complex, this large, new hotel has the best
views in town.

Sylvia Hotel, 1154 Gilford Street, Vancouver, BC V6G 2P6, tel (604) 681–9321.
This old, ivy-covered favorite on English Bay has been modernized without loosing
the charming atmosphere. Excellent beach views from the bar, restaurant and south-
facing rooms.

Waterfront Center Hotel, 900 Canada Place Way, Vancouver, BC V6C 3L5, tel (604)
691–1991.
An attractive addition to the once industrial seafront, has a modern, uncluttered feel,
subtle earth tones and West Coast artwork throughout the public areas. Sixty per
cent of the rooms have views of the Burrard Inlet.

Wedgewood Hotel, 845 Hornby Street, Vancouver, BC V6Z 1V1, tel (604) 689–7777.
A small, privately-run European-style hotel tastefully decorated in antiques is a favorite of those who avoid the chain hotels.

A number of companies offer a selection of Bed & Breakfast homes in Vancouver,
Victoria and throughout the province. Contact **BC Bed & Breakfast Association**, Box
593, 810 West Broadway, Vancouver BC V5Z 4E2, tel (604) 276–8616.

Alberta

Calgary
Delta Bow Valley Inn, 209–4 Avenue, S E Calgary, Alberta T2G 0C6, tel (403) 266–
1980, toll free 1–800–268–1133.
A first-class, centrally located hotel with all amenities, including exercise facilities.

Elbow River Inn & Casino, 1919 Macleod Trail, S E Calgary, Alberta T2G 4S1, tel
(403) 269–6771, toll free 1–800–661–463.
The city's only hotel on the banks of the Elbow River, it is conveniently located with an
underpass walkway to the Stampede Park and near Calgary's largest shopping mall.

The International Hotel, 220–4 Avenue, S W Calgary, T2P 4H5, tel 265–9600, toll
free 1–800 223–0888.
A centrally located, all-suite hotel with reasonable rates and no charge for children.

The Palliser, 133–9 Avenue, S W Calgary, Alberta T2P 2M3, tel (403) 262–1234, toll free 1–800–268–9411.
This railway hotel sits right over the station (perfect for those arriving on VIA Rail). Rambunctious local fans once rode horses through the grand lobby during the wild Calgary Stampede. Nice bar.

Skyline Plaza Hotel, 110–9 Avenue, S E Calgary, Alberta T2G 5A6, tel (403) 266–7331, toll free 1–800–648–7776.
New, elegant, and located near the city's spacious indoor public gardens.

Westin Hotel, 320–4 Avenue, S W Calgary, Alberta T2P 2S6, tel (403) 266–1611, toll free 1–800–228–3000.
One of the city's top hotels is appreciated locally for its fine Owl's Nest dining room.

EDMONTON
Best Western City Center Inn, 11310–109 Street, Edmonton, Alberta T5G 2T7, tel (403) 479–2042, toll free 1–800–5281234.
Centrally located, indoor pool and jacuzzi, a reliable medium price hotel.

Fantasyland Hotel, 17700–87 Avenue, Edmonton, Alberta T5T 4V4, tel (403) 444–3000, toll free 1–800–661–6454.
Part of the West Edmonton Mall, you have to see it to believe it. Theme rooms include beds in a pick-up truck, Victorian coach, railway sleeper or in Polynesian, Roman or Arabian setting. A matter of taste.

Hilton Interational Hotel (formerly the Four Seasons), 10235–101 Street, Edmonton, Alberta T5J 3E9, tel (403) 428–7111, toll free 1–800–268–6282.
Fine dining, luxury accommodation and good location, forming part of Edmonton Center complex.

Holiday Inn Crowne Plaza (formerly the Chateau Lacombe), 101 Street, at Bellamy Hill, Edmonton, Alberta T5J 1N7, tel (403) 428–6611, toll free 1–800–HOLIDAY.
Centrally-located, on the Saskatchewan River, cozy bar with good view of the river.

The Hotel McDonald, 10065–100 Street, Edmonton, Alberta T5J 0N6, tel (403) 424–5181, toll free 1–800–268–9411.
This classic chateau-style railway hotel built in 1915 was closed for many years. The beautiful stone building scenically perched on the North Saskatchewan River reopened in the early 1990s after a $20 million renovation and is again one of the city's best.

Westin Hotel, 10135–100 Street, Edmonton, Alberta T5J ON7, tel (403) 426–3636, toll free 1–800–228–3000.
A top hotel with award-winning Carvery Restaurant, good lounge and indoor swimming pool.

Saskatchewan

REGINA
Delta Regina, 1818 Victoria Avenue, Regina, Saskatchewan S4P OR1, tel (306) 569–1666, toll free 1–800–268–1133.
This first class hotel is like a city-center 'resort', with indoor pool, sauna and whirlpool.

Hotel Saskatchewan, 2125 Victoria Avenue, Regina, Saskatchewan S4P OS3, tel (306) 522–7691, toll free 1–800–667–5828.
Solid, historic, with a vintage ambience to match its place as the city's original grand hotel.

Journey's End, 3221 E Eastgate Drive, Regina, Saskatchewan S4Z 1A4, tel (306) 789–5522, toll free 1–800–668–4200.
A good choice for low budget, and 'rubber tire' travelers, and worth the patronage for the name alone.

Ramada Renaissance, 1919 Saskatchewan Drive, Regina, Saskatchewan S4P 4H2, tel (306) 525–5255, toll free 1–800–268–8998.
Indoor pool, whirlpool and a three-story waterslide complex. Conveniently located near the Galleria shopping mall.

Regina Inn, 1975 Broad Street, Regina, Saskatchewan S4P 1Y2, tel (306) 525–6767, toll free 1–800–667–8162.
First-class downtown hotel with an outdoor whirlpool.

SASKATOON
Delta Bessborough, 601 Spadina Crescent E, Saskatoon, Saskatchewan S7K 3G8, tel (306) 244–5521, toll free 1–800–268–1133.
The imposing riverside chateau hotel, a kind of palace on the plains with five acres of gardens, is a major feature of the small city's skyline.

The House of Aird, 1005 Aird Street, Saskatoon Saskatchewan S7N 0S9, tel (306) 668–6198.
This two-story 'character home' with only three rooms has the personal touch of a bed and breakfast. Guests get a continental breakfast with home baking and jams.

King George Hotel, 157–2 Avenue N, Saskatoon, Saskatchewan S7N 0S6, tel (306) 244–6133, toll free 1–800–667–1234.
An entertainment center as well as a hotel, with bowling alley, karaoke and night club.

Ramada Renaissance, 405–20 Street E, Saskatoon, Saskatchewan S7K 6X6, tel (306) 665–3322, toll free 1–800–268–9889.
The best rooms in this new hotel have river views. The hotel features two water slides in the recreation complex.

Saskatoon Inn, 2002 Airport Drive, Saskatoon, Saskatchewan S7L 6M4, tel. (306) 242–1440, toll free 1–800–667–8789.
Airport hotel with tropical plants in central courtyard (a soothing sight in Prairie winters) and nightly entertainment.

Senator Hotel, 243–21 Street E, Saskatoon, Saskatchewan S7K 0B7, tel (306) 244–6141.
This is an older, 'European'-style hotel in the heart of the city, with reasonable rates.

Sheraton-Cavalier, 612 Spadina Crescent E, Saskatoon, Saskatchewan S7K 3G9, tel (306) 652–6770, toll free 1–800–325–3535.
Full service, deluxe hotel includes swimming pool, sauna and two indoor waterslides.

Manitoba

WINNIPEG
Assiniboine Gordon Inn on the Park, 1975 Portage Avenue, Winnipeg, MB R3J 0J9, tel (204) 888–4806.
Budget accommodation with all standard facilities, located some distance from downtown, not far from the airport and Winnipeg's large Assiniboine Park.

The Charterhouse Hotel, 330 York Avenue, Winnipeg, MB R3C 0N9, tel (204) 942–0101, toll free 1–800–782–0175.
An affordable, centrally located motor inn, but with all services, including a good dining room.

Fort Garry, 222 Broadway, Winnipeg, MB R3C OR3, tel (204) 942–8251 or 1–800–665–8088.
This venerable, railway chateaux-type hotel across the street from the VIA Rail station is part of Winnipeg's history.

The Norwood Hotel, 122 Marion Street, Winnipeg, MB R2H OT1, tel (204) 233–4475.
Located across the River in St Boniface, the hotel is in an old brick building, refurbished and with a new wing added. Moderately priced coffee shop with excellent cuisine.

Sheraton Winnipeg, 161 Donald Street, Winnipeg, MB R3C 1M3, tel (204) 942–5300 or 1–800–325–3535.
Overlooking Canada's widest and windiest corner, the famous Portage and Main intersection. Good views down Portage from the upper floors. One of Winnipeg's newest quality hotels.

Westin Hotel, 2 Lombard Place, Winnipeg, MB R3B OY3, tel (204) 957–1350 or 1–800–228–3000.
One of the city's top hotels, with dinner theater and indoor swimming pool.

Winnipeg Marlborough, 331 Smith Street, Winnipeg, MB R3B 2G9, tel (204) 942–6411, toll free 1–800–667–7666.
An old-time, four-star hotel with plenty of character in a beautiful heritage building (1912) that has been renovated and upgraded.

For budget accommodation in private homes, write the non-government run **Bed & Breakfast of Manitoba**, 533 Sprague Street, Winnipeg, Manitoba MB R3G 1J9, tel (204) 783–9797.

Ontario

OTTAWA
Australis Guest House, 35 Marlborough Avenue, Ottawa, Ontario K1N 8E6, tel (613) 235–8461.
Oldest established B&B in downtown Ottawa area. Beautiful period house including unique eight foot high stained-glass window. Recommended by *Newsweek*.

Chateau Laurier Hotel, 1 Rideau Street, Ottawa, Ontario K1N 8S7, tel (613) 232–6411.
Next to the Parliament buildings, and one of the most interesting and ornate of the great railway inns.

Minto Place Suite Hotel, 433 Laurier Avenue W, Ottawa, Ontario K1R 7Y1, tel (613) 232–2200.
This reputable apartment hotel which caters to civil servants accommodates long stayers.

Ottawa Hilton (formerly the Four Seasons), 150 Albert Street, Ottawa, Ontario K1P 5G2, tel (613) 238–1500.
This hotel has long been popular with Ottawa mandarins on expense accounts.

Westin Hotel, 11 Colonel By Dr, Ottawa, Ontario K1N 9H4, tel (613) 560–7000.
This hotel connected to the Rideau Center has the chain's reliable standards. Good exercise facilities for the conscientious business traveler.

Toronto
Accommodation Toronto, 2560 Matheson Boulevard E, Ste 220, Mississauga, Ontario L4W 4Y9, tel (416) 629–3800, fax (416) 629–0035 is a free hotel reservations service.
Operated by the **Hotel Association of Metropolitan Toronto**, it represents 120 properties, from economical to luxury.

Econo-Lodging Services, 101 Nymark Avenue, Willowdale, Ontario M2J 2H1, tel (416) 494–0541, fax (416) 493–1629 is also a free reservation service.
It offers moderate and deluxe hotels, furnished apartments and tourist homes.

Four Seasons Hotel, 21 Avenue Road, Toronto, Ontario M5R 2G1, tel (416) 964–0411.
One of Toronto's leading hotels, located in trendy Yorkville, where fashionable locals go for shopping and power lunching.

Royal York, 100 Front Street W, Toronto, Ontario M5J 1E3, tel (416) 368–2511.
The largest of the railway hotels—in fact, at 1,600 rooms, this great stone place claims to be the largest hotel in the British Commonwealth. A little faded perhaps but still the grand old lady of Toronto inns.

Sheraton Center Hotel & Towers, 123 Queen Street W, Toronto, Ontario M5H 2M9, tel (416) 361–1000.
Large, fully-serviced and centrally located, the Sheraton is almost a city unto itself. Conveniently connected to Toronto's Underground City.

Sheraton Toronto East Hotel & Towers, 2035 Kennedy Road, Scarborough, Ontario M1T 3G2, tel (416) 299–1500.
The best bet for those doing business in this eastern suburb. Located near one of Toronto's new Chinese districts, this is popular with business travelers and tourists from Asia.

The Sutton Place Grande Hotel Le Meridien Toronto, 955 Bay Street Toronto, Ontario M5S 2A2, tel (416) 924–9221.
A long name for a relatively small (208 room, 72 suite) place. Formerly the Sutton Place Kempinski, the hotel merges the elegance of old Europe with modern amenities. Tastefully decorated with original oil paintings, hardwood floors, crystal chandeliers and antiques.

The Toronto Bed and Breakfast Inn, Box 269, 253 College Street, Toronto, Ontario M5T 1R5, tel (416) 588–8800 or 961–3676, fax (416) 5964–1756.
Represents B&Bs in private homes in Metro Toronto, Ottawa, Kingston and Niagara Falls.

Westin Harbor Castle, 1 Harbor Square, Toronto, Ontario M5J 1A6, tel (416) 869–1600.
Its big, big twin towers overlook the harbor and lake, with fine views from the upper floors and the rooftop revolving restaurant, the 36th-story Lighthouse.

Quebec

MONTREAL
L'Auberge de La Fontaine, 1301 Rachel E, Montreal, Quebec H2J 2K1, tel (514) 597–0166.
One of Montreal's most charming little inns. An award winner, recommended by some of the leading newspapers in the US.

The Four Seasons (or, as they say here, Les Quatre Saisons), 1050 Sherbrooke Ouest, Montreal, Quebec. H3A 2R6, tel (514) 284–1110, toll free 1–800–268–6282.
A very elegant member of the deluxe Canadian hotel chain. Fine dining, heated outdoor pool and a full fitness center.

Hospitality Montreal Relay, 3977 Laval Avenue, Montreal, Quebec H2W 2H9, tel (514) 287–9635 is a booking agency for bed and breakfasts or furnished apartments in downtown Montreal.

Hôtel La Résidence du Voyageur, 847 Sherbrooke E, Montreal, Quebec H2L 1K6, tel (514) 527–9515.
Near Old Montreal, the Latin Quarter and entertainment districts, this moderately priced hotel is good value. Multi-lingual staff and free morning coffee and biscuits.

Hôtel Terrasse Royale, 522 Côte-des-Neiges, Montreal, Quebec H3T 1Y1, tel (514)514 739-6391.
Apartment hotel for longer stay (weekly or monthly rates), fully equipped kitchens.

Le Méridien Montréal, 4 Place Des Jardins, Montreal, Quebec H5B 1E5, tel (514) 285–1450.
Conveniently located near the business district (with direct access to the Montreal Convention Center) and the lively St Catherine's nightlife area. Both hotel and restaurant maintain that elegant French chain's high standards.

The Queen Elizabeth (La Reine Elizabeth), 900 Rene Levesque Boulevard, Montreal, Quebec H3B 4A5, tel (514) 861–3511, toll free 1–800–268–9420.
Montreal's version of the railway hotel, and despite its offensive (to Quebecoise) name, is part of city life with its connection to the central railway station and the subway. The excellent Beaver Club is a well-known local restaurant recalling a group of powerful 19th-century fur merchants.

Ritz-Carlton Kempinski, 1228 Sherbrooke Ouest, Montreal, Quebec H3G 1H6, tel (514) 842–4212, toll free 1–800–363–0366.
Five stars, and the height of Montreal elegance.

Welcome Bed & Breakfast, 3950 Laval Avenue, Montreal Quebec H2W 2J2, tel (514) 844–5897
Books accommodation in downtown, French Quarter and Sherbrooke. Bicycle rental available.

QUEBEC CITY

Château Frontenac, 1 Rue des Carrières, Quebec City, Quebec G1R 5J5, tel (418) 692–3861.
The most palatial, and certainly the most dramatically set, of the chateau hotels, the Frontenac sits like a Gothic castle overlooking the St Lawrence River, an impressive sight winter or summer.

Hôtel le Cottage, 3135 Chemin Saint-Louis Sainte-Foy, Quebec G1W 1R9, tel (418) 653–4941.
An economical hotel near old Quebec, with free shuttle service to the old city, 'family' restaurant and heated pool.

There are three commendable hotels within walking distance of the Old City:
Hilton Québec, 3 Place Québec, Quebec City, Quebec G1R 4X3, tel (418) 647–2411, toll free 1–800–445–8667.
Hilton's reliable service and standards, with a good location connected to the convention center.

Loews Le Concorde, 1225 Place Montcalm, Quebec City, Quebec G1R 4W6, tel (418) 647–2222.
Views of the Battlefield Park and the city, especially from the 28th-floor revolving restaurant.

Radisson Auberge des Gouverneurs, 690 Boulevard René-Levesque, Quebec City, Quebec G1R 5A8, tel (418) 647–1717.
Renovated, with indoor and outdoor pools.

Réservation Québec is a free booking service for all types of accommodation, including hotels, bed and breakfasts, country houses or full board farm lodging. Free phone 1–800–363–7372, in Montreal 1–800–878–1000 .

New Brunswick

FREDERICTON

Sheraton Inn Fredericton, 225 Woodstock Road, Fredericton, NB E3B 2H8, tel (506) 457–7000.
Overlooking the Saint John River, with an indoor and outdoor pools, sauna and whirlpools. The lounge has a pleasant view. Nice new Sheraton, set right on the river.

Lord Beaverbrook Hotel, 659 Queen Street PO Box 545, Fredericton, NB E3B 4A6, (506) 455–3371.
Centrally located, with in-house art gallery, the hotel does interesting theme packages.

MONCTON
Hotel Beausejour, 650 Main Street, Moncton NB E1C 1E6, tel (506) 854–4344, toll free 1–800–441–1414.
A Canadian Pacific Hotel & Resorts city-center hotel with a big pool and fine dining.

SAINT JOHN
Courtney Bay Inn-City Center, 350 Haymarket Square, Saint John, NB E2L 3P1, tel (506) 657–3610, toll free 1–800–565–7666.
Heated outdoor pool.

Delta Brunswick Inn, 39 King Street, Saint John, NB E2L 4W3, tel (506) 648–1981, toll free 1–800–268–1133.
A new hotel on Market Square, joined by a walkway to Market Square. With full feature Health Club and a Children's Creative and Activity Center

The Parkerhouse Inn, 71 Sydney Street, Saint John, New Brunswick, E2L 2L5, tel (506) 652–5054.
This is a comfortable four-star inn, furnished in a pleasant, Victorian style.

Saint John Hilton, One Market Square, Saint John, NB E2L 4Z6, tel (506) 693–8484.
On the waterfront, part of Market Square with good views of the harbor. Pleasantly furnished with a Brigantine lounge and Turn of the Tide restaurant serving maritime cuisine.

Nova Scotia

HALIFAX
Chateau Halifax, 1990 Barrington Street, Halifax, NS B3J 1P2, tel (902) 425–6700.
A CP hotel, though not in the grand chateau tradition. Conveniently located as part of the Scotia Square commercial complex.

The Delta Barrington, 1875 Barrington, Halifax, NS B3J 3L6, tel (902) 429–7410.
Part of old Halifax, in the shopping and convention complex in the reconstructed historic city block.

Halifax Sheraton, 1919 Upper Water Street, Halifax, NS B3J 3J5, tel (902) 421–1700, toll free 1–800–325–3535.
You can't get much closer to the waterfront than this very elegant hotel which has docking space for visiting yachts.

Holiday Inn Halifax Center, 1980 Robie Street, Halifax, NS B3H 3G5, tel (902) 423–1161, toll free 1–800–465–4329.
Reliable, economical accommodation with seniors discounts, exercise equipment, pool, whirlpool, sauna and sun deck.

Inn on the Lake, Box 29 Waverley, NS, B0N 2S0, tel (902) 861–3480.
A pleasant little 45-room inn half way between the airport and the city. Most rooms have balconies.

Ramada Renaissance, 240 Brownlow Ave, Dartmouth, NS B3B 1X6, tel (902) 468–8888.
This is a family oriented hotel with indoor waterslide and other recreational facilities, in Dartmouth, across the harbor from Halifax.

Check In is a computerized reservation and information service representing more than 95 per cent of available rooms in the province. In Canada, call 1–800–565–0000 and in the continental US, 1–800–341–6096.

Prince Edward Island

CHARLOTTETOWN
The Charlottetown Hotel, A Rodd Classic Hotel. Box 159, Charlottetown, PEI C1A 7K4, tel (902) 894–7371.
In downtown Charlottetown, noted for its indoor, tropical pool and lounge with live entertainment.

Dundee Arms Motel and Inn, 200 Pownal Street, Charlottetown, PEI C1A 3W8, tel (902) 892–2496.
A historic mansion in a residential area furnished with antiques, surrounded by modern motel units. The Colonial Dining Room is excellent.

The Inn on the Hill, Box 1720, 150 Euston Street, Charlottetown, PEI C1A 1W5, tel (902) 894–8572.
At University and Euston, near shopping and theaters.

The Kirkwood Motor Hotel, 455 University Avenue, Charlottetown PEI C1A 44N8, tel (902) 892–4206.
A small and personal motor hotel with indoor pool and outdoor patio.

Prince Edward Hotel and Convention Center, 18 Queen Street, Charlottetown PEI C1A 8B9, tel (902) 566–2222.
A Canadian Pacific Hotels and Resort hotel, with full recreational facilities, harborside pub and harbor cruises.

Newfoundland

St John's

The Battery Hotel, 100 Signal Hill Road, St John's, Newfoundland A1A 1B3, tel (709) 576–0040, toll free 1–800–563–8181.
An older hotel, somewhat reminiscent of an airplane hangar and a little removed from the city center, but well worth it for the harbor-side rooms. Scenic vistas of the city from the lounge and restaurant.

Best Western Travellers Inn, 199 Kenmount Road, St John's, Newfoundland A1B 3P9, tel (709) 722–5540, toll free 1–800–528–1234.
Good, comfortable accommodation. Dining room, lounge and night club.

Captain's Quarters Hotel,19 Merrymaking Road, St John's, Newfoundland A1C 6H4, tel (709) 576–7173/7468.
A small 20-room budget hotel near the downtown area.

Hotel Newfoundland, Box 5637 Cavendish Square, St John's, Newfoundland A1C 5W8, tel (709) 726–4980, toll free 1–800–441–1414.
A Canadian Pacific property and the city's major hotel, complete with pool, sauna and squash courts.

The Olde Inn, 157 LeMarchant Road, St John's, Newfoundland A1C 2H4, tel (709) 722–1171.
This 15 room budget hotel has laundry facilities, shared bathrooms.

Radisson Plaza Hotel & Convention Center, 120 New Gower Street, St John's, Newfoundland A1C 1J3, tel (709) 739–6404.
The conventioneers' choice, with indoor pool, sauna, whirlpool, a piano bar, with corporate and senior's rates.

Yukon

WHITEHORSE

Capital Hotel, 103 Main Street, Whitehorse, Yukon Y1A 2A7, tel (403) 667–2565.
A small hotel decorated with Goldrush decor, where live music in the lounge goes on until 2 am.

Edgewater Hotel, 101 Main Street, Whitehorse, Yukon Y1A 2A7, tel (403) 667–2572.
Good accommodation, downtown, adjacent to the Yukon River, with the Gallery Lounge and Cellar dining room.

Fort Yukon Hotel, 2163–2 Avenue, Whitehorse, Yukon Y1A 2A7, tel (403) 667–2595).
Open all year round, with RV (recreational vehicle) sites May to October. Private bath, public showers, cafe and lounge.

High Country Inn, 4051–4 Avenue, Whitehorse, Yukon Y1A 1H1 tel (403) 667–4471.
Northern hospitality in comfortable and affordable lodging, totally renovated. Some suites have kitchenettes.

DAWSON CITY

Downtown Hotel, 2nd Avenue and Queen Street, Box 780, Dawson City, Yukon Y0B 1G0, tel (403) 993–5346.
A modern, 60-room hotel with all of the facilities found in the south.

Gold Nugget Motel, 5th Avenue and Dugas Street, Box 86, Dawson City, Yukon Y0B 1G0, tel (403) 993–5445.
Open 24 hours, June 1 to early September.

Midnight Sun Hotel, 3rd Avenue and Queen Street, Box 840, Dawson City, Yukon Y0B 1G0, tel (403) 993–5495.
Open May to September. In the heart of the historic city. Coffee shop, dining room, cocktail lounge, pub and Gertie's Gourmet Sandwich Bar.

Northern Network of Bed & Breakfasts, Box 954–T, Dawson City, Yukon, Y0B 1G0, tel (403) 993–5649. This association represents more than 80 places in Northwest Territories, Yukon, BC and Alaska. Write for a free brochure.

Triple 'J' Hotel, 5th Avenue and Queen Street, Box 359, Dawson City, Yukon Y0B 1G0, tel (403) 993–5323.
Rooms, executive suites and cabins with kitchenette. Next door to Diamond Tooth Gerties, so easy access to the nightlife.

White Ram Manor Bed & Breakfast, 7th Avenue & Harper Street, Box 302, Dawson City, Yukon Y0B 1G0, tel (403) 993–5772.
This year-round hotel, within walking distance to most attractions, has hot tub, barbecue and picnic area

Northwest Territories

YELLOWKNIFE
Captain Ron's Bed & Breakfast, 8 Lessard Drive, Yellowknife, NWT X1A 2G5, tel (403) 873–3746.
On the shores of Great Slave Lake in the heart of the picturesque Old Town, a short walk from city center.

The Executive, Box 1960 Yellowknife, NWT X1A 2P5, tel (403) 920-5710.
Furnished suites for long stayers, available by day, week or month.

Explorer Hotel, Postal Service 7000, Yellowknife, NWT X1A 2R3, tel (403) 873–3531. Toll free 1–800–661–0892.
The best in town. Get a room with a view over the museum set on the lake. Good restaurant, by northern standards.

Yellowknife Inn, Box 490, Yellowknife, NWT X1A 2N4, tel (403) 873–2601.
In the heart of town, with full facilities. Complimentary Continental breakfasts.

Useful Addresses

For further detailed information on each province, you can write or visit the following tourist offices who will gladly answer your questions and supply you with local timetables, maps etc.

■ ALBERTA
Alberta Economic Development and Tourism, PO Box 2500, Edmonton, Alberta, Canada T5J 2Z4, tel (403) 427-4321, toll free 1–800–661-8888.

■ BRITISH COLUMBIA
Tourism British Columbia, Parliament Buildings, Victoria, British Columbia, Canada V8V 1X4, tel (604) 387-1642, toll free 1–800–663-6000.

■ MANITOBA
Travel Manitoba, Dept 3083, 7th Floor, 155 Carlton Street, Winnipeg, Manitoba, Canada R3C 3H8, tel (204) 942–2535, toll free 1–800–665-0040.

■ NEW BRUNSWICK
Tourism New Brunswick, PO Box 12345, Fredericton, New Brunswick, Canada E3B 5C3, tel (506) 453-2377, toll free 1–800–561-0123.

■ NEWFOUNDLAND AND LABRADOR
Department of Development and Tourism, PO Box 8730, St John's, Newfoundland, Canada A1C 5R8, tel (709) 729-2830, toll free 1–800–563-6353.

■ NORTHWEST TERRITORIES
TravelArctic, Yellowknife, Northwest Territories, Canada X1A 2L9, tel (403) 873-7200, 1–800–661-0788.

■ NOVA SCOTIA
Department of Tourism, PO Box 456, Halifax, Nova Scotia, Canada B3J 2R5, tel (902) 424–4709, toll free US 1–800–341-6096, Canada 1–800–565–0000.

■ ONTARIO
Travel Ontario, Queen's Park, Toronto, Ontario, Canada M7A 2E5, tel (416) 965-4008, toll free 1–800–ONTARIO–668–2746.

■ PRINCE EDWARD ISLAND
Department of Tourism and Parks, Visitor Services Division, PO Box 940, Charlottetown, Prince Edward Island, Canada C1A 7M5, tel (902) 368-4444, toll free 1–800–565-0267.

■ QUEBEC
Tourisme Québec, PO Box 20 000, Québec (Quebec), Canada G1K 7X2, tel (514) 873-2015 from Montreal, 1–800–363-7777.

■ SASKATCHEWAN
Tourism Saskatchewan, 1919 Saskatchewan Drive, Regina, Saskatchewan, Canada S4P 3V7, tel (306) 787-2300, toll free 1–800–667-7191.

■ YUKON
Tourism Yukon, PO Box 2703, Whitehorse, Yukon, Canada Y1A 2C6, tel (403) 667-5340.

Recommended Reading

Canadians have been writing fiction set in their country since Susanna Moodie's *Roughing it in the Bush* (1852), a popular account of a gentle English woman's encounter with the harsh Canadian wilderness. Canada's raw and untamed setting thenceforth became a common theme in the country's literature, though it has been balanced by satirists such as Thomas Chandler Haliburton and his *Sam Slick; the Clockmaker* (1836) and, later, Stephen Leacock. Leacock's more than 60 books, including the comic *Sunshine Sketches of a Little Town* (1912) and *Arcadian Adventures with the Idle Rich* (1914), made him the English-speaking world's best-known humorist in the early part of the century.

Hugh MacLennan, a later novelist whose work provides a sense of place, was the first major writer in English to portray Canada's national character. His internationally popular *Two Solitudes* (1945) dealt with the profound differences and tensions between the French and English in Montreal. Other typically Canadian themes include the rapid transition of the 20th century in small communities and the contrast between Canadian and American societies.

More recently, Mordecai Richler, novelist and critic of Canadian manners and society, depicted life in Montreal in a sharp, witty style. *The Apprenticeship of Duddy Kravitz* (1959), the profile of a brash Montreal Jewish boy-entrepreneur set along Montreal's bustling, ethnic Main Street, was made into a popular movie. More recent works by Richler include novels *St Urbain's Horseman* (1971) and *Joshua Then and Now* (1980), and essays and journalistic pieces in *Shoveling Trouble* (1972), *Notes on an Endangered Species* (1974) and *Home Sweet Home: My Canadian Album* (1983).

W O Mitchell's *Who Has Seen the Wind*, a touching account of growing up on the Prairies, is a Canadian classic, as are Margaret Laurence's *The Stone Angel* (1964), set in the fictional Manitoba town Manawaka, and *The Fire Dwellers* (1969), set in Vancouver. Canada's history has been well chronicled by both learned and popular writers. Good basic works available in paperback are the recently revised *Short History of Canada* by Desmond Morton and Kenneth McNaught's *A History of Canada*.

Pierre Berton is the best known and most prolific chronicler of popular Canadian history. He has produced dozens of books of which the railway histories, *The National Dream* (1970) and *The Last Spike* (1971), and *Klondike: The Last Great Gold Rush*, the story of the north, are especially compelling. Other Berton works include: *My Country* (1976) and *The Wild Frontier* (1978), sketches of characters and events; *Hollywood's Canada* (1975) looking at how the California movie factories misrepresent Canada; and *The Promised Land* (1984) a history of the settlement of the west. In *Arctic Grail* (1988), he turned his attention to the Canadian north and its unique problems. Journalist and author Peter Newman is fascinated by Canada's business elite. His popular two-volume *The Canadian Establishment* (1975, 1981) looks at the lives of those who wield financial power in both the east and west. *Sometimes a Great Nation* (1988), is a collection of his essays from the mid 70s to the present dealing with all things Canadian. Newman has also completed a three-volume history of the Hudson's Bay Company, *Company of Adventurers* (1985), *Caesar's of the Wilderness* (1987) and *Merchant Princes* (1991).

Barry Broadfoot, a former newspaper reporter, tapes hundreds of interviews with ordinary Canadians to create social portraits of small periods of history. His books include *The Pioneer Years: 1895–1914*, memories of settlers who opened the west, *Ten Lost Years: 1929–1939* about the Depression, and *Six War Years: 1939–1945*. In his current work, *Next Year Country* (1988), he looks at the lives of Prairie farmers and their questionable future. Canada's most widely read author today is perhaps controversial Farley Mowat (or, as his detractors call him, Hardly Know-it), with more than 25 books published in 40 countries. Mowat, who espouses the causes of native peoples and the environment, captures the spirit of Canada's remote regions. Among his best known works are *The Rock Within the Sea* (1968), *The Boat Who Wouldn't Float* (1969) and *A Whale For the Killing* (1972), all dealing with the lives of his Newfoundland neighbors. *Sea of Slaughter* (1984) records the destruction of North Atlantic marine species. On a lighter note, *Back to Black* (1987), a collection of comic sketches by popular CBC radio host Arthur Black, offers a whimsical insight into this odd country. Another popular CBC Radio show host, Peter Gzowski of the long-running Morningside program, presents amusing vignettes of Canadian life in *Canadian Living* (1993).

American Andrew Malcolm, who was *New York Times* bureau chief for Canada for four years, visited every province and territory. His work, *The Canadians*, provides an informed, lively, and sometimes tough perspective on Canada, the US, and the differences between them. British travel writer Stephen Brook crossed Canada from sea to shining sea by plane, train and bus to produce *Maple Leaf Rag* (1987). His highly personal, sometimes humerous account of every region and most cities suffers from what Canadians would see as British prissiness and superciliousness in books.

With so much space, it is perhaps natural that Canadian authors produce 'road books'. Recent efforts include George Galt's *Whistlestop*, an account of rail travel across Canada, well written in parts, but the author seems intimidated by ordinary, earthy Canadians. Better is *Last Train to Toronto, a Canadian Rail Odyssey* (1992). This sympathetic work by American author Terry Pindell looks at Canada's declining rail system, and the people who depended on it. Kildare Dobbs took to the road by bus, concentrating on the cities, producing the amusing and insightful *Ribbon of Highway* (1992). Stuart Maclean's *Welcome Home* (1993) looks at Canadian small towns. The award-winning *Occupied Canada* by Robert Hunter and Robert Calihoo is a unique, and somewhat sobering, look at Canada from the native Indians perspective. Mordechai Richler's *O God O Canada* concern's Quebec and its relationship. Canada. *Stranger Music* is a selection of poems and songs by Leonard Cohen, one of Canada's best known authors and song writers.

On a practical level, those taking the train should pack Bill Coo's excellent *Scenic Guide to Western Canada* and *Scenic Guide to Central and Atlantic Canada*, mile by mile guides to 43,700 kilometers (12,600 miles) of the country's rail journeys.

Index

Abbey of St-Benoit-du-Lac 204, 210
Acadia (see also Nova Scotia) 22, 27, 231
Acadian Pioneer Village, PEI 220
Acadians 27, 215, 219, 226, 231, 234
Adventure 46–55
Agawa Canyon, Ontario 181, 182
Alert Bay, BC 93
Amundsen, Roald 141
Annapolis Royal, NS 22, 215, 234
Annapolis Valley, NS 243, 245
Anne of Green Gables 220, 223
L'Anse aux Meadows, Nfld 21, 243
arctic 41
Arctic Circle, NWT 146
Argentia, Nfld 250
Art Gallery of Ontario, Toronto 166
Athabasca Valley, Alta 107
Atlantic Ocean 11
Avalon Wilderness Area, Nfld 250–1
Avenue LaPorte, Quebec City 201

Baffin Island, NWT 143
Baie St Paul, Quebec 207
Baker Lake, NWT 147
Basilica of St John the Baptist,
   St John's, Nfld 259
Battle at Batoche 34
Bay Bulls, Nfld 255
Bay of Fundy, Saint John, NB
   .... 22, 228, 229, 234
Bay Street, Toronto, Ontario 162
beaches area, Toronto, Ontario 158
Beaupre/Charlevoix, Quebec 207
Beaver Lake, Quebec 191
Beaverbrook Art Gallery, Fredericton,NB
   228
Beechey Island, NWT 146
Belfast, PEI 226
Bering Strait 21
Bird Islands, Nfld 258
Black Creek Pioneer Village, Toronto,
   Ontario 166
Bloor Street, Toronto, Ontario 161
Bluenose ship 238
Bonanza Creek, Yukon 153

Bonaventure Island, Quebec 214
Boyce Farmer's Market, Fredericton, NB . 229
Britain/the British
   26, 38, 215, 223, 233, 235,247, 254
British Columbia 67–94
British Columbia Hall of Fishes 77
British North America 235
Brockton Point Lighthouse, Vancouver 76
Bromont, Quebec 204
Brule, Etienne 158
By, Lieutenant Colonel John 170
Bylot Island, NWT 145
Bylot Island Bird Sanctuary, NWT 146
Byward Market, Ottawa, Ontario 174

Cabin of Sam Mc Gee 151
Cabot, John 22, 249
Cabot Tower, St John's, Nfld 254
Calgary, Alta 109–11
Calgary Stampede 112, 266
Calgary Tower 111
Cambridge Bay, NWT 141
Campobello Island, NB 233
Canada Place, Vancouver, BC 77–8
Canada's Sports Hall of Fame,
   Toronto, Ontario 162
Canada's Wonderland, Toronto, Ontario 167
Canadian Cuisine 268–72
Canadian National Exhibition Grounds,
   Toronto, Ontario 162
Canadian National Railway 109
Canadian National Tower, Toronto, Ontario
   162
Canadian Opera Company 167
Canadian Pacific Railway 35, 212
Canadian Shield 34, 155
Canadiana Village, Quebec 204
Cap-Egmont, PEI 222
Cap Sable Island, NS 243
Cap Traverse, PEI 224
Cape Breton Island, NS 241–43
Cape Columbia, NWT 41, 145
Cape Dorset, NWT 41, 145
Cape Spear, Nfld 41, 241
Cape Wolfe, PEI 220

Capilano Trading Post, BC 42
Capital City Recreation Park, Edmonton,
    Alta 110
Carberry Desert, Manitoba 127
Carcross, Yukon 153
Cariboo Chilcotin, BC 42
Cartier, Jacques 22, 219
Casa Loma, Ontario 161
Castle-Craigdarroch Castle, Victoria, BC .. 86
Cathedral of St John the Baptist, St John's,
    Nfld 251
Cathedral of the Holy Trinity, Quebec City ..
    199
Celidh Trail, Cape Breton, NS 241
Centre Culturel Franco-Manitobain, St Boni-
    face, Manitoba 126
Center for the Performing Arts, Calgary,
    Alta 111
Center Stage, Toronto, Ontario 162
Champlain, Samuel de 22, 183, 191, 226
Charlottetown, PEI 219
Chateau de Ramesay, Montreal, Quebec . 190
Chemainus, Vancouver Island, BC 89
Chesterfield Inlet, NWT 151
Chicoutimi, Quebec 209
Chilkoot Trail, Yukon 153
Chinatown
    Toronto 158–9
    Vancouver 68
Chinatown Gate, Edmonton, Alta 109
Christ Church Cathedral, Fredericton,NB
    229
Church Point, NS 243
Churchill, Manitoba 127, 131
Citadel, Quebec City 199
Citadel Fortress, Halifax, NS 235
City Hall, Toronto 159
Civic Centre, Calgary, Alta 111
Clear Lake, Manitoba 127
Clinton, BC 96
Cochrane, Ontario 182
Colonial Building, St John's, Nfld 250
Columbia Icefield, Alta 106
Confederation 33, 220, 223

Confederation Center of the Arts, Charlotte .
    town, PEI 220
Confederation Square, Ottawa, Ontario .. 170
Constitution Act of 1982 38
Convention Centre, Edmonton, Alta 109
Cook, James 34
Coombs, Vancouver Island, BC 92
Coppermine River, NWT 142
Coral Harbor, Southampton Island, NWT147
Cordillera (mountain range) 42, 43
Cornwallis Island, NWT 146
coureurs de bois 122
Courtenay, Vancouver Island, BC 92
Cowichan Bay, Vancouver island, BC 89
Craigflower Manor, Victoria, BC 86
Cypress Bowl, BC 80
Cypress Hills, Alta 114

Dartmouth, Halifax, NS 238
Dawson City, Yukon 41
Deer Island, NB 233
Delkatia Wildlife Sanctuary, Masset, BC ... 97
Dempster Highway, NWT and Yukon 141
Depression, the 38
Devonian Gardens, Calgary, Alta 109
Dewy Soper Bird Sanctuary, NWT 145
Diamond Tooth Gertie's Gambling Hall,
    Yukon 153
Digby, NS 245
Dinosaur Trail, Alta 114
Domed Stadium, Toronto 163
Dresden, Ontario 176
Drumheller, Alta 114
Dufferin Terrace, Quebec City 200

East Point Lighthouse, PEI 224
Eastern Townships, Quebec 204–6
Eaton's Center, Toronto 159
Edmonton, Alta 107–9, 140
Eldorado Creek, Yukon 153
Ellesmere Island, NWT 42, 146
Ericson, Leif 21, 249
Exchange District, Winnipeg, Manitoba .. 124

Factory Theater, Toronto 167
Fairmont Hot Springs Resort, BC 98
Fairview Cemetery, Halifax, NS 238
Fédération de Libération de Québec ....
    (FLQ) 39, 185
Food, see Canadian Cuisine
Fort Conger, NWT 147
Fort Edmonton Park 108
Fort George, Ontario 176
Fort Herschmer, Dawson City, Yukon 153
Fort Langley, BC 83
Fort Needham, Halifax, NS 238
Fort Rodd Hill National Historic Park.......88
Fort Steele, BC..................98
Franklin, Sir John 146
Franklin District, NWT 143–7
Fraser River 83
Fraser Valley 83
Fredericton, NB 228–9
Free Meeting House, Moncton, NB 229
French Pavilion, Quebec 194
Frobisher, Sir Martin 143
Fur trade 39

Galerie d'Art, Moncton, NB 231
Gaspé 210–14
Gastown, BC..................72–3
Gibbet Hill, St John's, Nfld 254
Glass Castle, Vancouver Island, BC 89
Golden Boy Statue, Winnipeg, Manitoba 124
Government House, Regina, Sask..........174
Granby, Quebec 204
Grand Banks, Nfld 21
Grand Manan, NB 233
Grand Pelerin, Quebec 211
Granville Island, Vancouver, BC 74
Great Clay Belt, Ontario 182
Great Lakes, Ontario 41
Great Slave Lake, NWT 142
Grey Mountain, Whitehorse, Yukon 151
Grise Fjord, NWT 146
Grouse Mountain, BC..................78, 79
Halifax, NS 33, 234–8
Halifax Explosion 238–9
Harbour Castle Hotel, Toronto..............163

Harborfront, Toronto 163
Hazelton Avenue, Toronto 161
Head-Smashed-In Buffalo Jump, Alta 114
Heritage Park, Calgary, Alta 111
Hidden Lake, Yukon 151
High Arctic Islands, NWT 143
High Level Bridge, Edmonton, Alta 108
Historic Properties, Halifax, NS 235
Horton River, NWT 141
Hotels 274-91
Hudson Bay 25, 43, 129
Hull, Quebec 175
Ile d'Orleans, Quebec 201
Ile Notre Dame, Montreal, Quebec..........194
The Interior, BC 93–99
Iqaluit (formerly Frobisher Bay), NWT ...143

James Bay, NWT 43
Jasper, Alta 106

Kananaskis resort area, Alta 107
Keewatin District, NWT 147
Kenora, Ontario 179
Kensington, PEI 223
Kensington Market, Toronto 158
Kent House, Quebec City 199
Kimberley , BC 99
King, William Lyon Mackenzie 38, 41
King Square, Saint John, NB 230
Kings Landing Historical Settlement, NB
   228–9
Kingston, Ontario 178–9
Kingston Mills, Ontario 178
Kipling, Rudyard 85
Kitchener-Waterloo, Ontario 176
Klondike, Yukon 154
Klondike Days, Edmonton, Alta 108, 259
Klondike River, Yukon 152

La Have River, NS 243
La Malbaie, Quebec 207
La Ronde, Montreal, Quebec 195
Labrador 209, 247
Lac la Hache, BC 96
Lac Mercier, Quebec 204

Lac-Massawippi, Quebec 206
Lachine Rapids, Montreal, Quebec 195
Lake Beauvert, Alta 106
Lake Erie, Ontario 179
Lake Hazen, NWT 146
Lake Huron, Ontario 179
Lake Louise, Alta 106, 249
Lake Minnewanka, Banff, Alta 106
Lake of the Woods, Ontario 179
Lake Okanagan, BC 98
Lake Okanagan Resort, BC 98
Lake Ontario 158
Lake Simcoe, Ontario 180
Lake Superior, Ontario 25, 180
Lake Winnipeg, Manitoba 126
Lanaudiere Region, Quebec 204
Last Mountain Lake, Sask 121
Laurentians, Quebec 203–4
Laurier, Sir Wilfred 35, 171
Lennox Island Micmac Nation Reserve, PEI
.... 21
Liard Highway, NWT 140
Lilloet, BC 96
Long Beach, Vancouver Island 92
Longfellow, Henry Wadsworth 215, 234
Louisbourg Fortress, NS 26, 242
Lower Fort Garry, Winnipeg, Manitoba 130
Lunenburg, NS 243

Macdonald, Sir John A 33, 179, 207
Mackenzie, William Lyon 31
Mackenzie District, NWT 141
Mackenzie Highway, NWT 141
H R MacMillan Planetarium, Vancouver, BC
.... 79
Magnetic Hill, Moncton, BC 231
Magog, Quebec 204
Mahone Bay, NS 247
Malahat Summit, Vancouver Island 89
Maligne Lake and Canyon, Alta 107
Malpeque Bay, PEI 222
Manitoba 34, 122–131
Manitoba Centennial Centre, Winnipeg .. 125
Manitoba Theater Center 125
Manitoulin Island, Ontario 180

Maple Leaf Gardens, Toronto 161, 167
Marble Island, NWT 147
Marconi, Guglielmo 250
Marineland, Niagara Falls, Ontario 170
Maritimes 215-245
Market Square, Saint John, NB 230
Massey Hall, Toronto 167
McMichael Gallery, Toronto 166
Mennonite Home, Ontario 176
Mennonite Heritage Village, Steinbech, ...
    Manitoba 127
Merritt, BC 92
Metis 33, 114–16, 134–35
Metro Toronto Zoo, Ontario 166
Middle Island, Lake Erie, Ontario 41
Miles Canyon, Whitehorse, Yukon 151
Military Compound, Fredericton, NB 228
Moncton, NB 231–33
Mont Royal, Montreal 191
Mont Ste Anne, Quebec 211
Mont Tremblant, Quebec 203
Montague, PEI 224
Montmorency Falls, Quebec 201
Montreal 25, 30, 33, 185–198
Moose Factory, Ontario 176
Mooosehide Village, Yukon 153
Moosonee, Ontario 176
Mount Cain, BC 90
Mount Robson, Alta 107
Mount Seymour, BC 77, 79, 80
Museums
    Alberta
        Provincial Museum 109
        Tyrell Museum of Paleontology 114

    British Columbia
        British Columbia Forest Museum 89
        Cape Mudge Indian Village Museum .. 93
        Fort George Regional and Railway
            Museum 96
        Fort Victoria Museum 88
        Maritime Museum 79, 85
        Museum of Anthropology 77
        Provincial Museum 85
        Queen Charlotte Islands Museum 97

Railway Museum 81, 99
Royal London Wax Museum 86
Vancouver Museum 79

Manitoba
Museum of Man 124
St Boniface Museum 126
Western Canadian Aviation Museum 127

New Brunswick
Acadian Museum 231
Moncton Museum 231
New Brunswick Museum 230
St Martins' Quaco Museum 230
York-Sunbury Historical Society
    Museum 228

Northwest Territories
Prince of Wales Northern Heritage
    Museum 142

Nova Scotia
Giant MacAskill Highland Pioneers
    Museum 241
Lunenburg Fisheries Museum 242
Yarmouth County Historical Society
    Museum 243

Ontario
Bytown Museum 171
Canadian Ski Museum 174
Canadian War Museum 174
Marine Museum of Upper Canada 162
Museum of Canadian Scouting 174
National Aeronautic Collection 174
National Museum of Man and Natural
    Sciences 174
National Museum of Science and
    Technology 174
Royal Ontario Museum 166

Prince Edward Island
Acadian Museum 220
Elmira Railway Station 224
Fisheries Museum 224

PEI Museum and Heritage
    Foundation 220
Port Hill's Green Park Provincial Park
    Museum 223

Quebec
Granby Car Museum 204
Maritime Museum 211

Saskatchewan
Museum of Natural History 117
RCMP Centennial Museum 117
Tyrell Museum of Paleontology 114
Ukrainian Museum 118
Western Development Museum 118

Yukon
Macbride Museum 151
Dawson City Museum 152
Yukon Museums and Historical
    Association 151

Muskokas 180
Muttart Conservatory, Edmonton,
    Alberta 109

Nahanni River, NWT 140
Nanaimo, Vancouver Island 89, 92
Nathan Phillips Square, Toronto 159
National Arts Center, Ottawa 175
National Ballet of Canada 167
National Film Board Gallery, Ottawa 175
National Gallery of Canada, Ottawa 175
National Library and Public Archives,
    Ottawa 175
Native Art Gallery, Prince George, BC 96
Native Arts and Cultural Center Native Point,
    NWT 147
New Brunswick 215, 226–33
Newfoundland 21, 27, 33, 38, 245–55
Niagara Falls 169–70
Niagara-on-the-Lake, Ontario 176
Norman Mackenzie Art Gallery, Regina,
    Sask 117
North Bay, Ontario 182

North Cape, PEI 222
North Lake, PEI 224
North Shore, Quebec 206–10
North York Performing Arts Center,
    Toronto 167
Northern Splendor Reindeer Farm,
    Yukon 151
Northwest Mounted Police 34, 98, 154
Northwest Passage 22, 71
North-West Rebellion 34, 115
Northwest Territories 18, 134-49
Notre Dame Basilica, Montreal 109
Notre Dame Basilica, Ottawa 174
Notre-Dame-des-Victories, Quebec City . 201
Nova Scotia (Acadia) 219, 233–45

Okanagan, BC 98
O'Keefe Center, Toronto 167
Old Chelsea Mall, Ottawa 174
Old Fort Erie, Ontario 175
Old Fort Henry, Kingston, Ontario 178
Old Fort William, Thunder Bay, Ontario 179
Old Montreal 190–91
Olde England Inne, Victoria, BC 86
Olympic Sites
    Calgary 111, 142
    Montreal 194, 195
Ontario (formerly Upper Canada) 18, 155–81
Ontario Place 162
Ontario Science Center 163
Orwell Corner 226, 263
Osgoode Hall, Toronto 159
Osoyoos, BC 98
Ottawa, Toronto 170–75

Palais de Justice, Quebec City 199
Palace Grande Theater, Yukon 153
Pangnirtung, NWT 143
Park Corner, PEI 223
Parks
    Alberta
        Banff National Park 102
        Dinosaur Provincial Park 114
        Jasper National Park 106
        Waterton Lakes National Park 107

Wood Buffalo Park 102, 107
British Columbia
    Barkerville Provincial Historic Park 96
    Cathedral Provincial Park 97, 98
    Fort Rodd Hill National Historic Park 88
    Glacier National Park 97
    Kootenay National Park 97
    Lynn Canyon Park 79
    MacMillan Provincial Park 92
    Mount Revelstoke National Park 97
    Naikoon Provincial Park 97
    Pacific Rim National Park 92
    Petroglyph Park 89
    Provincial Heritage Park 99
    Stanley Park 74–6
    Strathcona Provincial Park 88, 97
    Tweedsmuir Provincial Park 97
    Yoho National Park 99

Manitoba
    Fort Prince of Wales Park 131
    Grand Beach Provincial Park 127
    Museum of Man and Nature 124
    Riding Mountain National Park 126

New Brunswick
    Boreview Park 231
    Mount Carlton Provincial Park 228
    Rocks Provincial Park 231
    Roosevelt International Park 233

Newfoundland
    Cape Spear Park 258
    Gros Morne National Park 249
    Harborside Park 254
    L'Anse aux Meadows National Historic
        Park 249

Northwest Territories
    Auyuittuq National Park ... 134, 136, 145
    Nahanni National Park Reserve 134, 140
    Blackstone Park 141

Nova Scotia
Cape Breton Highlands
    National Park 241
Kejimkujik National Park 235
Point Pleasant Park 238

Ontario
Polar Bear Provincial Park 182

Quebec
Artillery Park 199
National Battlefields Park 199
Olympic Park 195
Orford Provincial Park 206
Park of the Luminous Cross 211

Prince Edward Island
Buffoland Provincial Park 226
Cedar Dunes Provincial Park 222
Fort Amherst Historic Park 223
Green Park Provincial Park 223
Jacques Cartier Provincial Park 220
Mount Carleton Provincial Park 228
Pinnette Provincial Park 226
Prince Edward Island
    National Park 223

Saskatchewan
Batoche National Park 115
Blackstrap Mountain
    Provincial Park 118
Buffalo Pound Provincial Park 121
Cannington Historic Park 122
Prince Albert Provincial Park 121
Steele Narrows Historic Park 115
Wenuskewin Heritage Park 118

Parliament Buildings, Ottawa 170
Parliament Hill, Ottawa 170
Peary, Admiral Robert 146
Peggy's Cove, NS 239
Perce Rock, Quebec 211
Peterborough, Ontario 178
Petty Harbor, Nfld 255

Place d'Armes, Montreal 191
Place des Arts, Montreal 189
Place Jacques Cartier, Montreal 191
Place Royale, Montreal 190
Place Royal, Quebec City 201
Place Ville Marie, Montreal 194
Placentia Bay, Nfld 247, 250
Plains of Abraham, Quebec City 199
Pond Inlet, NWT 145
Point Prim Lighthouse, PEI 226
Pointe-au-Pic, Quebec 207
Port Alberni, Vancouver island 92
Port aux Basques, Nfld 248, 250
Port Hardy 93
Portage and Main, Winnipeg, Manitoba .. 125
Post Office, Quebec City 200
Prince Arthur, BC 196
Prince Edward Island 33, 215–226
Prince George, BC 94
Prince Rupert, BC 94
Prince William Street, Saint John, BC 222
Princes of Wales Theater, Toronto 167
Privateer's Wharf, Halifax, NS 238
Province House, Charlottetown, PEI 219
Purcell Mountains, BC 94

Quadra Island, BC 93
Quebec (formerly Lower Canada)
    .... 25, 39,183–210
Quebec City 22, 183, 198–201
Queen Charlotte Islands, BC 97
Queen Maud Gulf Bird Sanctuary, NWT . 141
Queen's University, Kingston, Ontario 179
Quesnel, BC 96

Rainbow Stage, Winnipeg, Manitoba 125
Rama Grotto, Saskatchewan 121
Rankin Inlet, NWT 147
Regina, Saskatchewan 116
Resolute Bay, NWT 146
Reversing Falls Rapids, NB 230
Rideau Canal, Ontario 174
Rideau Hall, Ottawa 174
Riel House, Winnipeg, Manitoba 126

Rivière-du-Loup, Quebec 211
Rock Island, Quebec 206
Rocky Mountains 18, 25, 35, 102–107
Roy Thomson Hall, Toronto 167
Royal Alexandra Theater, Toronto 167
Royal Canadian Mounted Police 34, 100, 117
Rue Saint Genevieve, Quebec City 199

Sackville, NB 231
Saguenay Fjord, Quebec 209
Saguenay River, Quebec 207
St Amable Lane, Montreal 191
St Anne's, NS 241
St Boniface, Manitoba 126
St Boniface Basilica Cemetery, Manitoba .126
St Dunstan's Basilica, PEI 222
St Jean-Port-Joli, Quebec 210
Saint John, NB 229–33
Saint John River Valley, NB 229
St John's, Nfld 251–256
Saint-Joseph-de-la-Rive, Quebec 210
St Joseph's Oratory, Montreal 191
St Lawrence Blvd (formerly Main Street),
     Montreal 191
St Lawrence Market, Toronto 158–9
Saint-Louis-du-Ha! Ha!, Quebec 211
St Mary's Catholic Church, PEI 224
St Peter's Anglican Cathedral, PEI 220
St Sulpice Seminary, Montreal 190
Saint Vincent, Montreal 191
Ste Adele, Quebec 203
Ste Anne de Beaupré Shrine, Quebec 207
Ste Marie Among the Hurons, Ontario 174
Sam McGee's Cabin, Yukon 151
Saskatchewan 114–22
Saskatoon 118–21
Scollard Street, Toronto 161
Seacow Pound, PEI 222
Selkirk, Lord 122
Service, Robert W 149, 152
Shannon Falls, BC 81
Shuswap Lake, BC 101

Sicamous, BC 98

Signal Hill, St John's, Nfld 250, 254
Skeena, BC 96
Skinners Pond, PEI 220
South Saskatchewan River 118
South Shore International
     Exhibition Ox Pull, NS 243
Space Sciences Centre, Alta 108
Sparks Street Mall, Ottawa 171
Spirit Island, Alta 106
Sproat Lake, BC 92
Squamish, BC 81
Stampede Park, Calgary, Alta 111
Stanley Park, Vancouver, BC 74
Steveston, BC 80
Stowe Harriet Beecher 176
Stratford on Avon, Ontario 176
Sussex Drive, Ottawa 174

Tadoussac, Quebec 207–09
Takakkaw Falls, BC 99
Takhini Hotspring, Yukon 151
Temperance Street, St John's, Nfld 254
Thelon Game Sanctuary, NWT 147
Thunder Bay, Ontario 180
Toronto 33, 158–69
Toronto Islands, Ontario 159
Toronto's First Post Office 166
Trinity, Nfld 249
Trois Rivières, Quebec 25, 30
Trudeau, Pierre 19, 39

United Empire Loyalists 18, 30, 183, 215, 226
Union Station (railway), Toronto 162
University of British Columbia 76
University of New Brunswick 229
University of Saskatchewan 118
University of Toronto 161
Upper Canada Village, Ontario 178
Ursulines Convent, Quebec City 199

Val-David, Quebec 206
Vancouver 18, 19, 68–83
Vancouver, Captain George 67
Vancouver Island, BC 88–93
Vaults of the Maison des Vins, Quebec ...201

Victoria, BC 83–88
Victoria Glacier, Alta 18,106
Vikings 21, 247, 249
Village de Seraphin, Quebec 203
Visitor Reception Centre, Yukon 151

War of 1812 .... 18, 19, 180, 182
Wascana Center, Regina, Sakatchewan ... 116
Water Street, Halifax, NS 230
Water Street, St John's, Nfld 254, 255
Wells, BC 96
West Baffin Eskimo Cooperative, NWT .. 145
West Edmonton Mall, Alta 109
West End, Vancouver 72
Whirlpool Rapids Bridge, Niagara Falls,
    Ontario 170
Whistler-Blackcomb Mountain, BC ... 80, 107
Whitehorse, Yukon 151
Williams Lake, BC 96

Winnipeg, Manitoba 124–7
Winnipeg Art Gallery 124
Wolfe, Major General James 27, 198, 220
Wood Islands, PEI 226
Wood Mountain Post, Saskatchewan 121
World Wars 35, 38–40
Wreck Beach, BC 77

Yarmouth, NS 243–5
Yellowhead Pass, Alta 107
Yellowknife, NWT 136, 142
Yonge Street, Toronto 159
Yorkville, Ontario 161
York, PEI 224
Yukon 18, 149–53
Yukon Historical and Museums
    Association 151
Yukon River 151